Engineering Long-Lasting Software: An Agile Approach Using SaaS and Cloud Computing
Alpha Edition

Armando Fox and David Patterson

January 10, 2012

Book version: 0.8.0

The cover background is a photo of the Aqueduct of Segovia, Spain. We chose it as an example of a beautiful, long-lasting design. The full aqueduct is about 20 miles (32 km) long and was built by the Romans in the 1st or 2nd century A.D. This photo is from the half-mile (0.8 km) long, 92 feet (28 m) high above ground segment built using unmortared, granite blocks. The Roman designers followed the architectural principles in the ten volumes series De Architectura ("On Architecture"), written in 15 B.C. by Marcus Vitruvius Pollio. It was untouched until the 1500s, when King Ferdinand and Queen Isabella performed the first reconstruction of these arches. The aqueduct is still in use and delivering water today.

Both the print book and ebook were prepared with LaTeX, tex4ht, and Ruby scripts employing Nokogiri. Additional Ruby scripts automatically keep the Pastebin excerpts and screencast URIs up-to-date in the text.

Arthur Klepchukov designed the iOS and Android versions and provided the cover and design graphics for all versions.

Contents

1 Engineering Software is Different from Hardware   **15**

To help understand the nature of engineering software, we contrast it with hardware engineering with regards to product lifetimes, development processes, productivity, and assurance. The similarities and differences led to two popular processes for software development: Waterfall and Agile. We show the synergy between Software as a Service (SaaS), Cloud Computing, and Agile software development. We conclude with a tour of the remainder the book.

2 SaaS Architecture   **41**

Whether creating a new system or preparing to modify an existing one, understanding its architecture at multiple levels is essential. Happily, good software leverages patterns at many levels—proven solutions to similar architectural problems, adapted to the needs of a specific problem. Judicious use of patterns helps simplify design, reveal intent, and compose software components into larger systems. We'll examine the patterns present at various logical layers of SaaS apps, discuss why each pattern was chosen, and where appropriate, note the opportunity cost of not choosing the alternative. Patterns aren't perfect for every problem, but the ability to separate the things that change from those that stay the same is a powerful tool for organizing and implementing large systems.

3   Ruby & Rails Basics   69

This quick introduction will get you up to speed on idiomatic Ruby and Rails. We focus on the unique productivity-enhancing features of Ruby and Rails that may be unfamiliar to Java programmers, and we omit many details that are well covered by existing materials. As with all languages, becoming truly comfortable with Ruby's powerful features will require going beyond the material in this introduction to the materials listed in Section 3.19.

4   Validating Requirements: BDD and User Stories   129

The first step in the Agile cycle, and often the most difficult, is a dialogue with each of the stakeholders to understand the requirements. We first derive ***user stories***, which are short narratives each describing a specific interaction between some stakeholder and the application. The ***Cucumber*** tool turns these stylized but informal English narratives into acceptance and integration tests. As SaaS usually involves end-users, we also need a user interface. We do this with ***low-fidelity (Lo-Fi)*** drawings of the Web pages and combine them into ***storyboards*** before creating the UI in HTML.

5   Verification: Test-Driven Development   153

In test-driven development, you first write failing tests for a small amount of nonexistent
code and then fill in the code needed to make them pass, and look for opportunities to
refactor (improve the code's structure) before going on to the next test case. This cycle is
sometimes called Red–Green–Refactor, since many testing tools print failed test results in
red and passing results in green. To keep tests small and isolate them from the behavior of
other classes, we introduce mock objects and stubs as examples of *seams*—places where
you can change the behavior of your program at testing time without changing the source
code itself.

6   Improving Productivity: DRY and Concise Rails   187

7   Software Maintenance: Using Agile Methods on Legacy Software   189

8   Working In Teams vs. Individually   191

9   Software Design Patterns for SaaS   193

10 Operations: Performance, Scaling, and Practical Security   195

11 Looking Backwards and Looking Forwards   197

In this chapter we give perspectives on the big ideas in this book—Agile, Cloud Computing, Rails, SaaS, and SOA—and show how Berkeley students who have graduated and
taken jobs in industry rank their importance.

Foreword

Introduction

This book is an opinionated path through the bewildering array of methodologies, languages, tools, and artifact types that collectively make up "software engineering." The goal is to instill good software habits in students—testability, software architecture, modularity, and reusability—while providing them the gratification of building a working deployed artifact that they themselves (and their peers) would use and find compelling.

The particular choice we make is to teach agile development using a methodology similar to extreme programming (XP) in the context of building and deploying a software-as-a-service (SaaS) application implemented using Ruby on Rails. Each choice has a good reason.

Why Agile?

We use the IEEE SWEBOK framework[1] (Software Engineering Body of Knowledge, stewarded by the Institute of Electrical and Electronics Engineers) to introduce agile ideas and methods, and specifically how to use them to create SaaS, which we believe is important to the future of software. While agile might not be suitable for building safety-critical or lights-out systems, its iteration-based, short-planning-cycle approach is a great fit for the reality of crowded undergraduate schedules and fast-paced courses. Busy students will by nature procrastinate and then pull several all-nighters to get a demo cobbled together and working by the project deadline; agile not only thwarts this tactic (since students are evaluated on progress being made each iteration) but in our experience actually leads to real progress using responsible discipline on a more regular basis.

Within each iteration, we are able to address the major issues of the software lifecycle in microcosm—requirements gathering with the customer, transforming requirements to user stories, driving the class-level architecture of the software using behavior-driven development, driving the implementation using test-driven development, and evaluating both unit/regression test coverage and acceptance/integration test results. That is, rather than first evaluating students on requirements gathering, then on good design, then on development and finally on test coverage and a working demo, *all* of these elements are evaluated on *every iteration*, encouraging the students to see the concepts and techniques as part of an integrated ongoing process rather than as isolated stages in a pipeline.

Why Software as a Service?

To motivate students, it's helpful to use a platform that lets them create compelling apps. As of 2010, there are more than 3.5 billion mobile phones deployed worldwide, or approximately 1 phone for every other person on the planet; combined with the explosive growth of SaaS, we believe the future of software is "client + cloud" applications that are split between a tablet or smart phone and a cluster of servers to do heavy computation and persist data.

Therefore, both mobile applications for smart phones and tablets and Software as a Service (SaaS) for cloud computing are compelling targets for teaching students. As you can teach the principles with either target, given the time constraints of a one-semester course, we choose in favor of the platform with the most productive tools. Our experience is that it is no contest: the programming and testing frameworks for SaaS and cloud computing are dramatically more productive than those for mobile apps, and the client part of many SaaS apps can be adapted to mobile devices using the HTML/CSS/JavaScript skills learned in creating SaaS.

In addition, beyond the commercial promise of SaaS and the "hireability" of students who know how to create it, SaaS projects can be deployed inexpensively using public cloud computing, which means students' course artifacts are on display for the whole world to see. The exposure and "look what I made" factor of public deployment are hard to match.

Why Rails?

We want students to understand that in the real world, programmers are rewarded not for the number of lines of code written or for how quickly they can "bash out" a feature, but for functionality delivered with high assurance of stability and while keeping the codebase beautiful and maintainable for continued growth. To many students, especially "hotshot" coders who come into a software engineering course with nontrivial programming experience, the methodologies and techniques we use to do this—design patterns, refactoring, test-first development, behavior-driven design—seem a strange and a dubious use of time. We have found that students are more likely to gradually embrace these practices if given the best possible tools to support the practices. The Rails community has created by far the most seamless, elegant, and comprehensive tool set to support Agile and XP, and the idea of constantly refining and inventing tools that support testing as well as helping produce beautiful application code is a distinguishing characteristic of the Ruby developer ecosystem. While learning Ruby and Rails will be new to most students, juniors and seniors seem to learn it without difficulty, and far superior tools outweigh the learning costs.

Finally, even if our students never use Ruby again, they will have learned how to *reduce to practice* such important ideas as metaprogramming, higher-order programming, functional programming, and use of closures in the service of higher productivity and more maintainable code. We believe these skills will transfer to new languages, framework, and programming systems. Our early survey of alumni of the course that led to this book (see Chapter 11) suggests that this is happening.

Lastly, if you're reading this on a Kindle Classic, some tables, code examples, and figures may be easier to read if you rotate the device to landscape mode or zoom in on the table or figure. If any tables or figures are too hard to read, just navigate to the book's website, http://www.saasbook.info[2], where you'll find high-resolution images of every figure cross-referenced to the figure numbers in the text.

History of this Book

The material in this book started as a byproduct of a Berkeley research project[3] that was developing technology to make it easy to build the next great Internet service. We decided that young people were more likely to come up with such a service, so we started teaching Berkeley undergraduates about Software as a Service using Agile techniques in 2008. Each year the course improved in scope and ambition, embracing the rapid improvements in the Rails tools along the way.

A colleague suggested that this would be excellent material for the software engineering course that has long been taught at Berkeley, so one of us (Fox) taught that course with this new content in 2010. The results were so impressive that the other of us (Patterson) suggested that writing a textbook would let other universities benefit from this powerful curriculum.

These ideas crystallized with the emerging viability of electronic textbooks and the possibility of avoiding the costs and delays of a traditional publisher. In March 2011 we made a pact to write the book together. We were equally excited by making the material more widely available and about rethinking what an electronic textbook should be, since up until then they were essentially just the PDFs of print books.

The first step was to read related textbooks and professional books, and there is no shortage of books on each topic. Figures 1 and 2 show just 24 of the 30+ books we consulted, representing more than 10,000 pages! The sheer mass of these books can intimidate beginners. Therefore, a second reason to write the book is simply to offer a coherent introduction and overview of all these important topics within a single slim volume.

We also talked to others about the content. We attended conferences such as SIGCSE (Computer Science Education), the Conference on Software Engineering Education and Training, and the Federated Research Computing Conference to both talk to colleagues and to send them a survey to get their feedback. Also, since industry often complains about weaknesses in software education, we spoke to representatives from a half-dozen leading software companies including Amazon, eBay, Facebook, Google, and Microsoft. We were struck by the unanimity of the number one request from each company: that students learn how to enhance sparsely-documented legacy code. In priority order, other requests were making testing a first-class citizen, working with non-technical customers, performing design reviews, and working in teams. We believe the social skills needed to work effectively with nontechnical customers, work well in teams, and to perform effective design reviews surely are helpful for the developers' whole careers; the question is how to fit them into one book. Similarly, no one questions the value of emphasizing testing; the question is how to get students to embrace it.

Given the perspective of educators and industrial colleagues, we proposed an outline that we think addressed all these concerns, and started writing in June 2012. Given Fox's much greater expertise on the subject, he is writing roughly two-thirds of the chapters and Patterson the rest. Both of us collaborated on the organization and were first reviewers for each other's chapters. Fox also created the LaTex pipeline that let us produce the many formats of the book for the various electronic and print targets. (We suspect other authors may want to follow Fox's lead, and so this pipeline will likely eventually become an open source software project.)

The original plan was to bring out an Alpha edition of the textbook for 100 Berkeley students for the Spring semester 2012. Based on students' feedback, we'd revise it over the summer and class test the Beta version of the textbook in the Fall semester 2012, ideally at other universities in addition to Berkeley. After that final round of feedback, we'd bring out the first edition for real in early 2013.

These plans were altered in November 2011 when we were recruited to offer the Spring 2012 course online (for free) via saas-class.org[4]. As of this writing, more than 40,000 people have signed up for a course starting in February 2012, meaning that this book will receive a much bigger Alpha test than we have ever could have envisioned!   Since this online course covers just the first half of the Berkeley course, to lower book cost and to save trees, this Alpha edition does *not* include chapters from the last part of the Berkeley course: DRY and Concise Rails, Using Agile Methods on Legacy Software, Working in Teams, Software Patterns for SaaS, and Operations. (We will distribute them separately to the 100 Berkeley students, and to the extent timing permits, we will make them available as free upgrades to ebook purchasers.) In addition to Beta testing in the classroom, we plan to cover the full curriculum as part of a two-part online course in the Fall, so the Beta edition will include all chapters.

Hence, we apologize in advance for the problems you find in the Alpha edition, and look forward to your feedback on how to improve this material. It should be an interesting experience, and sure to be highly educational for everyone involved!

Armando Fox and David Patterson

January, 2012

Berkeley, California

Armando Fox

David Patterson

Disclaimer

Throughout the book we use specific Web sites, tools, products, or trade names to ground examples in reality. Unless specifically noted, the authors have no formal connection to any of these sites, tools, or products, and the examples are for informational purposes only and not meant as endorsements. Any trademarked names mentioned are the property of their respective owners and mentioned here for informational purposes only. Where possible, we focus on free and/or open-source software so that students can get hands-on ability related to the examples without incurring additional out-of-pocket costs.

The authors' opinions are their own and not necessarily those of their employer.

Acknowledgments

We thank our industrial colleagues who gave us feedback on our ideas about the course and the book outline, especially Tracy Bialik, Google Inc.; Brad Green, Google Inc.; Jim Larus, Microsoft Research; Rob Mee, Pivotal Labs; Tony Ng, eBay; Russ Rufer, Google Inc.; Peter Van Hardenberg, Heroku; and Peter Vosshall, Amazon Web Services.

We thank our academic colleagues for their feedback on our approach and ideas, especially Timothy Lethbridge, University of Ottawa, and Mary Shaw, Carnegie-Mellon University.

Part of the "bookware" is the collection of excellent third-party sites supporting SaaS development. For their help in connecting us with the right products and services that could be offered free of charge to students in the class, and valuable discussion on how to use them in an educational setting, we thank Maggie Johnson, Google Inc.; Dana Le, Heroku (Salesforce); James Lindenbaum, Heroku; Rob Mee, Pivotal Labs; Kurt Messersmith, Amazon Web Services; and Chris Wanstrath, GitHub.

Figure 1: These 12 books contain more than 5000 pages. Your authors read more than 30 books to prepare this text. Most of these books are listed in the To Learn More sections at the end of the appropriate chapters.

Figure 2: Another 12 books your authors read also contain more than 5000 pages. Most of these books are listed in the To Learn More sections at the end of the appropriate chapters.

Finally, for helping us reinvent the on-campus class that led to this effort, we thank our graduate student instructors Kristal Curtis and Shoaib Kamil, and our undergraduate lab staff over four iterations of the class: Aaron Beitch, Allen Chen, David Eliahu, Amber Feng, Karl He, Brandon Liu, Sunil Pedapudi, Omer Spillinger, Tim Yung, and Richard Zhao.

(And we thank in advance the students of CS 169, Spring 2012, for being the guinea pigs!)

1 Engineering Software is Different from Engineering Hardware

It was on one of my journeys between the EDSAC room and the punching equipment that "hesitating at the angles of stairs" the realization came over me with full force that a good part of the remainder of my life was going to be spent finding errors in my own programs.
— Maurice Wilkes, Memoirs of a Computer Pioneer, 1985

To help understand the nature of engineering software, we contrast it with hardware engineering with regards to product lifetimes, development processes, productivity, and assurance. The similarities and differences led to two popular processes for software development: Waterfall and Agile. We show the synergy between Software as a Service (SaaS), Cloud Computing, and Agile software development. We conclude with a tour of the remainder the book.

Maurice Wilkes (1913–2010) received the 1967 Turing Award for designing and building EDSAC in 1949, one of the first stored program computers. The Turing Award[5] is the highest award in computing, which ACM has bestowed the annually since 1966. Named after computing pioneer Alan Turing, it is known informally as the Nobel Prize of Computer Science.
(This book uses sidebars to include what your authors think are interesting asides or short biographies of computing pioneers that supplement the primary text, which we hope readers will enjoy.)

1.1   Introduction

Since the UNIVAC I in 1951, which was the first commercial computer, we have made tremendous advances in hardware design. Thanks in large part to Moore's Law, today's computers have 100 billion times the UNIVAC I's price-performance. (Patterson and Hennessy 2008)

Over these six decades there have been so many software disasters that they are clichés, captured by short phrases that software engineers have memorized since they've heard the stories so many times: Ariane 5 rocket explosion[7], Therac-25 lethal radiation overdose[8], Mars Climate Orbiter disintegration[9], FBI Virtual Case File project abandonment[10], and so on. However, it is hard to recall a single comparable computer hardware disaster.

Why hasn't software engineering been as successful as hardware engineering?

The reasons have to do with differences in nature of the two media and the subsequent cultures that have grown up around them. Let us start with the one major difference—product lifetimes—and the resulting development processes for hardware and software, before discussing two big ideas that are similar for software and hardware: assurance and productivity.

Ariane 5 flight 501. On June 4, 1996, an overflow occurred 37 seconds after liftoff in a guidance system, with spectacular consequences[6], when a floating point number was converted to a shorter integer. This exception could not occur on the shorter flight path of the Ariane 4 rocket, so reusing successful components without thorough system testing was expensive: satellites worth $370M were lost.

1.2   Product Lifetimes: Independent Products vs. Continuous Improvement

Unlike hardware, software is expected to grow and evolve over time. Whereas hardware designs must be declared finished before they can be manufactured and shipped, initial software designs can easily be shipped and later upgraded over time. Basically, the cost of upgrade in the field is astronomical for hardware and affordable for software.

Hence, software can achieve a high-tech version of immortality, potentially getting better over time while generations of computer hardware decay into obsolescence.

This fundamental difference in the two media has led to different customer expectations, business models, and engineering development processes. Since a hardware product is not going to get any better over time, customers expect it to be basically bug-free when it arrives. If it's not working properly, the assumption is there had to have been a flaw in manufacturing of this particular item, and so it should be returned and replaced. If too many customers return products, the company loses money.

The Oldest Living Program might be MOCAS[11] ("Mechanization of Contract Administration Services"), which was originally purchased by the US Department of Defense in 1958 and was still in use as of 2005.

Customers are considerably more forgiving for software, assuming if there are problems when software is installed, they just need to get the latest version of it, presumably with their bugs fixed. Moreover, they expect to get notices about and install improved versions of the software over the lifetime that they use it, perhaps even submitting bug reports to help developers fix their code. They may even have to pay an annual maintenance fee for this privilege!

Just as novelists fondly hope that their brainchild will be read long enough to be labeled a classic—which for books is 100 years!—software engineers should hope their creations would also be long-lasting. Of course, software has the advantage over books of being able to be improved over time. In fact, a long software life often means that others maintain and enhance it, even letting the creators of original code off the hook.

This brings us to a few terms we'll use throughout the book. The term *legacy code* refers to software that, despite its old age, continues to be used because it meets customers' needs. Sixty percent of software maintenance costs are for adding new functionality to legacy software, vs. only 17% for fixing bugs, so legacy software is successful software.

The term "legacy" has a negative connotation, however, in that it indicates that the code is difficult to evolve because of inelegance of its design or use of antiquated technology. To contrast to legacy code, we use the term ***beautiful code*** to indicate long-lasting code that is easy to evolve. The worst case is not legacy code, however, but ***unexpectedly short-lived code*** that is soon discarded because it doesn't meet customers' needs. We'll highlight examples that lead to beautiful code with the Mona Lisa icon in the page margin. Similarly, we'll highlight text that deals with legacy code using an abacus icon in the page margin, which is certainly a long-lasting but little changed calculating device.

Surprisingly, despite the widely accepted importance of enhancing existing software, this topic is traditionally ignored in college courses and textbooks. We feature such software in this book for two reasons. First, you can reduce the effort to build a program by finding existing code that you can reuse. One supplier is open source software. Second, it's advantageous to learn how to build code that makes it easier for successors to enhance, as that increases software's chances of a long life. In the following chapters, we show both examples of both beautiful code and legacy code that we hope will inspire you to make your designs simpler to evolve.

Summary: Successful software can live decades and is expected to evolve and improve, unlike computer hardware that is finalized at time of manufacture and can be considered obsolete within just a few years. One goal of this book is to teach you how to increase the chances of producing beautiful code so that your software lives a long and useful life.

While software development processes initially followed hardware development processes, the potential to evolve over time has led to new development processes for software.

1.3 Development Processes: Waterfall versus Agile

Measure twice, cut once.   —English proverb

The hardware community developed a rigid development process that starts, sensibly enough, with a thorough, detailed, written specification of what the product should do. What follows are a series of refinements that descend through levels of abstraction until there is description of the design at a low enough level that it can be manufactured. A great deal of time and effort is then expended to test that the low-level design matches the high level specification until it passes acceptance tests. Indeed, given the cost of mistakes, as much effort can be spent on verification as was spent on design.

The software version of this hardware development process is also a sequence of phases:

1. Requirements analysis and specification

2. Architectural design

3. Implementation and Integration

4. Verification

5. Operation and Maintenance

Given that the earlier you find an error the cheaper it is to fix, the philosophy of this process is to complete a phase before going on to the next one, thereby removing as many errors as early as possible. Getting the early phases right can also prevent unnecessary work downstream. This approach also expects extensive documentation with each phase, to make sure that important information is not lost if a person leaves the project and so that new people can get up to speed quickly when they join the project. Because it flows from the top down to completion, it is called the ***Waterfall*** software development process or Waterfall software development ***lifecycle***.

In the Waterfall lifecycle, the long life of software is acknowledged by a maintenance phase that repairs errors as they are discovered. New versions of software developed in the Waterfall model go through the same several phases, and take typically between 6 and 18 months. We will refer to the software processes like Waterfall that involve a great deal of planning and major phase changes with the term ***Big Design Up Front***, abbreviated ***BDUF)***.

The Waterfall model can work well with well-defined tasks like NASA space flights, but it runs into trouble when customers are unclear on what they want. A Turing Award winner captures this observation:

> *Plan to throw one [implementation] away; you will, anyhow.* —Fred Brooks, Jr.

That is, it's easier for customers to understand what they want once they see a prototype and for engineers to understand how to build it better once they've done it the first time.

While a variety of software development lifecycles were developed over the years to better match the nature of software versus hardware, perhaps the Reformation moment for software engineering was the Agile Manifesto in February 2001. A group of software developers met to develop a lighter-touch software lifecycle. Here is what the ***Agile Alliance*** nailed to the door of the "Church of Big Design Up Front":

"We are uncovering better ways of developing software by doing it and helping others do it. Through this work we have come to value:

- **Individuals and interactions** *over processes and tools*

- **Working software** *over comprehensive documentation*

- **Customer collaboration** *over contract negotiation*

- **Responding to change** *over following a plan*

That is, while there is value in the items on the right, we value the items on the left more."

> **Variants of Agile** There are many variants of Agile software development (Fowler 2005). The one we use in this book is ***Extreme Programming***, which is abbreviated ***XP***.

This alternative development model is based on embracing change as a fact of life: developers should continuously refine a working but incomplete prototype until the customer is happy with result, with the customer offering feedback on each iteration. Agile emphasizes ***Test-Driven Development (TDD)*** to reduce mistakes, ***user stories*** to reach agreement and validate customer requirements, and ***velocity*** to measure progress. We'll cover these topics in detail in later chapters.

Regarding software lifetimes, the Agile software lifecycle is so quick that new versions are available every two weeks, so they are not even special events as in the Waterfall model. The assumption is one of basically continuous improvement over its lifetime.

Summary: The Waterfall software development process or *lifecycle* is characterized by much of the design being done in advance in coding, completing each phase before going on to the next one. In contrast, the Agile lifecycle works with customers to continuously add features to working prototypes until the customer is satisfied.

Self-Check 1.3.1 *True or False: A big difference between Waterfall and Agile development is that Agile does not use requirements.*
◇ False: While Agile does not develop extensive requirements documents as does Waterfall, the interactions with customers to lead to creation of requirements as user stories, as we shall see in Chapter 4. ∎

Having highlighted the difference in product lifetimes and the impact on development processes, we now show how hardware and software take similar approaches to making sure the artifacts meet their specifications.

1.4 Assurance

We start this topic with definitions of two terms that are commonly interchanged but have subtle distinctions:

- *Verification*: Did you build the thing *right*? (Did you meet the specification?)

- *Validation*: Did you build the right *thing*? (Is this what the customer wants? That is, is the specification correct?)

Generally, hardware prototypes aim at verification—ensuring that hardware meets the spec—while software prototypes more typically help with validation, since customers could not change hardware even if they wanted to, but they can demand and receive changes to software.

The two main approaches to verification and validation are *testing* and *formal analysis*. The motivation for both approaches is that the earlier developers find mistakes, the cheaper it is to repair them. Given the substantial costs of repair, both testing and formal analysis involve large communities of researchers and practitioners with many books on the topics. We highlight just some of the main issues here, starting with testing.

Given the vast number of different combinations of inputs, testing cannot be exhaustive. One way to reduce the space is to perform different tests at different phases of software development. Starting bottom up, *unit testing* makes sure that a single procedure or method does what was expected. The next level up is *module testing* or *functional testing*, which tests across individual units. For example, unit testing works within a single class and functional testing works across classes. Above this level is *integration testing*, which ensures that the interfaces between the units have consistent assumptions and communicate correctly. This level does not test the functionality of the units. At the top level is *system testing* or *acceptance testing*, which tests to see if the integrated program meets its specifications.

The many levels of testing, from unit tests to acceptance tests, need an indication of the fraction of the possible paths have been tested. If we represent the paths as a graph, the term *test coverage* means what fraction of the paths is covered by the test. Note that

Infeasibility of exhaustive testing
Suppose it took just 1 millisecond to test a program and it had just one 64-bit input that we wanted to test exhaustively. (Obviously, most programs take longer to run and have more inputs.) Just this simple case would take 2^{64} milliseconds, or 500M years!

even 100% test coverage is no guarantee of design reliability, however, since it says nothing about the quality of the tests that were run.

Given the long development time of hardware and the long lifetime of software, another concern is whether later changes in design will cause failures in tests that it previously passed. To prevent such a backwards step, computer engineers use *regression testing* to automatically rerun old tests to ensure that the current version still works at least as well as it used to. A related term is *continuous integration* or *CI* testing, which means the program is tested as the code is developed versus a separate phase after completing development.

Given the quick tour of issues in testing, we can see how assurance is performed in our lifecycles. For the Waterfall development process, testing happens after each phase is complete and in a final verification phase that includes acceptance tests. Assurance for Agile comes from test-driven development, in that the tests are written *before* the code when coding from scratch. When enhancing with existing code, TDD means writing the tests before writing the enhancements. The amount of testing depends on whether you are enhancing beautiful code or legacy code, with the latter needing a lot more.

While testing is widely relied upon, quoting another Turing Award winner:

> *Program testing can be used to show the presence of bugs, but never to show their absence!*
> —Edsger W. Dijkstra

Edsger W. Dijkstra (1930–2002) received the 1972 Turing Award for fundamental contributions to developing programming languages.

Thus, there has been a great deal of research investigating approaches to verification beyond testing. Collectively, these techniques are known as *formal methods*. The general strategy is to start with a formal specification and prove that the behavior of the code follows the behavior of that spec. These are mathematical proofs, either done by a person or done by a computer using either *automatic theorem proving* or *model checking*. Theorem proving uses a set of inference rules and a set of logical axioms to produce proofs from scratch. Model checking verifies selected properties by exhaustive search of all possible states that a system could enter during execution.

Because formal methods are so computationally intensive, they tend to be used only when the cost to repair errors is very high, the features are very hard to test, and the item being verified is not too large. Examples include vital parts of hardware (like network protocols) or safety critical software systems (like medical equipment). For formal methods to actually work, the size of the design must be limited: the largest formally verified software is an operating system kernel that is less than 10,000 lines of code, and its verification cost about $500 per line of code. (Klein et al. 2010)

Hence, formal methods are *not* good matches to high-function software that changes frequently, as is the case for Cloud Computing applications of this book. Consequently, we will not cover formal methods further.

NASA software lifecycle costs NASA spent $35M per year to maintain 420,000 lines of code[12] for the space shuttle, or about $80 per line of code per year.

Summary: Testing and formal methods reduce the risks of errors in designs.

- In its many forms, testing helps *verify* that software meets the specification and *validates* that the design does what the customer wants.

- Attacking the infeasibility of exhaustive testing, we divide to conquer by focusing on *unit testing*, *module testing* or *functional testing*, *integration testing*, and full *system testing* or *acceptance testing*. Each higher level test delegates more detailed testing to lower levels.

- By mapping designs to graphs and recording which nodes and arcs are traversed, *test coverage* indicates what has and has not been tested.

- *Regression testing* reapplies old tests to reduce the chance of new revisions breaking designs that have worked in the past.

- *Formal methods* rely on formal specifications and automated proofs or exhaustive state search to verify more than what testing can do, but they are so expensive to perform that today they are only applicable to small, stable, critical portions of hardware or software.

Self-Check 1.4.1 *While all of the following help with verification, which form of tests is most likely to help with validation: Unit, Module, Integration, or Acceptance?*
◇ Validation is concerned with doing what the customer really wants versus whether code met the specification, so acceptance testing is most likely to point out the difference between doing the thing right and doing the right thing. ∎

Given this review of hardware and software development processes and approaches to assurance, we are ready to how we make developers more productive.

1.5 Productivity

Moore's Law means that hardware resources double every 18 months. Thus, computers would take increasingly long to design unless hardware engineers improved *their* productivity. In turn, these faster computers with much larger memories could run much larger programs. Similarly, to build bigger applications that could take advantage of the more powerful computers, software engineers needed to improve their productivity.

Both hardware and software engineers developed four fundamental mechanisms to improve their productivity:

1. Clarity via conciseness

2. Synthesis

3. Reuse

4. Automation and Tools

One of the driving assumptions of improving productivity of programmers is that if programs are easier to understand, then they will have fewer bugs as well as to be easier to evolve. A closely related corollary is that if the program is smaller, it's generally easier to understand. We capture this notion with our motto of "clarity via conciseness".

Programming languages do this two ways. The first is simply offering a syntax that lets programmers express ideas naturally and in fewer characters. For example, below are two ways to express a simple assertion:

assert_greater_than_or_equal_to(a, 7)
a.should be >= 7

Unquestionably, the second version (which happens to be legal Ruby) is shorter and easier to read and understand, and will likely have fewer bugs and be easier to maintain. It's easy to imagine momentary confusion about the order of arguments in the first version in addition to the higher cognitive load of reading twice as many characters (see Chapter 3).

The second way to improve clarity is to raise the level of abstraction. For hardware engineers, it meant going from designing rectangles to transistors to gates to adders and so on up the hierarchy. With the design of whole systems on a single chip today, building blocks are whole processors or caches.

John Backus (1924–2007) received the 1977 Turing Award in part for "profound, influential, and lasting contributions to the design of practical high-level programming systems, notably through his work on Fortran," which was the first widely used HLL.

Raising the level of abstraction for software engineers initially meant the invention of higher-level programming languages such as Fortran and COBOL. This step raised the engineering of software from assembly language for a particular computer to higher-level languages that could target multiple computers simply by changing the compiler.

As computer hardware performance continued to increase, more programmers were willing to delegate tasks that they formerly performed themselves to the compiler and run-time system. For example, Java and similar languages took over memory management from the earlier C and C++ languages. Scripting languages like Python and Ruby have raised the level of abstraction even higher. Examples are ***reflection***, which allows programs to observe themselves, and ***metaprogramming***, which allows programs to modify their own structure and behavior at runtime. To highlight examples that improve productivity via conciseness, we will use this "Concise" icon.

The second productivity mechanism is synthesis. Logic synthesis for hardware engineers meant that they could describe hardware as Boolean functions and receive highly optimized transistors that implemented those functions. The classic software synthesis example is Bit Blit[13]. This graphics primitive combines two bitmaps under control of a mask. Including a conditional statement in the innermost loop was too slow, so instead special-purpose code would be generated in each instance to perform the exact bitmap combination desired. We'll highlight examples that improve productivity by generating code with this "CodeGen" gears icon in the page margin.

The third productivity mechanism is to re-use portions from past designs rather that write everything from scratch. (We highlight examples that improve productivity by via reuse with this "Reuse" recycling icon in the page margin.) As it is easier to make small changes in software than in hardware, software is even more likely than hardware to reuse a component that is almost but not quite a correct fit.

Procedures and functions were invented in the earliest days of software so that different parts of the program could re-use the same code with different parameter values. These were soon followed by standardized libraries for input/output and for mathematical functions, so that programmers could re-use code developed by others. Hardware engineers also had the equivalent of procedures and design libraries.

Procedures in libraries let you reuse implementations of individual tasks. But more commonly programmers want to reuse and manage ***collections*** of tasks. The next step in software reuse was ***object oriented programming***, where you could reuse the same tasks with different objects via the use of inheritance in languages like C++ and Java.

While inheritance supported reuse of implementations, another opportunity for reuse is a general strategy for doing something even if the implementation varies. ***Design patterns***, inspired by (Alexander et al. 1977) work in civil architecture, arose to address this need. Language support for reuse of design patterns includes ***dynamic typing***, which facilitates composition of abstractions, and ***mix-ins***, which offers ways to collect functionality from multiple methods without some of the pathologies of multiple inheritance found in some object oriented programming. Python and Ruby are examples of languages with features that help with re-use of design patterns.

Note that reuse does *not* mean copying and pasting code so that you have very similar code in many places. The problem with cutting and pasting code is that you may not change all the copies when fixing a bug or adding a feature. Hunt and Thomas 1999 offer a software engineering guideline that guards against repetition:

> *Every piece of knowledge must have a single, unambiguous, authoritative representation within a system.* —Andy Hunt and Dave Thomas, 1999

This guideline has been captured in the motto and acronym: ***Don't Repeat Yourself (DRY)***. We'll use a towel as the "DRY" icon in page margins to show examples of DRY in the following chapters.

A core value of computer engineers is finding ways to replace tedious manual tasks with automation to save time, improve accuracy, or both. Examples for lay people include word processors to simplify typing and editing, spreadsheets for make accounting easier, and email to make exchanging messages much lower overhead than letters. (We highlight automation examples with the robot icon.)

Not surprisingly, we also automate tedious tasks to help ourselves, giving us our fourth productivity enhancer. Electronic Computer Aided Design (ECAD) tools kept pace with the hardware designers' ascension in abstraction. New ECAD tools were also invented as new problems presented themselves with the march of Moore's Law, such as concerns about energy and power. Obvious CAD tools for software development are compilers and interpreters that raise the level of abstraction and generate code as mentioned above, but there also more subtle productivity tools like makefiles and version control systems that automate tedious tasks.

The tradeoff is always the time it takes to learn a new tool versus the time saved in applying it. Other concerns are the dependability of the tool, the quality of the user experience, and how to decide which one to use if there are many choices. Nevertheless, one of the software engineering tenets of faith is that a new tool can make our lives better.

Your authors embrace the value of automation and tools. That is why we show you several tools in this book to make you more productive. (We highlight tool examples with the hammer icon.) For example, Chapter 4 shows how ***Cucumber*** automates turning user stories into integration tests, Chapter 5 introduces ***RSpec*** that automates the unit testing process, and Chapter 8 demonstrates how ***Pivotal Tracker*** automatically measures ***Velocity***, which is a measure of the rate of adding features to an application.

The good news is that any tool we show you will have been vetted to ensure its dependability and that time to learn will be paid back many times over in reduced development time and in the improved quality of the final result. The bad news is that you'll need to learn several new tools. However, we think the ability to quickly learn and apply new tools is a requirement for success in engineering software, so it's a good skill to cultivate.

Learning new tools
Proverbs 14:4 in the King James Bible discusses improving productivity by taking the time to learn and use tools: *Where there are no oxen, the manger is clean; but abundant crops come by the strength of oxen.*

Returning to a development lifecycles, productivity is measured in the people-hours to implement a new function. The difference is the cycles are much longer in Waterfall vs. Agile—on the order of 6 to 18 months vs. 1/2 a month—so much more work is done between releases that the customer sees, and the hence chances are greater for Waterfall that more work will ultimately be rejected by the customer.

Summary: Moore's Law inspired software engineers to improve their productivity by:

- Coveting conciseness, in using compact syntax and by raising the level of design by using higher-level languages. Recent advances include *reflection* that allows programs to observe themselves and *metaprogramming* that allows programs to modify their own structure and behavior at runtime.

- Synthesizing implementations.

- Reusing designs by following the principle of *Don't Repeat Yourself (DRY)* and by relying upon innovations that help reuse, such as procedures, libraries, object-oriented programming, and design patterns.

- Using (and inventing) CAD tools to automate tedious tasks.

Self-Check 1.5.1 *Which mechanism does is the weakest argument for productivity benefits of compilers for high-level programming languages: Clarity via conciseness, Synthesis, Reuse, or Automation and Tools?*

◇ Compilers make high-level programming languages practical, enabling programmers to improve productivity via writing the more concise code in a HLL. Compilers do synthesize lower-level code based on the HLL input. Compilers are definitely tools. While you can argue that HLL makes reuse easier, it is the weakest of the four for explaining the benefits of compilers. ∎

Having reviewed how to improve software productivity, we now introduce a new way to ship software.

1.6   Software as a Service

Software as a Service (SaaS) delivers software and data as a service over the Internet, usually via a thin program such as a browser that runs on local client devices instead of binary code that must be installed and runs wholly on that device. Examples that many of us use everyday include searching, social networking, and watching videos. The advantages for the customer and for the software developer are widely touted, including:

1. Since customers do not need to install the application, they don't have to worry whether their hardware is the right brand or fast enough nor whether they have the correct version of the operating system.

2. The data associated with the service is generally kept with the service, so customers don't need to worry about backing up the data, losing the data due to a local hardware malfunction, or even losing the data by losing the whole device, such as a phone or tablet.

SaaS Programming Framework	Programming Language
Active Server Pages (ASP.NET)	Common Language Runtime (CLR)
Django	Python
Enterprise Java Beans (EJB)	Java
JavaServer Pages (JSP)	Java
Rails	Ruby
Sinatra	Ruby
Spring	Java
Zend	PHP

Figure 1.1: Examples of SaaS programming frameworks and the programming languages they are written in.

3. When a group of users want to collectively interact with the same data, SaaS is a natural vehicle.

4. When a data is large and/or updated frequently, it may make more sense to centralize data and offer remote access via SaaS.

5. Only a single copy of the software runs in a uniform, tightly-controlled hardware and operating system environment selected by the developer, which avoids the compatibility hassles of distributing binaries that must run on wide-ranging computers and operating systems. In addition, developers can test new versions of the application on a small fraction of the real customers temporarily without disturbing most customers.

6. Since developers are the only ones with a copy of the software, they can upgrade the software and underlying hardware frequently as long as they don't violate the user-facing application program interfaces (API). Moreover, they don't need to annoy users with the seemingly endless requests for permission to upgrade their applications.

Multiplying the advantages to the customer and the developer together explains why SaaS is rapidly growing and why traditional software products are increasingly being transformed to offer SaaS versions. An example of the latter is Microsoft Office 365, which allows you to use the popular Word, Excel, and PowerPoint productivity programs as a remote service by paying for use instead of software that must be purchased in advance and installed on your local computer. Another example is TurboTax Online, which offers the same deal for another shrink-wrap standard-bearer.

Note that the last item in the list above—frequent upgrades due to only one copy of the software—perfectly aligns itself with the Agile software lifecycle. SaaS companies compete regularly on bringing out new features to help ensure that their customers do not abandon them for a competitor who offers a better service. Hence, Amazon, eBay, Facebook, Google, and other SaaS providers all rely on the Agile lifecycle, and traditional software companies like Microsoft are increasing using Agile in their product development.

SaaS: Innovate or Die? Lest you think the perceived need to improve a successful service is just software engineering paranoia, the most popular search engine used to be Alta Vista and the most popular social networking site used to be MySpace.

Unsurprisingly, given the popularity of SaaS, Figure 1.1 shows that there are many programming frameworks that claim to help. In this book we use Ruby on Rails ("Rails"), although the ideas we cover will work with other programming frameworks as well. We chose Rails because it came from a community that had already embraced the Agile lifecycle, so the tools support Agile particularly well.

Ruby is typical of modern scripting languages in including automatic memory management and dynamic typing. By including important advances in programming languages, Ruby goes beyond languages like Perl in supporting multiple programming paradigms such as object oriented and functional programming.

Useful addition features that help productivity via reuse include ***mix-ins***, which collects related behaviors and makes it easy to add them to many different classes, and ***metaprogramming***, which allows Ruby programs to synthesize code at runtime. Reuse is also enhanced with Ruby's support for ***closures*** via ***blocks*** and ***yield***. Chapter 3 is a short description of Ruby for those who already know Java, as well as an introduction to Rails.

In addition to our view of Rails being technically superior for Agile and SaaS, Ruby and Rails are widely used. For example, Ruby routinely appears among top 10 most popular programming languages. Probably the best-known SaaS using Rails is Twitter, which was invented in 2006 and grew from 20,000 tweets per day in 2007 to 200,000,000 in 2011.

If you are not already familiar with Ruby or Rails, this gives you a chance to practice an important software engineering skill mentioned above: use the right tool for the job, even if it means learning a new tool or new language! Indeed, an attractive feature of the Rails community is that they routinely improve productivity by inventing new tools to automate tasks that were formerly done manually.

Summary: ***Software as a Service (SaaS)*** is attractive to both customers and providers because the universal client (the Web browser) makes it easier for customers to use the service and the single version of the software at a centralized site makes it easier for the provider to deliver and improve the service. Given the ability and desire to frequently upgrade SaaS, the Agile software development process is popular for it, and so there are many frameworks to support them. This book uses Ruby on Rails.

Self-Check 1.6.1 *Which of the following examples of SaaS examples from Google is the best match to the six arguments given above: Search, Maps, News, Gmail, Calendar, YouTube, and Documents.*

◇ While you can argue the mappings, below is our answer. (Note that we cheated and put some apps in multiple categories)

1. No user installation: Documents

2. Can't lose data: Gmail, Calendar.

3. Users cooperating: Documents.

4. Large/changing datasets: Search, Maps, News, and YouTube.

5. Software centralized in single environment: Search.

6. No field upgrades when improve app: Documents.

∎

Self-Check 1.6.2 *True or False: If you are using the Agile development process to develop SaaS apps, you could use Python and Django or languages based on the Microsoft CLR and ASP.NET instead of Ruby and Rails.*

◇ True. There are several programming frameworks for Agile and SaaS, including Django and ASP.NET. ∎

1.7 Service Oriented Architecture

> *SOA had long suffered from lack of clarity and direction.... SOA could in fact die - not due to a lack of substance or potential, but simply due to a seemingly endless proliferation of misinformation and confusion.* —Thomas Erl, *About the SOA Manifesto*, 2010

> **SOA confusion** At the time of this writing, Wikipedia has independent entries for *Service-oriented Architecture*, *Service Oriented Architecture Fundamentals*, and *Service-Oriented Architecture Types*. The Wikipedia authors can't even agree on the capitalization and hyphenation!

SaaS is actually a special case of a more general software architecture where all components are designed to be services: a ***Service Oriented Architecture (SOA)***. Alas, SOA is one of those terms that is so ill defined, over used, and over hyped that some think it is just an empty marketing phrase, like ***modular***. SOA actually means that components of an application act as interoperable services, and can be used independently and recombined in other applications. The contrasting implementation is considered a "software silo", which rarely has APIs to internal components. If you mis-estimate what the customer really wants, the cost of recovering from that mistake and trying something else, or producing a similar-but-not-identical variant to please a subset of users, is much lower with SOA than with siloed software.

For example, Amazon started in 1995 with "siloed" software for its online retailing site. According to former Amazonian Steve Yegge[14], in 2002 the CEO and founder of Amazon mandated a change to what we would today call SOA. He broadcast an email to all employees along these lines:

1. *All teams will henceforth expose their data and functionality through service interfaces.*

2. *Teams must communicate with each other through these interfaces.*

3. *There will be no other form of interprocess communication allowed: no direct linking, no direct reads of another team's data store, no shared-memory model, no backdoors whatsoever. The only communication allowed is via service interface calls over the network.*

4. *It doesn't matter what technology they use. HTTP, Corba, Pubsub, custom protocols—doesn't matter. [Amazon CEO Jeff] Bezos doesn't care.*

5. *All service interfaces, without exception, must be designed from the ground up to be externalizable. That is to say, the team must plan and design to be able to expose the interface to developers in the outside world. No exceptions.*

6. *Anyone who doesn't do this will be fired.*

7. *Thank you; have a nice day!*

A similar software revolution happened at Facebook in 2007—three years after the company went online—when ***Facebook Platform*** was launched. Relying on SOA, Facebook Platform allowed third party developers to create applications that interact with core features of Facebook such as what people like, who their friends are, who is tagged in their photos, and so. For example, the New York Times was one of the early Facebook Platform developers. Facebook users reading the New York Times online on May 24, 2007 suddenly noticed that they could see which articles their friends were reading and which articles their friends liked.

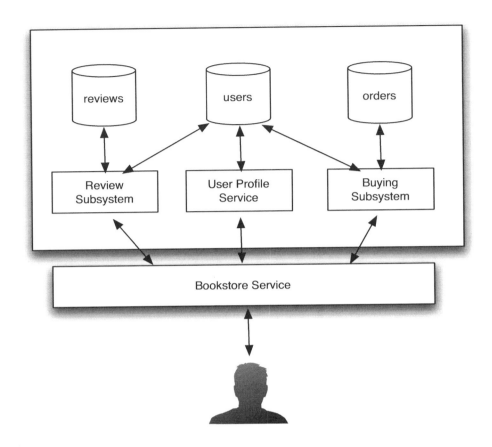

Figure 1.2: Silo version of a fictitious bookstore service, with all subsystems behind a single API.

As a contrasting example of a social networking site using a software silo, Google+ had no APIs when it was launched on June 28, 2011 and had just one heavyweight API three months later: following the complete stream of everything a Google+ user sees.

To make these notions more concrete, suppose we wanted to create a bookstore service as first a silo and then as a SOA. Both will contain the same three subsystems: reviews, user profiles, and buying.

Figure 1.2 shows the silo version. The silo means subsystems internally can share access to data directly in different subsystems. For example, the reviews subsystem can get user profile info out of the users subsystem. However, all subsystems are inside a single external API ("the bookstore").

Figure 1.3 shows the SOA version of the bookstore service, where all subsystems are separate and independent. Even though all are inside the "boundary" of the bookstore's datacenter, which is shown as a dotted rectangle, the subsystems interact with each other as if they were in separate datacenters. For example, if the reviews subsystem wants information about a user, it can't just reach directly into the users database. Instead, it has to ask the users *service*, via whatever API is provided for that purpose. A similar restriction

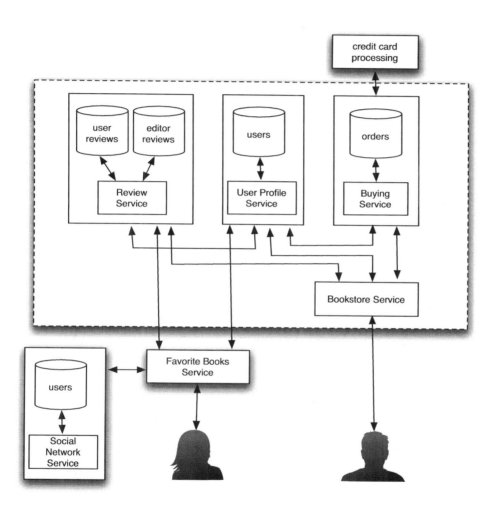

Figure 1.3: SOA version of a fictitious bookstore service, where all three subsystems are independent and available via APIs.

is true for buying.

The "bookstore app" is then just one particular composition of these services. Consequently, others can recombine the services with others to create new apps. For example, a "my favorite books" app might combine the users service and reviews service with a social network, so you can see what your social-network friends think about the books you have reviewed (see Figure 1.3).

The critical distinction of SOA is that no service can name or access another service's data; it can only make requests for data thru an external API. If the data it wants is not available thru that API, then too bad. SOA usually means a bit more work compared to building a siloed service, but the payback is tremendous reusability.

Yegge's discussion of SOA at Amazon vs. Google points out two potential disadvantages that may partially offset the advantages to external developers. The first is debugging. Fortunately, a good testing environment reduces the amount of debugging. Practices like RESTful interfaces from Chapter 2, Behavior Driven Design from Chapter 4, Test Driven Development from Chapter 5, and Rails tools that support these practices like Cucumber and RSpec provide a testing environment for SOA that we believe is superior to those for software silos. Due to the many APIs to internal subsystems that are absent with siloed software, the second perceived weakness of SOA is security. Although a much stiffer challenge than debugging, Chapter 10 introduces security techniques that help with SOA for SaaS.

Summary: Although the term was nearly lost in a sea of confusion, *Service Oriented Architecture (SOA)* just means an approach to software development where all the subsystems are only available as external services, which means others can recombine them in different ways. Following the tools and guidelines in this book ensures that your SaaS apps will be a good fit to SOA.

Self-Check 1.7.1 *Another take on SOA is that it is just a common sense approach to improving programmer productivity. Which productivity mechanism does SOA best exemplify: Clarity via conciseness, Synthesis, Reuse, or Automation and Tools?*

◇ Reuse! The purpose of making internal APIs visible is so that programmers can stand on the shoulders of others. ∎

Given the case for SaaS and the understanding that it relies on a Service Oriented Architecture, we are ready to see the underlying hardware that makes SaaS possible.

1.8   Cloud Computing

> *If computers of the kind I have advocated become the computers of the future, then computing may someday be organized as a public utility just as the telephone system is a public utility ... The computer utility could become the basis of a new and important industry.*   —John McCarthy, at MIT centennial celebration in 1961

SaaS places three demands on our information technology (IT) infrastructure:

1. Communication, to allow any customer to interact with the service.

John McCarthy (1927–2011) received the Turing Award in 1971 and is the inventor of Lisp. As a pioneer of timesharing large computers, as early as 1961 he envisioned an "ecosystem" foreshadowing today's Software as a Service in which large computers provide continuous service to large numbers of users with a utility-pricing-like model. Clusters of commodity hardware and the spread of fast networking have helped make this vision a reality.

2. Scalability, in that the central facility running the service must deal with the fluctuations in demand during the day and during popular times of the year for that service as well as a way for new services to add users rapidly.

3. Dependability, in that both the service and the communication vehicle must be continuously available: every day, 24 hours a day ("24×7").

The Internet and broadband to the home easily resolve the communication demand of SaaS. Although some early web services were deployed on expensive large-scale computers—in part because such computers were more reliable and in part because it was easier to operate a few large computers—a contrarian approach soon overtook the industry. Collections of commodity small-scale computers connected by commodity Ethernet switches, which became known as *clusters*, offered several advantages over the "big iron" hardware approach:

- Because of their reliance on Ethernet switches for the interconnect, clusters are much more scalable than conventional servers. Early clusters offered 1000 computers, and today's datacenters contain 100,000.

- Careful selection of the type of hardware to place in the datacenter and careful control of software state made it possible for a very small number of operators to successfully run thousands of servers. In particular, some datacenters rely on *virtual machines* to simplify operation. A virtual machine monitor is software that imitates a real computer so successfully that you can even run an operating system correctly on top of the virtual machine abstraction that it provides. The goal is to imitate with low overhead, and one popular use is to simplify software distribution within a cluster.

- Barroso and Hoelzle 2009 show that the cost of the equivalent amount of processors, memory, and storage is much less for clusters than "big iron," perhaps by a factor of 20.

- Although the cluster components are less reliable than conventional servers and storage systems, the cluster software infrastructure makes the whole system dependable via extensive use of redundancy. The low hardware cost makes the redundancy at the software level affordable. Modern service providers also use multiple datacenters that are distributed geographically so that a natural disaster cannot knock a service offline.

As Internet datacenters grew, some service providers realized that their per capita costs were substantially below what it cost others to run their own smaller datacenters, in large part due to economies of scale when purchasing and operating 100,000 computers at a time. They also benefit from higher utilization given that many companies could share these giant datacenters, which Barroso and Hoelzle 2009 call *Warehouse Scale Computers*, as smaller datacenters often run at only 10% to 20% utilization. Thus, these companies realized they could profit from making their datacenter hardware available on a pay-as-you-go basis.

The result is called *public cloud services* or *utility computing*, which offers computing, storage, and communication at pennies per hour (see Armbrust et al. 2010). Moreover, there is no additional cost for scale: Using 1000 computers for 1 hour costs no more than using 1 computer for 1000 hours. Leading examples of "infinitely scalable" pay-as-you-go computing are Amazon Web Services, Google App Engine, and Microsoft Azure. The public cloud means today that anyone with a credit card and a good idea can start a SaaS company that can grow to millions of customers without first having to build and operate a datacenter.

Today, we call this long held dream of computing as a utility **Cloud Computing**. We believe that Cloud Computing and SaaS are transforming the computer industry, with the full impact of this revolution taking the rest of this decade to determine. Indeed, this revolution is one reason we decided to write this book, as we believe engineering SaaS for Cloud Computing is radically different from engineering shrink-wrap software for PCs and servers.

Summary

- The Internet supplies the communication for SaaS.

- ***Cloud Computing*** provides the scalable and dependable hardware computation and storage for SaaS.

- Cloud computing consists of ***clusters*** of commodity servers that are connected by local area network switches, with a software layer providing sufficient redundancy to make this cost-effective hardware dependable.

- These large clusters or ***Warehouse Scale Computers*** offer economies of scale.

- Taking advantage of economies of scale, some Cloud Computing providers offer this hardware infrastructure as low-cost ***utility computing*** that anyone can use on a pay-as-you-go basis, acquiring resources immediately as your customer demand grows and releasing them immediately when it drops.

Self-Check 1.8.1 *True or False: Internal datacenters could get the same cost savings as Warehouse Scale Computers if they embraced SOA and purchased the same type of hardware.*

◇ False. While imitating best practices of WSC could lower costs, the major cost advantage of WSCs comes from the economies of scale, which today means 100,000 servers, thereby dwarfing internal datacenters. ∎

1.9 Fallacies and Pitfalls

We include this section near the end of chapters to explain the ideas once again from another perspective and to give readers a chance to learn from the mistakes of others. ***Fallacies*** are statements that seem plausible (or are actually widely held views) based on the ideas in the chapter, but they are not true. ***Pitfalls***, on the other hand, are common dangers associated with the topics in the chapter that are difficult to avoid even when you are warned.

 Fallacy: If a software project is falling behind schedule, you can catch up by adding more people to the project.

The main theme of Fred Brooks's classic book, *The Mythical Man-Month*, is that not only does adding people not help, it makes it worse. The reason is twofold: it takes a while

---

Rapid growth of FarmVille The prior record for number of users of a social networking game was 5 million. FarmVille had 1 million players within 4 days after it was announced, 10 million after 2 months, and 28 million daily players and 75 million monthly players after 9 months. Fortunately, FarmVille used the Elastic Compute Cloud (EC2) from Amazon Web Services, and kept up with its popularity by simply paying to use larger clusters.

for new people to learn about the project, and as the size of the project grows, the amount of communication increases, which can reduce the time to available for people to get their work done. His summary, which some call Brooks's Law, is

Adding manpower to a late software project makes it later. —Fred Brooks, Jr.

 Pitfall: **Ignoring the cost of software design.**

Since there is no cost to manufacture software, the temptation is to believe there is almost no cost to changing it so that it can be remanufactured the way the customer wants. However, this perspective ignores the cost of design and test, which can be a substantial part of the overall costs for software projects. Zero manufacturing costs is also one rationalization used to justify pirating copies of software and other electronic data, since pirates apparently believe no one should pay for the cost of development, just for manufacturing.

1.10 Guided Tour of the Book

I hear and I forget. I see and I remember. I do and I understand. —Confucius

With this introduction behind us, we can now explain what follows and what paths you might want to take.

To do and understand, as Confucius advises, begin by reading Appendix A. It explains how to obtain and use the "bookware", which is our name for the software associated with the book.

Chapter 2 explains the architecture of a SaaS application, using an altitude analogy of going from the 100,000-foot view to the 500-foot view. During the descent you'll learn the definition of many acronyms that you may have already heard—APIs, CSS, IP, REST, TCP, URLs, URIs, and XML—as well as some widely used buzzwords: cookies, markup languages, port numbers, and three-tier architectures. It also demonstrates the importance of design patterns, particularly Model-View-Controller that is at the heart of Rails.

Chapter 3 introduces Ruby and Rails. The Ruby introduction is short because it assumes you already know another object-oriented programming language well, in this case Java. As mentioned above, we believe successful software engineers will need to routinely learn new languages and tools over their careers, so learning Ruby and Rails is good practice. Readers already familiar with Ruby and Rails should skip this chapter.

Figure 1.4 shows one iteration of the Agile lifecycle, which we use as a framework on which to hang the next chapters of the book.

Chapter 4 discusses how to talk to the customer. ***Behavior-Driven Design (BDD)*** advocates writing tests that customers without a programming background can read, called **user stories**, and Chapter 4 shows how to write user stories so that they can be turned into integration tests as well as acceptance tests. It introduces the ***Cucumber*** tool to help automate this task. As SaaS apps are often user facing, the chapter also covers how to prototype a useful user interface using "Lo-Fi" prototyping.

Chapter 5 covers ***Test-Driven Development (TDD)***. The chapter demonstrates how to write good, testable code and introduces the ***RSpec*** testing tool for writing unit tests, the ***Autotest*** tool for automating test running, and the ***SimpleCov*** tool to measure test coverage.

(The Alpha edition does not include the next five chapters, since the large online class using the Alpha edition does not cover this material, which allowed us to lower the costs for the print book for 99% of the potential readers.)

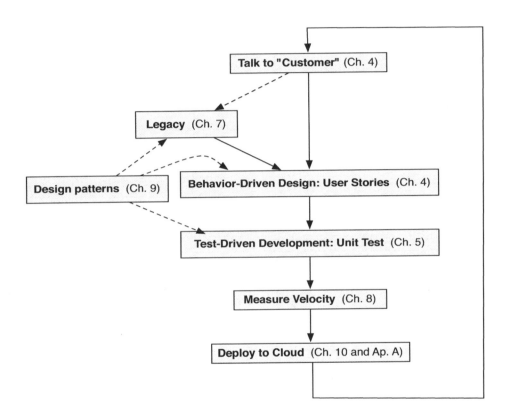

Figure 1.4: An iteration of the Agile software lifecycle and its relationship to the chapters in this book. The dashed arrows indicate a more tangential relationship between the steps of an iteration, while the solid arrows indicate the typical flow. Note that the Agile process applies equally well to existing legacy applications and new applications, although the customer may play a smaller role with legacy apps.

Given the several chapters above to gain experience with Ruby and Rails basis, we return to Rails to explain more advanced features in Chapter 6. While more challenging to learn and understand, your application can be DRYer and more concise if you use concepts like partials, validations, lifecycle callbacks, filters, associations, and foreign keys. The chapter also explains how dynamic program synthesis (metaprogramming) in Rails improves productivity by automating the creation of JavaScript code for widely used AJAX scenarios, which are useful for enriching your SaaS app's user experience.

Chapter 7 describes how to deal with existing code, including how to enhance legacy code. Helpfully, it shows how to use BDD and TDD to both understand and refactor code and how to use the Cucumber and RSpec tools to make this task easier.

Chapter 8 gives advice on how to organize and work as part of an effective team versus doing it all by yourself. It explains the term *Velocity* and how to use it to measure progress in the rate that you deliver features, and introduces the SaaS-based tool *Pivotal Tracker* to simplify such measurements. It also describes how the version control system *Git* and the corresponding services *GitHub* and *ProjectLocker* can let team members work on different features without interfering with each other or causing chaos in the release process.

To help you practice Don't Repeat Yourself, Chapter 9 introduces design patterns, which are proven structural solutions to common problems in designing how classes work together, and shows how to exploit Ruby's language features to adopt and reuse the patterns. The chapter also offers guidelines on how to write good classes. It introduces just enough UML (Unified Modeling Language) notation to help you notate design patterns and to help you make diagrams that show how the classes should work.

Note that Chapter 9 is about software architecture whereas prior chapters are about the Agile development process. We placed this chapter after the Agile process chapters as we believe in a college course setting that this order will let you start an Agile iteration sooner, and we think the more iterations you do, the better you will understand the Agile lifecycle. However, as Figure 1.4 suggests, knowing design patterns will be useful when writing or refactoring code as part of the BDD/TDD process.

Chapter 10 offers practical advice on how to first deploy and then to improve performance and scalability in the cloud, and briefly introduces some security techniques that are uniquely relevant to deploying SaaS.

Chapter 11 summarizes the book, presents a survey from Berkeley alumni now in industry on the usefulness of the ideas in this book, and projects what is next.

1.11 How *NOT* to Read this Book

The temptation is to skip sidebars, elaborations, and screencasts to just skim the text to until you find what you want to answer your question.

While elaborations are typically for experienced readers who want to know more about what is going on behind the curtain, and sidebars are just short asides that we think you'll enjoy, screencasts are *critical* to learning this material. While we wouldn't say you could skip the text and just watch the screencasts, we would say that they are some of the most important parts of the book. They allow us to express a lot of concepts, show how they interact, and demonstrate you can do the same tasks yourself. What would take many pages and be difficult to describe can come alive in a two to five minute video. Screencasts allow us to follow Confucius' advice: "I see and I remember."

In our view, screencasts are the most important advantage of ebooks over print books, and they contain important information not found elsewhere in the book. So please watch

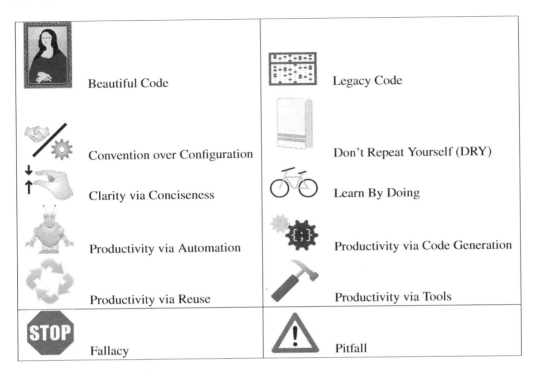

Beautiful Code	Legacy Code
Convention over Configuration	Don't Repeat Yourself (DRY)
Clarity via Conciseness	Learn By Doing
Productivity via Automation	Productivity via Code Generation
Productivity via Reuse	Productivity via Tools
Fallacy	Pitfall

Figure 1.5: Summary of Icons used in the book.

them!

The second point is to have your computer open with the Ruby interpreter ready so that you can try the examples in the screencasts and the text. We even make it easy to copy-and-paste the code using the service Pastebin[15], (If you're reading the ebook, the link accompanying each code example will take you to that code example on Pastebin.) This practice follows Confucius' advice of "I do and I understand."

Our third point is that however wonderful listening to lectures can be, there are topics that you need to study to learn, especially in our buzzword-intensive ecosystem of Agile + Ruby + Rails + SaaS + Cloud Computing. Indeed, Figure 11.2 in Chapter 11 lists nearly 120 new terms introduced in just the first three chapters. To help you learn them, each term is linked to the appropriate *Wikipedia* article the first time it appears. We also use icons to remind you of the common themes throughout the book, which Figure 1.5 summarizes as a single handy place to look them up.

Depending on your background, we suspect you'll need to read some chapters more than once before you get the hang of it. To help you focus on the key points, each section includes *self-check questions* with answers and a *summary* of the key concepts in that section, and each chapter ends with *Fallacies and Pitfalls* explaining common misconceptions or problems that are easy to experience if you're not vigilant. *Exercises* at the end of each chapter are more open-ended than the self-check questions; some have solutions posted at the book's website, saasbook.info[16]. *Sidebars* highlight what we think are interesting asides about the material. In particular, to give readers a perspective about who came up with these big ideas that they are learning and that information technology relies upon, we

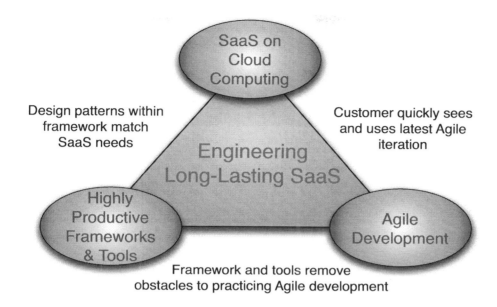

Figure 1.6: The Virtuous Triangle of Engineering long-lasting SaaS is formed from the three software engineering crown jewels of (1) SaaS on Cloud Computing, (2) Highly Productive Framework and Tools, and (3) Agile Development.

use sidebars to introduce 20 Turing Award winners. (As there is no Nobel Prize in IT, our highest honor is known as the "Nobel Prize of Computing".)

We deliberately chose to keep the book concise, since different readers will want additional detail in different areas. **Links** are provided to the Ruby and Rails online documentation for built-in classes or methods, to Wikipedia for definitions of important concepts you may be unfamiliar with, and to the Web in general for further reading related to the material. If you're using the Interactive Edition or the Kindle edition, the links should be live if you're connected to the Internet; in the print version, the link URIs appear at the end of each chapter.

Lastly, since this Alpha Edition will likely have errors and is missing some content that will be in the final version, as resources permit we will provide *free updates* to the Interactive and Kindle Editions until the Alpha Edition is replaced by a Beta Edition in late 2012. At this time we don't know whether we will generate revised print versions of the Alpha Edition; errata will be online at http://saasbook.info[17].

1.12 Concluding Remarks: Engineering Software is More Than Programming

> *Most software today is very much like an Egyptian pyramid with millions of bricks piled on top of each other, with no structural integrity, but just done by brute force and thousands of slaves.*
> —Alan Kay, *ACM Queue*, 2005

Engineering software shares the assurance and productivity goals and techniques of engineering hardware. However, the long-lasting and evolvable nature of successful software versus the relatively short life of successful computer hardware has led to different development processes. Inspired by hardware development, the Waterfall lifecycle can be best for well-defined and slowly changing hardware and software products. The Agile lifecycle is a much better match to the rapidly changing nature of Software as a Service (SaaS) delivered via Cloud Computing. Following such a software development process increases the chances that your software will be dependable, pleasing to the customer, long lasting, and considered beautiful code by your peers.

Figure 1.6 shows the synergistic relationship between SaaS on Cloud Computing, Highly Productive Frameworks and Tools, and Agile Development, which are the three foundations of this book. SaaS on Cloud Computing is synergistic with Highly Productive Frameworks that exposes design patterns that help SaaS, such Model View Controller (see Chapter 2). Agile Development means continuous progress while working closely with the customer, and SaaS on Clouding Computing enables the customer to use the latest version immediately, thereby closing the feedback loop (see Chapter 4). Highly Productive Frameworks and Tools designed to support Agile development remove obstacles to practicing the methodology (see Chapters 5 and 8). We believe these three "crown jewels" form a "virtuous triangle" that leads to the engineering of beautiful, long-lasting Software as a Service.

This virtuous triangle also helps explain the innovative nature of the Rails community, where new important tools are frequently developed that further improve productivity, simply because it's so easy to do. We fully expect that future editions of this book will include tools not yet invented that are so helpful that we can't imagine how we got our work done without them!

We believe if you learn the contents of this book and use the "bookware" that comes with it, you can build your own (simplified) version of a popular software service like FarmVille or Twitter. Indeed, we're amazed that today you can learn this valuable technology in such a short time; the main reason we wrote this book is help more people become aware of and take advantage of this extraordinary opportunity. While being able to imitate currently successful services and deploy them in the cloud in a few months is impressive, we are even more excited to see what *you* will invent given this new skill set. We look forward to your beautiful code becoming long-lasting and to us becoming some of its passionate fans!

1.13 To Learn More

C. Alexander, S. Ishikawa, and M. Silverstein. *A Pattern Language: Towns, Buildings, Construction (Cess Center for Environmental).* Oxford University Press, 1977. ISBN 0195019199.

M. Armbrust, A. Fox, R. Griffith, A. D. Joseph, R. Katz, A. Konwinski, G. Lee, D. Patterson, A. Rabkin, I. Stoica, and M. Zaharia. A view of cloud computing. *Communications of the ACM (CACM)*, 53(4):50–58, Apr. 2010.

L. A. Barroso and U. Hoelzle. *The Datacenter as a Computer: An Introduction to the Design of Warehouse-Scale Machines (Synthesis Lectures on Computer Architecture).* Morgan and Claypool Publishers, 2009. ISBN 159829556X. URL http://www.amazon.com/Datacenter-Computer-Introduction-Warehouse-Scale-Architecture/dp/159829556X.

M. Fowler. The New Methodology. *martinfowler.com*, 2005. URL http://www.martinfowler.com/articles/newMethodology.html.

A. Hunt and D. Thomas. *The Pragmatic Programmer: From Journeyman to Master.* Addison-Wesley Professional, 1999. ISBN 020161622X. URL http://www.amazon. com/Pragmatic-Programmer-Journeyman-Master/dp/020161622X.

G. Klein, J. Andronick, K. Elphinstone, G. Heiser, D. Cock, P. Derrin, D. Elkaduwe, K. Engelhardt, R. Kolanski, M. Norrish, T. Sewell, H. Tuch, and S. Winwood. seL4: Formal verification of an OS kernel. *Communications of the ACM (CACM)*, 53(6):107–115, June 2010.

D. A. Patterson and J. L. Hennessy. *Computer Organization and Design, Fourth Edition: The Hardware/Software Interface (The Morgan Kaufmann Series in Computer Architecture and Design).* Morgan Kaufmann, 2008. ISBN 0123744938.

Notes

[1]http://swebok.org
[2]http://www.saasbook.info
[3]http://radlab.cs.berkeley.edu
[4]http://www.saas-class.org
[5]http://en.wikipedia.org/wiki/Turing_Award
[6]http://www.youtube.com/watch?v=kYUrqdUyEpI
[7]http://en.wikipedia.org/wiki/Ariane_5_Flight_501
[8]http://en.wikipedia.org/wiki/Therac-25
[9]http://en.wikipedia.org/wiki/Mars_Climate_Orbiter
[10]http://en.wikipedia.org/wiki/Virtual_Case_File
[11]http://developers.slashdot.org/story/08/05/11/1759213/
[12]http://www.fastcompany.com/magazine/06/writestuff.html
[13]http://en.wikipedia.org/wiki/Bit_blit
[14]https://plus.google.com/112678702228711889851/posts/eVeouesvaVX
[15]http://www.pastebin.com/u/saasbook
[16]http://saasbook.info
[17]http://saasbook.info

1.14 Exercises

Exercise 1.1 *(Discussion) In your opinion, how would you rank the software disasters in the first section from most terrible to the least? How did you rank them?*

Exercise 1.2 *(Discussion) The closest hardware failure to the software disasters mentioned in the first section is probably the Intel Floating Point Divide bug[1]. Where would you put this hardware problem in the ranked list of software examples from the exercise above?*

Exercise 1.3 *(Discussion) Measured in lines of code, what is the largest program in the world? For purposes of this exercise, assume it can be a suite of software that is shipped as a single product.*

Exercise 1.4 *(Discussion) Which programming language has the most active programmers?*

Exercise 1.5 *(Discussion) In which programming language is the most number of lines of code written annually? Which has the most lines of active code cumulatively?*

Exercise 1.6 *(Discussion) Make a list of, in your opinion, the Top 10 most important applications. Which would best be developed and maintained using a Waterfall lifecycle versus an Agile lifecycle? List your reasons for each choice.*

Exercise 1.7 *(Discussion) Given the list of Top 10 applications from the exercise above, how important are each of the four productivity techniques listed above?*

Exercise 1.8 *(Discussion) Given the list of Top 10 applications from the exercise above, what aspects might be difficult to test and need to rely on formal methods? Would some testing techniques be more important for some applications than others? State why.*

Exercise 1.9 *(Discussion) What are the top 5 reasons that SaaS and Cloud Computing will grow in popularity and the Top 5 obstacles to its growth?*

2 The Architecture of SaaS Applications

I think the major good idea in Unix was its clean and simple interface: open, close, read, and write.
—*Unix and Beyond: An Interview With Ken Thompson*, IEEE Computer 32(5), May 1999

Dennis Ritchie (left, 1941–2011) and Ken Thompson (right, 1943–) shared the 1983 Turing Award for fundamental contributions to operating systems design in general and the invention of Unix in particular.

Whether creating a new system or preparing to modify an existing one, understanding its architecture at multiple levels is essential. Happily, good software leverages patterns at many levels—proven solutions to similar architectural problems, adapted to the needs of a specific problem. Judicious use of patterns helps simplify design, reveal intent, and compose software components into larger systems. We'll examine the patterns present at various logical layers of SaaS apps, discuss why each pattern was chosen, and where appropriate, note the opportunity cost of not choosing the alternative. Patterns aren't perfect for every problem, but the ability to separate the things that change from those that stay the same is a powerful tool for organizing and implementing large systems.

> 1. A Web client (Firefox) requests the Rotten Potatoes home page from a Web server (WEBrick).
>
> 2. WEBrick obtains content from the Rotten Potatoes app and sends this content back to Firefox
>
> 3. Firefox displays the content and closes the HTTP connection.

Figure 2.1: 100,000-foot view of a SaaS client-server system.

2.1   100,000 Feet: Client-Server Architecture

Since the best way to learn about software is by doing, let's jump in right away. If you haven't done so already, turn to Appendix A and get this book's "bookware" running on your own computer or in the cloud. Once it is ready, Screencast 2.1.1 shows how to deploy and login to your Virtual Machine and try an interaction with the simple educational app Rotten Potatoes, which aspires to be a simplified version of the popular movie-rating Web site RottenTomatoes[2].

> **Screencast 2.1.1: Getting Started.**
> `http://vimeo.com/34754478`
> Once logged in to your VM, the screencast shows how to open a Terminal window, `cd` (change to) the directory `Documents/rottenpotatoes`, and start the Rotten Potatoes app by typing `rails server`. We then opened the Firefox web browser and entered `http://localhost:3000/movies` into the address bar and pressed Return, taking us to the Rotten Potatoes home page.

What's going on? You've just seen the simplest view of a Web app: it is an example of the *client-server architecture*. Firefox is an example of a client: a program whose specialty is asking a server for information and (usually) allowing the user to interact with that information. WEBrick, which you activated by typing `rails server`, is an example of a server: a program whose specialty is waiting for clients to make a *request* and then providing a *reply*. WEBrick waits to be contacted by a Web browser such as Firefox and routes the browser's requests to the Rotten Potatoes app. Figure 2.1 summarizes how a SaaS application works, from 100,000 feet.

Distinguishing clients from servers allows each type of program to be highly specialized to its task: the client can have a responsive and appealing user interface, while the server concentrates on efficiently serving many clients simultaneously. Firefox and other browsers (Chrome, Safari, Internet Explorer) are clients used by millions of people (let's call them *production clients*). WEBrick, on the other hand, is not a production server, but a "mini-server" with just enough functionality to let one user at a time (you, the developer) interact with your Web app. A real Web site would use a production server such as the Apache web server[3] or the Microsoft Internet Information Server[4], either of which can be deployed on hundreds of computers efficiently serving many copies of the same site to millions of users.

Before the Web's open standards were proposed in 1990, users would install separate and mutually-incompatible proprietary clients for each Internet service they used: Eudora (the ancestor of Thunderbird) for reading email, AOL or CompuServe for accessing proprietary content portals (a role filled today by portals like MSN and Yahoo!), and so on. Today, the Web browser has largely supplanted proprietary clients and is justifiably called the "universal client." Nonetheless, the proprietary clients and servers still constitute exam-

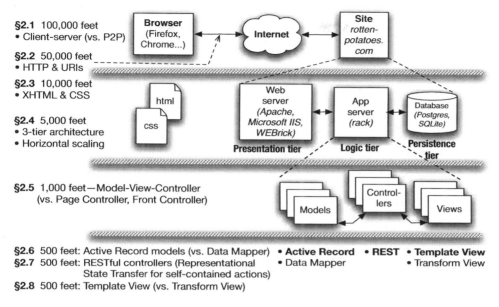

§2.1 100,000 feet
• Client-server (vs. P2P)

§2.2 50,000 feet
• HTTP & URIs

§2.3 10,000 feet
• XHTML & CSS

§2.4 5,000 feet
• 3-tier architecture
• Horizontal scaling

§2.5 1,000 feet—Model-View-Controller
(vs. Page Controller, Front Controller)

§2.6 500 feet: Active Record models (vs. Data Mapper)   • **Active Record**   • **REST**   • **Template View**
§2.7 500 feet: RESTful controllers (Representational   • Data Mapper   • Transform View
            State Transfer for self-contained actions)
§2.8 500 feet: Template View (vs. Transform View)

Figure 2.2: Using altitude as an analogy, this figure illustrates important structures in SaaS at various levels of detail and serves as an overall roadmap of the discussion in this chapter. Each level is discussed in the sections shown.

ples of client-server architecture, with clients specialized for asking questions on behalf of users and servers specialized for answering questions from many clients. Client-server is therefore our first example of a ***design pattern***—a reusable structure, behavior, strategy, or technique that captures a proven solution to a collection of similar problems by *separating the things that change from those that stay the same.* In the case of client-server architectures, what stays the same is the separation of concerns between the client and the server, despite changes across implementations of clients and servers. Because of the Web's ubiquity, we will use the term SaaS to mean "client-server systems built to operate using the open standards of the World Wide Web."

In the past, the client-server architecture implied that the server was a much more complex program than the client. Today, with powerful laptops and Web browsers that support animation and 3D effects, a better characterization might be that clients and servers are comparably complex but have been specialized for their very different roles. In this book we will concentrate on server-centric applications; although we cover some JavaScript client programming in Chapter 6, its context is in support of a server-centric application rather than for building complex in-browser applications such as Google Docs[5].

Of course, client-server isn't the only architectural pattern found in Internet-based services. In the ***peer-to-peer architecture***, used in BitTorrent, every participant is both a client and a server—anyone can ask anyone else for information. In such a system where a single program must behave as both client and server, it's harder to specialize the program to do either job really well.

Summary:

- SaaS Web apps are examples of the ***client-server architectural pattern***, in which client software is typically specialized for interacting with the user and making requests of the server on the user's behalf, and the server software is specialized for handling large volumes of such requests.

- Because Web apps use open standards that anyone can implement royalty-free, in contrast to proprietary standards used by older client-server apps, the Web browser has become the "universal client."

- An alternative to client-server is peer-to-peer, in which all entities act as both clients and servers. While arguably more flexible, this architecture makes it difficult to specialize the software to do either job really well.

Self-Check 2.1.1 *What is the primary difference between a client and a server in SaaS?*
◇ A SaaS client is optimized for allowing the user to interact with information, whereas a SaaS server is optimized for serving many clients simultaneously. ∎

Self-Check 2.1.2 *What element(s) in Figure 2.1 refer to a SaaS client and what element(s) refer to a SaaS server?*
◇ The **Browser** box in the upper-left corner refers to a client. The **html** and **css** document icons refer to content delivered to the client. All other elements are part of the server. ∎

2.2 50,000 Feet: Communication—HTTP and URIs

A ***network protocol*** is a set of communication rules on which agents participating in a network agree. In this case, the agents are Web clients (like Firefox) and Web servers (like WEBrick or Apache). Browsers and Web servers communicate using the ***HyperText Transfer Protocol***, or ***HTTP***. Like many Internet application protocols, HTTP relies on ***TCP/IP***, the venerable ***Transmission Control Protocol/Internet Protocol***, which allows a pair of agents to communicate ordered sequences of bytes. Essentially, TCP/IP allows the communication of arbitrary character strings between a pair of network agents.

Vinton E. "Vint" Cerf (left, 1943–) and Bob Kahn (right, 1938–) shared the 2004 Turing Award for their pioneering work on networking architecture and protocols, including TCP/IP.

In a TCP/IP network, each computer has an ***IP address*** consisting of four bytes separated by dots, such as 128.32.244.172. Most of the time we don't use IP addresses directly—another Internet service called ***Domain Name System*** (***DNS***), which has its own protocol based on TCP/IP, is automatically invoked to map easy-to-remember ***hostnames*** like www.eecs.berkeley.edu to IP addresses. Browsers automatically contact a DNS server to look up the site name you type in the address bar, such as www.eecs.berkeley.edu, and get the actual IP address, in this case 128.32.244.172. A convention used by TCP/IP-compatible computers is that if a program running on a computer refers to the name localhost, it is referring to the very computer it's running on. That is why typing localhost into Firefox's address bar at the beginning of Section 2.1 caused Firefox to communicate with the WEBrick process running on the same computer as Firefox itself.

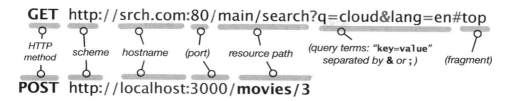

Figure 2.3: An HTTP request consists of an *HTTP method* plus a *URI*. A *full URI* begins with a scheme such as http **or** https **and includes the above components. Optional components are in parentheses. A *partial URI* omits any or all of the leftmost components, in which case those components are filled in or *resolved* relative to a *base URI* determined by the specific application. Best practice is to use full URIs.**

■ *Elaboration: Networking: multi-homing, IPv6 and HTTPS.*

We have simplified some aspects of TCP/IP: technically each ***network interface*** device has an IP address, and some ***multi-homed*** computers may have multiple network interfaces. Also, for various reasons including the exhaustion of the address space of IP numbers, the current version of IP (version 4) is slowly being phased out in favor of version 6 (IPv6), which uses a different format for addresses. However, since most computers have only one network interface active at a time and SaaS app writers rarely deal directly with IP addresses, these simplifications don't materially alter our explanations. We also defer discussion of the Secure HTTP protocol (HTTPS) until Chapter 10. HTTPS uses ***public-key cryptography*** to encrypt (encode) communication between an HTTP client and server, so that an eavesdropper sees only gibberish. From a programmer's point of view, HTTPS behaves like HTTP, but only works if the Web server has been configured to support HTTPS access to certain pages. "Mini" servers like WEBrick typically don't support it.

What about the :3000 we appended to localhost in the example? Multiple agents on a network can be running at the same IP address. Indeed, in the example above, both the client and server were running on your own computer. Therefore, TCP/IP uses ***port numbers*** from 1 to 65535 to distinguish different network agents at the same IP address. All protocols based on TCP/IP, including HTTP, must specify both the host and port number when opening a connection. When you directed Firefox to go to localhost:3000/movies, you were indicating that on the computer called localhost (that is, "this computer"), a server program was monitoring port 3000 waiting for browsers to contact it. If we didn't specify the port number (3000) explicitly, it would default to 80 for http or 443 for https (secure) connections.

> **The IANA.** The Internet Assigned Numbers Authority[6] assigns official default port numbers for various protocols and manages the top-level or "root" zone of DNS.

To summarize, communication in HTTP is initiated when one agent *opens a connection* to another agent by specifying a hostname and port number; an HTTP server process must be *listening for connections* on that host and port number.

The string http://localhost:3000/movies that you typed into Firefox's address bar is a ***URI***, or ***Uniform Resource Identifier***. A URI begins with the name of the communication *scheme* by which the information may be retrieved, followed by a hostname, optional port number, and a *resource* on that host that the user wants to retrieve. A resource generally means "anything that can be delivered to the browser": an image, the list of all movies in HTML format, and a form submission that creates a new movie are all examples of resources. Each SaaS application has its own rules for interpreting the resource name, though we will soon see one proposal called REST that strives for simplicity and consistency in resource naming across different SaaS apps.

> **URI or URL?** URIs are sometimes referred to as URLs, or Uniform Resource Locators. Despite subtle technical distinctions, for our purposes the terms can be used interchangeably. We use URI because it is more general and matches the terminology used by most libraries.

HTTP is a ***stateless protocol*** because every HTTP request is independent of and unre-

1. A Web client (Firefox) requests the Rotten Potatoes home page from a Web server (WEBrick).
   a) Firefox constructs an HTTP request using the URI *http://localhost:3000* to contact an HTTP server (WEBrick) listening on port 3000 on the same computer as Firefox itself (*localhost*).
   b) WEBrick, listening on port 3000, receives the HTTP request for the resource '/movies' (the list of all movies in Rotten Potatoes).

2. WEBrick obtains content from the Rotten Potatoes app and sends this content back to Firefox

3. Firefox displays the content and closes the HTTP connection.

Figure 2.4: At 50,000 feet, we can expand Step 1 from Figure 2.1.

lated to all previous requests. A web app that keeps track of "where you are" (Have you logged in yet? What step of the checkout process are you on?) must have its own mechanisms for doing so, since nothing about an HTTP request remembers this information. HTTP *cookies* associate a particular user's browser with information held at the server corresponding to that user's *session*, but it is the browser's responsibility, not HTTP's or the SaaS app's, to make sure the right cookies are included with each HTTP request. Stateless protocols therefore simplify server design at the expense of application design, but happily, successful frameworks such as Rails shield you from much of this complexity.

Screencast 2.2.1: Cookies.
`http://vimeo.com/33918630`
Cookies are used to establish that two independent requests actually originated from the same user's browser, and can therefore be thought of as part of a session. On the first visit to a site, the server includes a long string (up to 4 KBytes) with the `Set-Cookie:` HTTP response header. It is the browser's responsibility to include this string with the `Cookie:` HTTP request header on subsequent requests to that site. The cookie string, which is intended to be opaque to the user, contains enough information for the server to associate the request with the same user session.

We can now express what's happening when you load the Rotten Potatoes home page in slightly more precise terms, as Figure 2.4 shows.

To drill down further, we'll next look at how the content itself is represented.

Summary

- Web browsers and servers communicate using the ***HyperText Transfer Protocol***. HTTP relies on ***TCP/IP*** (Transmission Control Protocol/Internet Protocol), which lets computers of different types and on different networks reliably exchange ordered sequences of bytes.

- Each computer connected to a TCP/IP network has an ***IP address*** consisting of four numbers separated by dots, as in 128.32.244.172. The ***Domain Name System*** (DNS) allows the use of human-friendly names such as *fullsail.cs.berkeley.edu* in place of IP addresses. The special name `localhost` refers to the local computer and resolves to the special IP address 127.0.0.1.

- To distinguish which of many applications running on a particular computer is the intended recipient of a TCP/IP communication, each application *listens* on a particular ***TCP port***, numbered from 1 to 65535 ($2^{16} - 1$). Port 80 is used by HTTP (Web) servers.

- To run a SaaS app locally, you can activate an HTTP server listening on a port on `localhost`. WEBrick, the lightweight server included with Rails, uses port 3000 by default.

- A ***Uniform Resource Identifier*** (URI) names a resource available on the Internet, including the communication scheme that should be used to retrieve the resource (such as HTTP), the name of the server from which the resource is available, and the resource name, whose interpretation varies from application to application.

- HTTP is a stateless protocol in that every request is independent of every other request, even from the same user. ***HTTP cookies*** were invented to allow the association of HTTP requests from the same user. It is the browser's responsibility to accept a cookie from an HTTP server and ensure that the cookie is included with every future request sent to that server.

■ *Elaboration: Client Pull vs. Server Push.*

The Web is primarily a *client pull* client-server architecture because the client initiates all interactions—HTTP servers can only wait for clients to contact them. This is because HTTP was designed as a ***request-reply protocol***: only clients can initiate anything. Evolving standards, including WebSockets and HTML5, have some support for allowing the server to *push* updated content to the client. In contrast, true *server push* architectures, such as text messaging on cell phones, allow the server to initiate a connection to the client to "wake it up" when new information is available; but these cannot use HTTP. An early criticism of the Web's architecture was that a pure request-reply protocol would rule out such ***push-based*** applications, but in practice, the high efficiency of specialized server software supports creating Web pages that frequently *poll* (check in with) the server to receive updates, giving the user the illusion of a push-based application even without the features proposed in WebSockets and HTML5.

Self-Check 2.2.1 *What happens if we visit the URI* `http://google.com:3000` *and why?*

⋄ The connection will eventually "time out" unable to contact a server, because Google (like almost all Web sites) listens on TCP port 80 (the default) rather than 3000. ∎

Self-Check 2.2.2 *What happens if we try to access Rotten Potatoes at (say)* `http://localhost:3300` *(instead of* `:3000`*) and why?*

⋄ You get a "connection refused" since nothing is listening on port 3300. ∎

2.3   10,000 feet: Representation—HTML and CSS

If the Web browser is the universal client, ***HTML***, the HyperText Markup Language, is the universal language. A ***markup language*** combines text with markup (annotations about the text) in a way that makes it easy to syntactically distinguish the two. Watch Screencast 2.3.1 for some highlights of HTML 5, the current version of the language, then continue reading.

Screencast 2.3.1: HTML Introduction.
`http://vimeo.com/34754506`
HTML consists of a hierarchy of nested elements, each of which consists of an opening tag such as `<p>`, a content part (in some cases), and a closing tag such as `</p>`. Most opening tags can also have attributes, as in `<a href="http://...">`. Some tags that don't have a content part are self-closing, such as `<br clear="both"/>` for a line break that clears both left and right margins.

There is an unfortunate and confusing mess of terminology surrounding the lineage of HTML[7]. HTML 5 includes features of both its predecessors (HTML versions 1 through 4) and XHTML (eXtended HyperText Markup Language), which is a subset of ***XML***, an eXtensible Markup Language that can be used both to represent data and to describe other markup languages. Indeed, XML is a common data representation for exchanging information *between* two services in a Service-Oriented Architecture, as we'll see in Chapter 5 when we extend Rotten Potatoes to retrieve movie information from a separate movie database service. The differences among the variants of XHTML and HTML are difficult to keep straight, and not all browsers support all versions. Unless otherwise noted, from now on when we say HTML we mean HTML 5, and we will try to avoid using features that aren't widely supported.

> The use of angle brackets for tags comes from **SGML** (Standard Generalized Markup Language), a codified standardization of IBM's General Markup Language, developed in the 1960s for encoding computer-readable project documents.

Of particular interest are the HTML tag attributes `id` and `class`, because they figure heavily into connecting the HTML structure of a page with its visual appearance. The following screencast illustrates the use of Firefox's Web Developer toolbar to quickly identify the ID's and Classes of HTML elements on a page.

Screencast 2.3.2: Inspecting the ID and Class attributes.
`http://vimeo.com/34754568`
CSS uses ***selector notations*** such as `div#`*name* to indicate a `div` element whose `id` is *name* and `div.`*name* to indicate a `div` element with class *name*. Only one element in an HTML document can have a given `id`, whereas many elements (even of different tag types) can share the same `class`. All three aspects of an element—its tag type, its `id` (if it has one), and its `class` attributes (if it has any)—can be used to identify an element as a candidate for visual formatting.

As the next screencast shows, the ***CSS*** (***Cascading Style Sheets***) standard allows us to associate visual "styling" instructions with HTML elements by using the elements' classes

Selector	What is selected
h1	Any h1 element
div#message	The div whose ID is message
.red	Any element with class red
div.red, h1	The div with class red, or any h1
div#message h1	An h1 element that's a child of (inside of) div#message
a.lnk	a element with class lnk
a.lnk:hover	a element with class lnk, when hovered over

Attribute	Example values
font-family	"Times, serif"
font-weight	bold
font-size	14pt, 125%, 12px
font-style	italic
color	black
margin	4px
background-color	red, #c2eed6 (RGB values)
border	1px solid blue
text-align	right
text-decoration	underline
vertical-align	middle
padding	1cm

Figure 2.5: A few CSS constructs, including those explained in Screencast 2.3.3. The top table shows some CSS *selectors*, which identify the elements to be styled; the bottom table shows a few of the many attributes, whose names are usually self-explanatory, and example values they can be assigned. Not all attributes are valid on all elements.

and IDs. The screencast covers only a few basic CSS constructs, which are summarized in Figure 2.5. The Resources section at the end of the chapter lists sites and books that describe CSS in great detail, including how to use CSS for aligning content on a page, something designers used to do manually with HTML tables.

For an extreme example of how much can be done with CSS, visit the CSS Zen Garden[8].

Screencast 2.3.3: Introduction to CSS.
http://vimeo.com/34754607
There are four basic mechanisms by which a selector in a CSS file can match an HTML element: by tag name, by class, by ID, and by hierarchy. If multiple selectors match a given element, the rules for which properties to apply are complex, so most designers try to avoid such ambiguities by keeping their CSS simple. A useful way to see the "bones" of a page is to select *CSS>Disable Styles>All Styles* from the Firefox Web Developer toolbar. This will display the page with all CSS formatting turned off, showing the extent to which CSS can be used to separate visual appearance from logical structure.

Using this new information, Figure 2.6 expands steps 2 and 3 from the previous section's summary of how SaaS works.

1. A Web client (Firefox) requests the Rotten Potatoes home page from a Web server (WEBrick).
   a) Firefox constructs an HTTP request using the URI ***http://localhost:3000*** to contact an HTTP
      server (WEBrick) listening on port 3000 on the same computer as Firefox itself (***localhost***).
   b) WEBrick, listening on port 3000, receives the HTTP request for the resource '/movies' (the list of
      all movies in Rotten Potatoes).

2. WEBrick obtains content from the Rotten Potatoes app and sends this content back to Firefox
   a) WEBrick returns content encoded in HTML, again using HTTP. The HTML may contain references
      to other kinds of media such as images to embed in the displayed page. The HTML may also
      contain a reference to a CSS stylesheet containing formatting information describing the desired
      visual attributes of the page (font sizes, colors, layout, and so on).

3. Firefox displays the content and closes the HTTP connection.
   a) Firefox fetches any referenced assets (CSS, images, and so on) by repeating the previous four
      steps as needed but providing the URIs of the desired assets as referenced in the HTML page.
   b) Firefox displays the page according to the CSS formatting directives and including any referenced
      assets such as embedded images.

Figure 2.6: SaaS from 10,000 feet. Compared to Figure 2.4, step 2 has been expanded to describe the content returned by the Web server, and step 3 has been expanded to describe the role of CSS in how the Web browser renders the content.

Summary

- An ***HTML*** (HyperText Markup Language) document consists of a hierarchically nested collection of elements. Each element begins with a ***tag*** in <angle brackets> that may have optional ***attributes***. Some elements enclose content.

- A ***selector*** is an expression that identifies one or more HTML elements in a document by using a combination of the element name (such as body), element id (an element attribute that must be unique on a page), and element class (an attribute that need not be unique on a page).

- ***Cascading Style Sheets*** (CSS) is a markup language describing visual attributes of elements on a Web page. A stylesheet associates sets of visual properties with selectors. A special link element inside the head element of an HTML document associates a stylesheet with that document.

- The Firefox Web Developer toolbar is invaluable in peeking under the hood to examine both the structure of a page and its stylesheets.

Self-Check 2.3.1 *True or false: every HTML element must have an ID.*

◇ False—the ID is optional, though must be unique if provided. ∎

Self-Check 2.3.2 *Given the following HTML markup:*

```
<p class="x" id="i"> I hate <span>Mondays</span> </p>
<p> but <span class="y">Tuesdays</span> are OK. </p>
```

Write down a CSS selector that will select only *the word* Mondays *for styling.*

◇ Three possibilities, from most specific to least specific, are: **#i span**, **p.x span**, and

.x span. **p#i span** and **p#i.x span** are redundant since at most one element can have the ID **i**. ■

Self-Check 2.3.3 *In Self-Check 2.3.2, why are* **span** *and* **p span** *not* *valid answers?*
◇ Both of those selector also match *Tuesdays*, which is a **span** inside a **p**. ■

Self-Check 2.3.4 *What is the most common way to associate a CSS stylesheet with an HTML or HTML document? (HINT: refer to the earlier screencast example.)*

◇ Within the HEAD element of the HTML or HTML document, include a LINK element with at least the following three attributes: REL="STYLESHEET", TYPE="text/css", and HREF="*uri*", where *uri* is the full or partial URI of the stylesheet. That is, the stylesheet must be accessible as a resource named by a URI. ■

2.4 5,000 Feet: 3-Tier Architecture & Horizontal Scaling

So far we've seen how the client communicates with the server and how the information they exchange is represented, but we haven't said anything about the server itself. Moving back to the server side of Figure 2.2 and zooming in for additional detail on the second level, Web apps are structured as three logical *tiers*. The ***presentation tier*** usually consists of an ***HTTP server*** (or simply "***Web server***"), which accepts requests from the outside world (i.e., users) and usually serves static assets. We've been using WEBrick to fulfill that role.

The web server forwards requests for dynamic content to the ***logic tier***, where the actual application runs that generates dynamic content. The application is typically supported by an ***application server*** whose job is to hide the low-level mechanics of HTTP from the app writer. For example, an app server can route incoming HTTP requests directly to appropriate pieces of code in your app, saving you from having to listen for and parse incoming HTTP requests. Modern application servers support one or more ***Web application frameworks*** that simplify creation of a particular class of Web applications in a particular language. We will be using the Rails framework and the Rack application server, which comes with Rails. WEBrick can "speak" to Rack directly; other Web servers such as Apache require additional software modules to do so. If you were writing in PHP, Python, or Java, you would use an application server that handles code written in those languages. For example, Google AppEngine, which runs Python and Java applications, has proprietary middleware that bridges your app's Python or Java code to the Google-operated infrastructure that faces the outside world.

> Because application servers sit between the Web server (presentation tier) and your actual app code, they are sometimes referred to as ***middleware***.

Finally, since HTTP is stateless, application data that must remain stored across HTTP requests, such as session data and users' login and profile information, is stored in the ***persistence tier***. Popular choices for the persistence tier have traditionally been databases such as the open-source MySQL or PostgreSQL, although prior to their proliferation, commercial databases such as Oracle or IBM DB2 were also popular choices.

The "tiers" in the three-tier model are *logical* tiers. On a site with little content and low traffic, the software in all three tiers might run on a single physical computer. In fact, Rotten Potatoes has been doing just this: its presentation tier is just WEBrick, and its persistence tier is a simple open-source database called SQLite, which stores its information directly in files on your local computer. In production, it's more common for each tier to span one or more physical computers. As Figure 2.7 shows, in a typical site, incoming HTTP requests

> **LAMP.** Early SaaS sites were created using the Perl scripting language and PHP framework, whose availability coincided with the early success of Linux, an open-source operating system, and MySQL, an open-source database. Thousands of sites are still powered by the *LAMP Stack*—Linux, Apache, MySQL, PHP, or Perl.

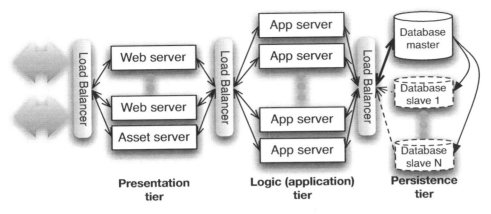

Figure 2.7: The 3-tier *shared-nothing* architecture, so called because entities within a tier generally do not communicate with each other, allows adding computers to each tier independently to match demand. *Load balancers*, which distribute workload evenly, can be either hardware appliances or specially-configured Web servers. The statelessness of HTTP makes shared-nothing possible: since all requests are independent, any server in the presentation or logic tier can be assigned to any request. However, scaling the persistence tier is much more challenging, as the text explains.

are directed to one of several Web servers, which in turn select one of several available application servers to handle dynamic-content generation, allowing computers to be added or removed from each tier as needed to handle demand.

However, as the Fallacies and Pitfalls section explains, making the persistence layer shared-nothing is much more complicated. Figure 2.7 shows the ***master-slave*** approach, used when the database is read much more frequently than it is written: any slave can perform reads, only the master can perform writes, and the master updates the slaves with the results of writes as quickly as possible. However, in the end, this technique only postpones the scaling problem rather than solving it. As one of Heroku's[9] founders wrote:

> *A question I'm often asked about Heroku is: "How do you scale the SQL database?" There's a lot of things I can say about using caching, sharding, and other techniques to take load off the database. But the actual answer is: we don't. SQL databases are fundamentally non-scalable, and there is no magical pixie dust that we, or anyone, can sprinkle on them to suddenly make them scale.* —Adam Wiggins, Heroku[10]

We can now add one more level of detail to our explanation; step 2a is new in Figure 2.8.

1. A Web client (Firefox) requests the Rotten Potatoes home page from a Web server (WEBrick).
   a) Firefox constructs an HTTP request using the URI ***http://localhost:3000*** to contact an HTTP
      server (WEBrick) listening on port 3000 on the same computer as Firefox itself (***localhost***).
   b) WEBrick, listening on port 3000, receives the HTTP request for the resource '/movies' (the list of
      all movies in Rotten Potatoes).

2. WEBrick obtains content from the Rotten Potatoes app and sends this content back to Firefox
   a) Via the Rack middleware (written in Ruby), WEBrick calls Rotten Potatoes code in the application
      tier. This code generates the page content using movie information stored in the persistence tier
      implemented by a SQLite database using local files.
   b) WEBrick returns content encoded in HTML, again using HTTP. The HTML may contain references
      to other kinds of media such as images to embed in the displayed page. The HTML may also
      contain a reference to a CSS stylesheet containing formatting information describing the desired
      visual attributes of the page (font sizes, colors, layout, and so on).

3. Firefox displays the content and closes the HTTP connection.
   a) Firefox fetches any referenced assets (CSS, images, and so on) by repeating the previous four
      steps as needed but providing the URIs of the desired assets as referenced in the HTML page.
   b) Firefox displays the page according to the CSS formatting directives and including any referenced
      assets such as embedded images.

**Figure 2.8: SaaS from 5,000 feet. Compared to Figure 2.6, step 2a has been inserted, describing the actions of the SaaS
server in terms of the three-tier architecture.**

Summary

- The three-tier architecture includes a presentation tier, which renders views and
  interacts with the user; a logic tier, which runs SaaS app code; and a persistence
  tier, which stores app data.

- HTTP's statelessness allows the presentation and logic tiers to be ***shared-
  nothing***, so cloud computing can be used to add more computers to each tier
  as demand requires. However, the persistence tier is harder to scale.

- Depending on the scale (size) of the deployment, more than 1 tier may be hosted
  on a single computer, or a single tier may require many computers.

■ Elaboration: Why Databases?

While the earliest Web apps sometimes manipulated files directly for storing data, there are
two reasons why databases overwhelmingly took over this role very early. First, databases
have historically provided high *durability* for stored information—the guarantee that once
something has been stored, unexpected events such as system crashes or transient data cor-
ruption won't cause data loss. For a Web app storing millions of users' data, this guarantee
is critical. Second, databases store information in a structured format—in the case of ***relational databases***, by far the most popular type, each kind of object is stored in a table whose
rows represent object instances and whose columns represent object properties. This organization is a good fit for the structured data that many Web apps manipulate. Interestingly,
today's largest Web apps, such as Facebook, have grown so far beyond the scale for which
relational databases were designed that they are being forced to look at alternatives to the
long-reigning relational database.

Self-Check 2.4.1 *Explain why cloud computing might have had a lesser impact on SaaS if most SaaS apps didn't follow the shared-nothing architecture.*

◇ Cloud computing allows easily adding and removing computers while paying only for what you use, but it is the shared-nothing architecture that makes it straightforward to "absorb" the new computers into a running app and "release" them when no longer needed. ∎

Self-Check 2.4.2 *In the ____ tier of three-tier SaaS apps, scaling is much more complicated than just adding computers.*

◇ Persistence tier ∎

2.5   1,000 Feet: Model-View-Controller Architecture

So far we've said nothing about the structure of the app code in Rotten Potatoes. In fact, just as we used the client-server architectural pattern to characterize the "100,000-foot view" of SaaS, we can use an architectural pattern called ***Model-View-Controller*** (usually shortened to MVC) to characterize the "1,000-foot view."

An application organized according to MVC consists of three main types of code. ***Models*** are concerned with the data manipulated by the application: how to store it, how to operate on it, and how to change it. An MVC app typically has a model for each type of entity manipulated by the app. In our simplified Rotten Potatoes app, there is only a Movie model, but we'll be adding others later. Because models deal with the application's data, they contain the code that communicates with the storage tier.

Views are presented to the user and contain information about the models with which users can interact. The views serve as the interface between the system's users and its data; for example, in Rotten Potatoes you can list movies and add new movies by clicking on links or buttons in the views. There is only one kind of model in Rotten Potatoes, but it is associated with a variety of views: one view lists all the movies, another view shows the details of a particular movie, and yet other views appear when creating new movies or editing existing ones.

Finally, ***controllers*** mediate the interaction in both directions: when a user interacts with a view (e.g. by clicking something on a Web page), a specific controller ***action*** corresponding to that user activity is invoked. Each controller corresponds to one model, and in Rails, each controller action is handled by a particular Ruby method within that controller. The controller can ask the model to retrieve or modify information; depending on the results of doing this, the controller decides what view will be presented next to the user, and supplies that view with any necessary information. Since Rotten Potatoes has only one model (Movies), it also has only one controller, the Movies controller. The actions defined in that controller can handle each type of user interaction with any Movie view (clicking on links or buttons, for example) and contain the necessary logic to obtain Model data to *render* any of the Movie views.

Given that SaaS apps have always been view-centric and have always relied on a persistence tier, Rails' choice of MVC as the underlying architecture might seem like an obvious fit. But other choices are possible, such as those in Figure 2.9 excerpted from Martin Fowler's *Catalog of Patterns of Enterprise Application Architecture*[11]. Apps consisting of mostly static content with only a small amount of dynamically-generated content, such as a weather site, might choose the *Template View* pattern. The *Page Controller* pattern works well for an application that is easily structured as a small number of distinct pages,

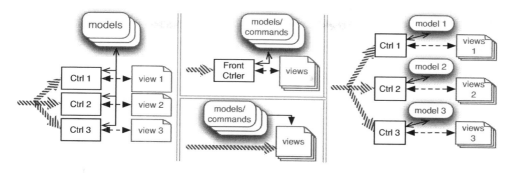

Figure 2.9: Comparing Web app architectural patterns. Models are rounded rectangles, controllers are rectangles, and views are document icons. Page Controller (left), used by Sinatra, has a controller for each logical page of the app. Front Controller (top center), used by Java 2 Enterprise Edition (J2EE) servlets, has a single controller that relies on methods in a variety of models to generate one of a collection of views. Template View (bottom center), used by PHP and Django, emphasizes building the app around the views, with logic in the models generating dynamic content in place of part of the views; the controller is implicit in the framework. Model-View-Controller (right), used by Rails and Java Spring, associates a controller and a set of views with each model type.

effectively giving each page its own simple controller that only knows how to generate that page. For an application that takes a user through a sequence of pages (such as signing up for a mailing list) but has few models, the *Front Controller* pattern might suffice, in which a single controller handles all incoming requests rather than separate controllers handling requests for each model.

Figure 2.10 summarizes our latest understanding of the structure of a SaaS app.

Summary

- The **Model-View-Controller** or MVC design pattern distinguishes *models* that implement business logic, *views* that present information to the user and allow the user to interact with the app, and *controllers* that mediate the interaction between views and models.

- In MVC SaaS apps, every user action that can be performed on a web page—clicking a link or button, submitting a fill-in form, or using drag-and-drop—is eventually handled by some controller action, which will consult the model(s) as needed to obtain information and generate a view in response.

- MVC is appropriate for interactive SaaS apps with a variety of model types, where it makes sense to situate controllers and views along with each type of model. Other architectural patterns may be more appropriate for smaller apps with fewer models or a smaller repertoire of operations.

Self-Check 2.5.1 *Which tier(s) in the three-tier architecture are involved in handling each of the following: (a) models, (b) controllers, (c) views?*

◇ (a) models: logic and persistence tiers; (b) controllers: logic and presentation tiers; (c) views: logic and presentation tiers. ∎

1. A Web client (Firefox) requests the Rotten Potatoes home page from a Web server (WEBrick).
   a) Firefox constructs an HTTP request using the URI *http://localhost:3000* to contact an HTTP
      server (WEBrick) listening on port 3000 on the same computer as Firefox itself (*localhost*).
   b) WEBrick, listening on port 3000, receives the HTTP request for the resource '/movies' (the list of
      all movies in Rotten Potatoes).

2. WEBrick obtains content from the Rotten Potatoes app and sends this content back to Firefox
   a) Via the Rack middleware (written in Ruby), WEBrick calls Rotten Potatoes code in the application
      tier. This code generates the page content using movie information stored in the persistence tier
      implemented by a SQLite database using local files.
      i) Rack routes the request to the *index* action of the Movies controller; the resource named by
          this route is the list of all movies
      ii) The Ruby function implementing the *index* action in the Movies controller asks the *Movie*
          model for a list of movies and associated attributes.
      iii) If successful, the controller identifies a View that contains the HTML markup for presenting the
          list of movies, and passes it the movie information so that an HTML page can be constructed.
          If it fails, the controller identifies a View that displays an error message.
      iv) Rack passes the constructed view to WEBrick, which sends it back to Firefox as the HTTP
          reply.
   b) WEBrick returns content encoded in HTML, again using HTTP. The HTML may contain references
      to other kinds of media such as images to embed in the displayed page. The HTML may also
      contain a reference to a CSS stylesheet containing formatting information describing the desired
      visual attributes of the page (font sizes, colors, layout, and so on).

3. Firefox displays the content and closes the HTTP connection.
   a) Firefox fetches any referenced assets (CSS, images, and so on) by repeating the previous four
      steps as needed but providing the URIs of the desired assets as referenced in the HTML page.
   b) Firefox displays the page according to the CSS formatting directives and including any referenced
      assets such as embedded images.

Figure 2.10: Step 2a has been expanded to show the role of the MVC architecture in fulfilling a SaaS app request.

id	title	rating	release_date	description
1	Gone with the Wind	G	1939-12-15	An American classic ...
2	Casablanca	PG	1942-11-26	Casablanca is a...

Figure 2.11: A possible RDBMS table for storing movie information. The `id` column gives each row's *primary key* or permanent and unique identifier. Most databases can be configured to assign primary keys automatically in various ways; Rails uses the very common convention of assigning integers in increasing order.

2.6 500 Feet: Active Record for Models

How do the models, views, and controllers actually do their jobs? Again, we can go far by describing them in terms of patterns.

Every nontrivial application needs to store and manipulate persistent data. Whether using a database, a plain file, or other persistent storage location, we need a way to convert between the data structures or objects manipulated by the application code and the way that data is stored. In the version of Rotten Potatoes used in this chapter, the only persistent data is information about movies. Each movie's *attributes* include its title, release date, MPAA rating, and short "blurb" summarizing the movie. A naive approach might be to store the movie information in a plain text file, with one line of the file corresponding to one movie and attributes separated by commas:

http://pastebin.com/5c3KvzSB

```
1 Gone with the Wind,G,1939-12-15,An American classic ...
2 Casablanca,PG,1942-11-26,Casablanca is a classic and...
```

To retrieve movie information, we would read each line of the file and splitting it into *fields* at the commas. Of course we will run into a problem with the movie *Food, Inc.* whose title contains a comma:

http://pastebin.com/sMc3i5ru

```
1 Food, Inc.,PG,2008-09-07,The current method of raw...
```

We might try to fix this by surrounding each field with quote marks:

http://pastebin.com/2uPcmpmm

```
1 "Food, Inc.","PG","2008-09-07","The current method of raw..."
```

...which will be fine until we try to enter the movie *Waiting for "Superman"*. As this example shows, devising even a simple storage format involves tricky pitfalls, and would require writing code to convert an in-memory object to our storage representation (called ***marshalling*** or ***serializing*** the object) and vice versa (*unmarshalling* or *deserializing*).

Fortunately, the need to persist objects is so common that several design patterns have evolved to fulfill it. A subset of these patterns makes use of ***structured storage***—storage systems that allow you to simply specify the desired structure of stored objects rather than writing explicit code to create that structure, and in some cases, to specify relationships connecting objects of different types. *Relational database management systems* (RDBMSs) evolved in the early 1970s as elegant structured storage systems whose design was based on a formalism for representing structure and relationships. We will discuss RDBMSs in more detail later, but in brief, an RDBMS stores a collection of *tables*, each of which stores entities with a common set of *attributes*. One row in the table corresponds to one entity, and the columns in that row correspond to the attribute values for that entity. The `movies` table for Rotten Potatoes includes columns for `title`, `rating`, `release_date`, and `description`, and the rows of the table look like Figure 2.11.

Since it is the responsibility of the Models to manage the application's data, some

Edgar F. "Ted" Codd (1923–2003) received the 1981 Turing Award for inventing the ***relational algebra*** formalism underlying relational databases.

correspondence must be established between the operations on a model object in memory (for example, an object representing a movie) and how it is represented and manipulated in the storage tier. The in-memory object is usually represented by a class that, among other things, provides a way to represent the object's attributes, such as the title and rating in the case of a movie. The choice made by the Rails framework is to use the *Active Record architectural pattern*. In this pattern, a single instance of a model class (in our case, the entry for a single movie) corresponds to a single row in a specific table of an RDBMS. The model object has built-in behaviors that directly operate on the database representation of the object:

- Create a new row in the table (representing a new object),

- Read an existing row into a single object instance,

- Update an existing row with new attribute values from a modified object instance,

- Delete a row (destroying the object's data forever).

This collection of four commands is often abbreviated **CRUD**. Later we will add the ability for moviegoers to indicate their favorite movies, so there will be a one-to-many relationship or *association* between a moviegoer and her favorites; Active Record exploits existing mechanisms in the RDBMS based on foreign keys (which we'll learn about later) to make it easy to implement these associations on the in-memory objects.

Summary

- One important job of the Model in an MVC SaaS app is to persist data, which requires converting between the in-memory representation of an object and its representation in permanent storage.

- Various design patterns have evolved to meet this requirement, many of them making use of structured storage such as Relational Database Management Systems (RDBMSs) to simplify not only the storage of model data but the maintenance of relationships among models.

- The four basic operations supported by RDBMSs are Create, Read, Update, Delete (abbreviated CRUD).

- In the ActiveRecord design pattern, every model knows how to do the CRUD operations for its type of object. The Rails ActiveRecord library provides rich functionality for SaaS apps to use this pattern.

Self-Check 2.6.1 *Which of the following are examples of structured storage: (a) an Excel spreadsheet, (b) a plain text file containing the text of an email message, (c) a text file consisting of names, with exactly one name per line.*

◇ (a) and (c) are structured, since an app reading those files can make assumptions about how to interpret the content based on structure alone. (b) is unstructured. ■

http://pastebin.com/rUdNKBRE

```
1 │ I    GET    /movies          {:action=>"index",   :controller=>"movies"}
2 │ C    POST   /movies          {:action=>"create",  :controller=>"movies"}
3 │      GET    /movies/new      {:action=>"new",     :controller=>"movies"}
4 │      GET    /movies/:id/edit {:action=>"edit",    :controller=>"movies"}
5 │ R    GET    /movies/:id      {:action=>"show",    :controller=>"movies"}
6 │ U    PUT    /movies/:id      {:action=>"update",  :controller=>"movies"}
7 │ D DELETE    /movies/:id      {:action=>"destroy", :controller=>"movies"}
```

Figure 2.12: The routes recognized by Rotten Potatoes, with the optional (`.:format`) tokens removed for clarity (see the Elaboration at the end of this section), showing which CRUD action each route represents. The additional I action is for Index, which lists members of collection. The rightmost column shows which Rails controller and which action (method) in that controller are called when a request matches the given URI and HTTP method.

2.7 500 feet: Routes, Controllers, and REST

Active Record gives each model the knowledge of how to create, read, update, and delete instances of itself in the database (CRUD). Recall from Section 2.5 that in the MVC pattern, controller actions mediate the user's Web browser interactions that cause CRUD requests, and in Rails, each controller action is handled by a particular Ruby method in a controller file. Therefore, each incoming HTTP request must be mapped to the appropriate controller and method. In Rails, this mapping is called a ***route***.

In an unfortunate collision of terminology, an HTTP request is characterized by both its URI and the ***HTTP method*** used for the request, as we saw in Figure 2.3. The HTTP standard defines various methods including GET, POST, PUT, and DELETE. When discussing routes and controllers, to avoid confusion we will use *method* to mean the HTTP method portion of a request and *controller action* or simply *action* to mean the Ruby code (method) that handles a particular kind of request.

A route, then, associates a URI plus an HTTP method with a particular controller file and action. The HTTP standard defines a number of methods including GET, POST, PUT, and DELETE, which Rails uses in defining routes. Although Web browsers only implement GET when you follow a link and POST when you click the Submit button on a fill-in form, Rails works around this inconvenience and allows using all four methods in our routes. The route mappings are generated by code in the file `config/routes.rb`, which we'll learn about in Chapter 3. In the Terminal window, make sure you are in the `rottenpotatoes` directory and type the command `rake routes` to show what routes are defined for Rotten Potatoes. Figure 2.12 explains the output. In a displayed URI such as `/movies/:id`, the tokens beginning with ':' act like wildcards, with `:id` representing the id attribute (primary key) of a model instance. For example, the route GET `/movies/8` will match line 5 of Figure 2.12 with `:id` having the value 8; therefore it is a request for an HTML page that shows details for the movie whose ID in the Movies table is 8, if such a movie exists.

> Actually, most browsers also implement HEAD, which requests metadata about a resource, but we needn't worry about that here.

> `rake` runs maintenance tasks defined in Rotten Potatoes' `Rakefile`. `rake --help` shows other options.

Similarly, the route GET `/movies` matches line 1, requesting an HTML page that lists all the movies (the Index action), and the route POST `/movies` matches line 2 and creates a new movie entry in the database. (The POST `/movies` route doesn't specify an `id` because the new movie won't have an ID until after it's created in the database.) Lines 1 and 2 illustrate that routes with the same URI but different HTTP methods can map to different controller actions.

Returning to Figure 2.12, observe that the `create` route (line 2) and the `new` route (line 3) both appear to be involved in handling the creation of a new movie. Why are two routes needed for this action? The reason is that in a Web app, two interactions are required to create a new movie, as Screencast 2.7.1 shows.

```
1                                 Non-RESTful Site      RESTful Site
2                                 ----------------      ------------
3   Login to site:              POST /login/dave       POST /login/dave
4   Welcome page:               GET  /welcome          GET  /user/301/welcome
5   Add item ID 427 to cart:    POST /add/427          POST /user/301/add/427
6   View cart:                  GET  /cart             GET  /user/301/cart
7   Pay:                        POST /checkout         POST /user/301/checkout
```

Figure 2.13: Non-RESTful and RESTful ways of mapping site functionality to HTTP methods and URIs. In a Service-Oriented Architecture, a client of the RESTful site could immediately request to view the cart (line 6), but a client of the non-RESTful site would first have to perform lines 3–5 to set up the implicit information on which line 6 depends.

Screencast 2.7.1: Create and Update each require two interactions.

http://vimeo.com/34754622

Creating a new movie requires two interactions with Rotten Potatoes, because before the user can submit information about the movie he must be presented with a form in which to enter that information. The empty form is therefore the resource named by the route in line 3 of Figure 2.12, and the submission of the filled-in form is the resource named by the route in line 2. Similarly, updating an existing movie requires one resource consisting of an editable form showing the existing movie info (line 4) and a second resource consisting of the submission of the edited form (line 6).

To summarize, routes are part of the middleware that connect URIs to specific controller methods in Rails. When a URI matching a defined route is received, the controller action indicated in the rightmost column is called to handle that request. In addition, wildcards such as :id that were matched in the URI are made available to the controller action as variables.

The routes in Figure 2.12 have an important property that is easy to overlook: they allow any CRUD request to be expressed by a URI that is self-contained, including all the information needed to satisfy that request. In particular, the result of a request, or the information needed to satisfy the request, does *not* depend on requests that have come before—a good fit to the statelessness of HTTP.

The philosophy that externally-visible Application Programming Interfaces (APIs) should expose only self-contained operations is called ***REpresentational State Transfer*** or REST. Services and APIs that follow this principle are said to be RESTful, so we can say that Figure 2.12 depicts RESTful routes and their corresponding RESTful URIs. Although simple to explain, REST is an unexpectedly powerful organizing principle for SaaS applications, because it makes the designer think carefully about exactly what conditions or assumptions each request depends on in order to be self-contained. A RESTful interface simplifies participating in a Service-Oriented Architecture because if every request is self-contained, interactions between services don't need to establish or rely on the concept of an ongoing session, as many SaaS apps do when interacting with human users.

As a concrete illustration of the REST principle, Figure 2.13 shows both a RESTful and non-RESTful way that an e-commerce site might implement the functionality of allowing a user to login, adding a specific item to his shopping cart, and proceeding to checkout. For the hypothetical non-RESTful site, every request after the login (line 3) relies on implicit information: line 4 assumes the site "remembers" who the currently-logged-in user is to show him his welcome page, and line 7 assumes the site "remembers" who has been adding items to their cart for checkout. In contrast, each URI for the RESTful site contains enough information to satisfy the request without relying on such implicit information: after Dave logs in, the fact that his user ID is 301 is present in every request, and his cart is identified explicitly by his user ID rather than implicitly based on the notion of a currently-logged-in user.

Summary

- An HTTP request consists of both a URI and an HTTP request method (GET, POST, PUT, or DELETE).

- A Rails route maps a request (URI+method) to a specific controller action that handles that request. In keeping with MVC terminology, the term "controller action" may refer either to the logical action itself or to the Ruby code in a controller that implements that action.

- If a URI is self-contained and includes all the information needed to satisfy the request, it's said to be RESTful (for REpresentational State Transfer). Rails generates RESTful routes by default, making it easy to integrate your user-facing Rails SaaS app into a Service-Oriented Architecture.

■ *Elaboration: PUT and DELETE.*

HTTP's PUT and DELETE methods, used in actions such as Update (line 6 of Figure 2.12), are not supported by Web browsers for historical reasons. To compensate, Rails includes a special mechanism that "decorates" submissions that should use PUT and DELETE in a special way and lets the Web browser submit the request using POST instead. A complementary mechanism "un-decorates" the specially-decorated request and internally changes the HTTP method "seen" by the controller to PUT or DELETE as appropriate. The result is that the Rails programmer can operate under the assumption that the PUT and DELETE methods are actually supported. Both mechanisms are part of the Rails code that implements route mappings.

■ *Elaboration: Optional* `:format` *in routes*

The raw output of `rake routes` includes a token (`.:format`) in most routes, which we omitted for clarity in Figure 2.12. If present, the format specifier allows a route to request resources in an output format other than the default of HTML—for example, GET `/movies.xml` would request the list of all movies as an XML document rather than an HTML page. Although in this simple application we haven't included the code to generate formats other than HTML, this mechanism allows a properly-designed existing application to be easily integrated into a Service-Oriented Architecture—changing just a few lines of code allows all existing controller actions to become part of an external RESTful API.

Self-Check 2.7.1 *True or false: If an app has a RESTful API, it must be performing CRUD operations.*

◇ False. The REST principle can be applied to any kind of operation. ■

Self-Check 2.7.2 *True or false: Supporting RESTful operations simplifies integrating a SaaS app with other services in a Service-Oriented Architecture.*

◇ True ■

Haml	HTML
%br{:clear => 'left'}	<br clear="left"/>
%p.foo Hello	<p class="foo">Hello</p>
%p#foo Hello	<p id="foo">Hello</p>
.foo	<div class="foo">...</div>
#foo.bar	<div id="foo" class="bar">...</div>

Figure 2.14: **Some commonly used Haml constructs and the resulting HTML. A Haml tag beginning with % must either contain the tag and all its content on a single line, as in lines 1–3 of the table, or must appear by itself on the line as in lines 4–5, in which case all of the tag's content must be indented by 2 spaces on subsequent lines. Notice that Haml specifies** class **and** id **attributes using a notation deliberately similar to CSS selectors.**

2.8 500 feet: Template Views

We conclude our brief tour with a look at Rails views. Because Web applications primarily deliver HTML pages, most frameworks provide a way to create a page of static markup (HTML or otherwise) interspersed with variables or very brief snippets of code. At runtime, the variable values or results of code execution are substituted or *interpolated* into the page. This architecture is known as Template View, and it is used by Rails' views subsystem as well as being the basis of frameworks such as PHP.

We will use a templating system called Haml (for HTML Abstraction Markup Language, pronounced "HAM-ell") to streamline the creation of HTML template views. We will learn more details and create our own views in Chapter 3, but in the interest of visiting all the "moving parts" of a Rails app, open app/views/movies/index.html.haml in the Rotten Potatoes directory. This is the view used by the Index controller action on movies; by convention over configuration, the suffixes .html.haml indicate that the view should be processed using Haml to create index.html, and the location and name of the file identify it as the view for the **index** action in the **movies** controller. Screencast 2.8.1 presents the basics of Haml, summarized in Figure 2.14.

> We prefer Haml's conciseness to Rails' built-in *erb* templating system, so Haml is preinstalled with the bookware.

Screencast 2.8.1: Interpolation into views using Haml.
http://vimeo.com/34754654
In a Haml template, lines beginning with % expand into the corresponding HTML opening tag, with no closing tag needed since Haml uses indentation to determine structure. Ruby-like hashes following a tag become HTML attributes. Lines **– beginning with a dash** are executed as Ruby code with the result discarded, and lines **= beginning with an equals sign** are executed as Ruby code with the result interpolated into the HTML output.

According to MVC, views should contain as little code as possible. Although Haml technically permits arbitrarily complex Ruby code in a template, its syntax for including a multi-line piece of code is deliberately awkward, to discourage programmers from doing so. Indeed, the only "computation" in the Index view of Rotten Potatoes is limited to iterating over a collection (provided by the Model via the Controller) and generating an HTML table row to display each element.

In contrast, applications written using the PHP framework often mingle large amounts of code into the view templates, and while it's possible for a disciplined PHP programmer to separate the views from the code, the PHP framework itself provides no particular support for doing this, nor does it reward the effort. MVC advocates argue that distinguishing the controller from the view makes it easier to think first about structuring an app as a set of RESTful actions, and later about rendering the results of these actions in a separate View step. Section 1.7 made the case for Service-Oriented Architecture; it should now be clear how the separation of models, views and controllers, and adherence to a RESTful controller style, naturally leads to an application whose actions are easy to "externalize" as standalone API actions.

■*Elaboration: Alternatives to Template View*

Because all Web apps must ultimately deliver HTML to a browser, building the output (view) around a static HTML "template" has always made sense for Web apps, hence the popularity of the Template View pattern for rendering views. That is, the input to the view-rendering stage includes both the HTML template and a set of Ruby variables that Haml will use to "fill in" dynamic content. An alternative is the Transform View pattern (Fowler 2002), in which the input to the view stage is *only* the set of objects. The view code then includes all the logic for converting the objects to the desired view representation. This pattern makes more sense if many different representations are possible, since the view layer is no longer "built around" any particular representation. An example of Transform View in Rails is a set of Rails methods that accept ActiveRecord resources and generate pure-XML representations of the resources—they do not instantiate any "template" to do so, but rather create the XML starting with just the ActiveRecord objects. These methods are used to quickly convert an HTML-serving Rails app into one that can be part of a Service-Oriented Architecture.

Self-Check 2.8.1 *In the Index view for Movies, why does the Haml markup in line 11 begin with −, while the markup in lines 13–16 begins with =?*

◇ In line 10 we just need the code to execute, to start the for-loop. In lines 13–16 we want to substitute the result of executing the code into the view. ■

Self-Check 2.8.2 *In Figure 3.12, why don't the helper methods for the New action (**new_movie_path**) and Create action (**movies_path**) take an argument, as the Show or Update helpers do?*

◇ Show and Update operate on existing movies, so they take an argument to identify which movie to operate on. New and Create by definition operate on not-yet-existing movies. ■

Self-Check 2.8.3 *In Figure 3.12, why doesn't the helper methods for the Index action take an argument? (HINT: The reason is different than the answer to Self-Check 2.8.2.)*

◇ The Index action just shows a list of all the movies, so no argument is needed to distinguish which movie to operate on. ■

2.9 Fallacies and Pitfalls

 Fallacy: **Rails doesn't scale (or Django, or PHP, or other frameworks).**

With the shared-nothing 3-tier architecture depicted in Figure 2.7, the Web server and app server tiers (where Rails apps would run) can be scaled almost arbitrarily far by adding computers in each tier using cloud computing. The challenge lies in scaling the database, as the next Pitfall explains.

 Pitfall: **Putting all model data in an RDBMS on a single server computer, thereby limiting scalability.**

The power of RDBMSs is a double-edged sword. It's easy to create database structures prone to scalability problems that might not emerge until a service grows to hundreds of thousands of users. Some developers feel that Rails compounds this problem because its Model abstractions are so productive that it is tempting to use them without thinking of the scalability consequences. Unfortunately, unlike with the Web server and app tiers, we cannot "scale our way out" of this problem by simply deploying many copies of the database because this might result in different values for different copies of the same item (the ***data consistency*** problem). Although techniques such as master-slave replication and database ***sharding*** help make the database tier more like the shared-nothing presentation and logic tiers, extreme database scalability remains an area of both research and engineering effort.

 Pitfall: **Prematurely focusing on per-computer performance of your SaaS app.**

Although the shared-nothing architecture makes horizontal scaling easy, we still need physical computers to do it. Adding a computer used to be expensive (buy the computer), time-consuming (configure and install the computer), and permanent (if demand subsides later, you'll be paying for an idle computer). With cloud computing, all three problems are alleviated, since we can add computers instantly for pennies per hour and release them when we don't need them anymore. Hence, until a SaaS app becomes large enough to require hundreds of computers, SaaS developers should focus on *horizontal scalability* rather than per-computer performance.

2.10 Concluding Remarks: Patterns, Architecture, and Long-Lived APIs

To understand the architecture of a software system is to understand its organizing principles. We did this by identifying patterns at many different levels: client-server, three-tier architecture, model-view-controller, Active Record, REST.

Patterns are a powerful way to manage complexity in large software systems. Inspired by Christopher Alexander's 1977 book *A Pattern Language: Towns, Buildings, Construction* describing design patterns for civil architecture, Erich Gamma, Richard Helm, Ralph Johnson and John Vlissides (the "Gang Of Four" or GOF) published the seminal book *Design Patterns: Elements of Reusable Object-Oriented Software* in 1995 (Gamma et al. 1994), which described what are now called the 23 GOF Design Patterns focusing on class-level structures and behaviors. Despite design patterns' popularity as a tool, they have been the subject of some critique; for example, Peter Norvig, currently Google's Director of Research, has argued that some design patterns just compensate for deficiencies in statically-typed programming languages such as C++ and Java, and that the need for them disappears in dynamic languages such as Lisp or Ruby. Notwithstanding some controversy, patterns of many kinds remain a valuable way for software engineers to identify structure in their work and bring proven solutions to bear on recurring problems.

Indeed, we observe that by choosing to build a SaaS app, we have predetermined the use of some patterns and excluded others. By choosing to use Web standards, we have predetermined a client-server system; by choosing cloud computing, we have predetermined the 3-tier architecture to permit horizontal scaling. Model–View–Controller is not predetermined, but we choose it because it is a good fit for Web apps that are view-centric and have historically relied on a persistence tier, notwithstanding other possible patterns such as those in Figure 2.9. REST is not predetermined, but we choose it because it simplifies integration into a Service-Oriented Architecture and can be readily applied to the CRUD operations, which are so common in MVC apps. Active Record is perhaps more controversial—as we will see in Chapters 3 and 6, its powerful facilities simplify apps considerably, but misusing those facilities can lead to scalability and performance problems that are less likely to occur with simpler persistence models.

If we were building a SaaS app in 1995, none of the above would have been obvious because practitioners had not accumulated enough examples of successful SaaS apps to "extract" successful patterns into frameworks like Rails, software components like Apache, and middleware like Rack. By following the successful footsteps of software architects before us, we can take advantage of their ability to *separate the things that change from those that stay the same* across many examples of SaaS and provide tools, frameworks, and design principles that support building things this way. As we mentioned earlier, this separation is key to enabling reuse.

In fact, Rails itself was originally extracted from a standalone app written by the consulting group 37signals.

Lastly, it is worth remembering that a key factor in the Web's success has been the adoption of well-defined protocols and formats whose design allows separating the things that change from those that stay the same. TCP/IP, HTTP, and HTML have all gone through several major revisions, but all include ways to detect which version is in use, so a client can tell if it's talking to an older server (or vice versa) and adjust its behavior accordingly. Although dealing with multiple protocol and language versions puts an additional burden on browsers, it has led to a remarkable result: A Web page created in 2011, using a markup language based on 1960s technology, can be retrieved using network protocols developed in 1969 and displayed by a browser created in 1992. Separating the things that change from those that stay the same is part of the path to creating long-lived software.

Tim Berners-Lee, a computer scientist at CERN[12], led the development of HTTP and HTML in 1990. Both are now stewarded by the nonprofit vendor-neutral World Wide Web Consortium (W3C)[13].

2.11 To Learn More

- W3Schools[14] is a free (advertising-supported) site with tutorials on almost all Web-related technologies.

- The World Wide Web Consortium (W3C)[15] stewards the official documents describing the Web's open standards, including HTTP, HTML, and CSS.

- The XML/XHTML Validator[16] is one of many you can use to ensure the pages delivered by your SaaS app are standards-compliant.

- The Object-Oriented Design web site[17] has numerous useful resources for developers using OO languages, including a nice catalog of the GoF design patterns with graphical descriptions of each pattern, some of which we will discuss in detail in Chapter 9.

M. Fowler. *Patterns of Enterprise Application Architecture.* Addison-Wesley Professional, 2002. ISBN 0321127420. URL http://martinfowler.coma/eaaCatalog/.

E. Gamma, R. Helm, R. Johnson, and J. M. Vlissides. *Design Patterns: Elements of Reusable Object-Oriented Software.* Addison-Wesley Professional, 1994. ISBN 0201633612.

Notes

[1] http://en.wikipedia.org/wiki/Pentium_FDIV_bug
[2] http://rottentomatoes.com
[3] http://projects.apache.org/projects/http_server.html
[4] http://www.iis.net
[5] http://docs.google.com
[6] http://iana.org
[7] http://www.w3.org/TR/html5/introduction.html#history-1
[8] http://csszengarden.com
[9] http://heroku.com
[10] http://adam.heroku.com/past/2009/7/6/sql_databases_dont_scale/
[11] http://martinfowler.com/eaaCatalog
[12] http://info.cern.ch
[13] http://w3.org
[14] http://w3schools.com
[15] http://w3.org
[16] http://validator.w3.org
[17] http://oodesign.com

2.12 Exercises

Exercise 2.1 *If the DNS service stopped working, would you still be able to surf the Web? Explain why or why not.*

◇ In practice, no. Even if you directly typed the IP address for a particular site into your Web browser, the very first page returned by visiting that site probably has a number of URIs embedded in it that will need DNS lookup. ■

Exercise 2.2 *Suppose HTTP cookies didn't exist. Could you devise another way to track a user across page views? (HINT: it involves modifying the URI and was a widely-used method before cookies were invented.)*

◇ On the user's first visit, construct whatever string you would normally send back as the cookie, and add it to every URI in the returned page. For example, if the cookie string was MyCookie, then an embedded link such as `<a href="page2.html">` would become `<a href="page2.html?cookie=MyCookie">`. On every incoming request, look for and strip out this parameter and use it to access the user's session state. This is sometimes called the "Fat URI" approach. ■

Exercise 2.3 *Find a Web page for which the W3C's online XHTML validator[1] finds at least one error. Sadly, this should be easy. Read through the validation error messages and try to understand what each one means.*

Exercise 2.4 *What port numbers are implied by each of the following URIs and why:*

1. *https://paypal.com*

2. `http://mysite.com:8000/index`

3. `ssh://root@cs.berkeley.edu/tmp/file` *(HINT: recall that the IANA establishes default port numbers for various network services.)*

◊

1. 443, the default port for https (secure HTTP) connections

2. 8000, given explicitly in the URI

3. 22, the default port for ssh (secure shell) connections

■

Exercise 2.5 *As described on Google's Search API documentation[2], you can do a Google search for a term by constructing a URI that includes the search query as a parameter named q, for example,* `http://www.google.com/search?q=saas` *to search for the term "saas". However, as Figure 2.3 showed, some characters are not allowed in URIs because they are "special," including spaces, '?', and '&'. Given this restriction, construct a legal URI that search Google for the terms "M&M" and "100%?".*

◊ Special characters can be included in a URI by including their ASCII codes expressed in hexadecimal and preceded by '%'. The ASCII code for '&' is 38 (hex 0x26), the code for '%' is 37 (hex 0x25), and the code for '?' is 63 (hex 0x3F).

Therefore we can write the search URIs as follows:

M&M → `http://google.com/search?q=M%26M`

100%? → `http://google.com/search?q=100%25%3F` ■

> **ASCII codes using Ruby.** Since the Ruby syntax for the character literal *x* is `?x`, you can verify these codes by typing `?%`, `??`, etc. in `irb`. You can print the hex equivalents with `?%.to_s(16)`.

Exercise 2.6 *Why do Rails routes map to controller actions but not model actions or views?*

◊ The controller handles all direct interaction with the user, so routes only point to controller actions. ■

3 Ruby and Rails Basics for Java Programmers

The best way to predict the future is to invent it.

—Alan Kay

This quick introduction will get you up to speed on idiomatic Ruby and Rails. We focus on the unique productivity-enhancing features of Ruby and Rails that may be unfamiliar to Java programmers, and we omit many details that are well covered by existing materials. As with all languages, becoming truly comfortable with Ruby's powerful features will require going beyond the material in this introduction to the materials listed in Section 3.19.

Alan Kay (1940–) received the 2003 Turing Award for pioneering many of the ideas at the root of contemporary object-oriented programming languages. He led the team that developed the Smalltalk language, from which Ruby inherits its approach to object-orientation. He also invented the "Dynabook" concept, the precursor of today's laptops and tablet computers, which he conceived as an educational platform for teaching programming.

3.1 Overview and Three Pillars of Ruby

Programming can only be learned by doing, so we've placed this icon in the margin in places where we strongly encourage you to try the examples yourself. Since Ruby is interpreted, there's no compile step—you get instant gratification when trying the examples, and exploration and experimentation are easy. Each example has a link to Pastebin[3], where you can copy the code for that example with a single click and paste it into a Ruby interpreter or editor window. (If you're reading the ebook, these links are live.) We also encourage you to check the official documentation for much more detail on many topics we introduce in Section 3.19.

Ruby is a minimalist language: while its libraries are rich, there are few mechanisms *in the language itself.* Three principles underlying these mechanisms will help you read and understand idiomatic code:

1. Everything is an object. In Java, some primitive types like integers must be "boxed" to get them to behave like objects.

2. Every operation is a method call on some object and returns a value. In Java, operator overloading is different from method overriding, and it's possible to have **void** functions that return no value.

3. All programming is metaprogramming: classes and methods can be added or changed at any time, even while a program is running. In Java, all classes must be declared at compile time, and base classes can't be modified by your app even then.

Each of these three principles will be covered in its own section. #1 and #2 are straightforward. #3 gives Ruby much of its productivity-enhancing power, but must be qualified with the admonition that with great power comes great responsibility. Using Ruby's metaprogramming features tastefully will make your code elegant and DRY, but abusing them will make your code brittle and impenetrable.

Ruby's basic syntax should be unsurprising if you're familiar with other modern scripting languages. Figure 3.1 shows the syntax of basic Ruby elements. Statements are separated by newlines (most commonly) or semicolons (rarely). Indentation is insignificant. While Ruby is concise enough that a single line of code rarely exceeds one screen line, breaking up a single statement with a newline is allowed if it doesn't cause a parsing ambiguity. An editor with good syntax highlighting can be very helpful if you're not sure whether your line break is legal.

A *symbol*, such as :octocat, is an immutable string whose value is itself; it is typically used in Ruby for enumerations, like an **enum** type in C or Java, though it has other purposes as well. However, a symbol is not the same as a string—it is its own primitive type, and string operations cannot be performed on it, though it can easily be converted to a string by calling **to_s**. For example, :octocat.to_s gives **"octocat"**, and **"octocat".to_sym** gives :octocat.

Regular expressions or *regexps* (often *regex* and *regexes* in order to be pronounceable) are part of every programmer's toolbox. A regular expression allows matching a string against a pattern containing possible "wildcards." Ruby's regular expression support resembles that of other modern programming languages: regexes appear between slashes and may be followed by one or more letters modifying their behavior, for example, */regex/*i

Variables	**local_variable, @@class_variable, @instance_variable**
Constants	**ClassName, CONSTANT, $GLOBAL_CONSTANT**
Booleans	**false, nil** are false; **true** and *everything else* (zero, empty string, etc.) is true.
Strings and Symbols	**"string", 'also a string', %q{like single quotes}, %Q{like double quotes}, :symbol** special characters (**\n**) expanded in double-quoted but not single-quoted strings
Expressions in *double-quoted* strings	**@foo = 3 ; "Answer is #{@foo}"; %Q{Answer is #{@foo+1}}**
Regular expression matching	**"hello" =~ /lo/** or **"hello".match(Regexp.new 'lo')**
Arrays	**a = [1, :two, 'three'] ; a[1] == :two**
Hashes	**h = {:a =>1, 'b' =>"two"} ; h['b'] == "two" ; h.has_key?(:a) == true**
Instance method	**def method(*arg, arg*)... end** (*use ***args** for variable number of arguments*
Class (static) method	**def ClassName.method(*arg, arg*)... end,** **def self.method(*arg, arg*)... end**
Special method names *Ending these methods' names in ? and !* *is optional but idiomatic*	**def setter=(*arg, arg*)... end** **def boolean_method?(*arg, arg*)... end** **def dangerous_method!(*arg, arg*)... end**

Conditionals	Iteration (see Section 3.6)	Exceptions

if *cond* (or **unless** *cond*)
   statements
 [**elsif** *cond*
   statements]
 [**else**
   statements]
 end
	while *cond* (or **until** *cond*)
	   statements
	 end
	 1.upto(10) do |i| ... **end**
	 10.times do... **end**
	 collection.**each do |elt|**... **end**
		begin
		   statements
		 rescue AnError => e
		   e *is an exception of class* **AnError**;
		   multiple **rescue** *clauses OK*
		 [**ensure**
		   this code is always executed]
		 end

Figure 3.1: Basic Ruby elements and control structures, with optional items in [square brackets].

	Symbol	Meaning	Example	Matches	Example	Mismatch
Count	*	0 or more	a*		aaaa	b
	+	1 or more	a+	a	aaaa	
	?	0 or 1	a?		a	aaaa
Anchors, Sets, Range, Append	^	start of line, also NOT in set	^a	a	ab	ba
	$	end of line	a$	a	dcba	ab
	()	group, also captures that group in Ruby	(ab)+	ababab	ab	b
	[]	set	[ab]	a	b	ab
	[x-y]	character range	[0-9]	3	9	a
	|	OR	(It's|It is)	It's	It is	Its
	[^]	NOT (opposite) in set	[^"]	b	9	"
	.	any character (except newline)	.{3}	abc	1+2	aa
	\	used to match meta-characters, also for classes	\.$	The End.	.	a
	i	append to pattern to specify case insensitive match	\ab\i	Ab	ab	a
Classes	\d	decimal digit ([0-9])	\d	3	9	a
	\D	not decimal digit ([^0-9])	\D	a	=	3
	\s	whitespace character	\s			a
	\S	not whitespace character	\S	a	=	
	\w	"word" character ([a-zA-Z0-9_])	\w	a	9	=
	\W	"nonword" character ([^a-zA-Z0-9_])	\W	=	$	a
	\n	newline	\n	--	--	a

Figure 3.2: Review of Ruby's regular expressions.

to indicate that the regex should ignore case when matching. As Figure 3.2 shows, special constructs embedded in the regex can match multiple types of characters and can specify the number of times a match must occur and whether the match must be "anchored" to the beginning or end of the string. For example, here is a regex that matches a time of day, such as "8:25pm", on a line by itself:

http://pastebin.com/kHhy9A9n
```
1 | time_regex = /^\d\d?:\d\d\s*[ap]m$/i
```

This regexp matches a digit at the beginning of a string (**^\d**), optionally followed by another digit (**\d?**), followed by a colon, exactly two digits, zero or more whitespace characters (**\s***), either **a** or **p**, then **m** at the end of the string (**m$**) and ignoring case (the **i** after the closing slash). Another way to match one or two digits would be **[0-9][0-9]?** and another way to match *exactly* two digits would be **[0-9][0-9]**.

Ruby allows the use of parentheses in regexes to *capture* the matched string or substrings. For example, here is the same regexp with three capture groups:

http://pastebin.com/JGBjHmyj
```
1 | x = "8:25 PM"
2 | x =~ /(\d\d?):(\d\d)\s*([ap])m$/i
```

The second line attempts to match the string **x** against the regex. If the match succeeds, the **=~** operator will return the position in the string (with 0 being the first character) at which the match succeeded, the global variable **$1** will have the value **"8"**, **$2** will be **"25"**, and **$3** will be **"P"**. The last-match variables are reset the next time you do another regex match. If the match fails, **=~** will return **nil**. Note that **nil** and **false** are not actually equal to each other, but both evaluate to "false" when used in a conditional expression (in fact, they are the *only* two values in Ruby that do so). Idiomatically, methods that are truly Boolean (that is, the only possible return values are "true" or "false") return **false**, whereas methods that return an object when successful return **nil** when they fail.

Lastly, note that =˜ works on both strings and **Regexp** objects, so both of the following are legal and equivalent, and you should choose whichever is easiest to understand in the context of your code.

http://pastebin.com/pZ0bF3N8

```
1  "Catch 22" =~ /\w+\s+\d+/
2  /\w+\s+\d+/ =~ "Catch 22"
```

Summary

- A distinguishing primitive type in Ruby is the symbol, an immutable string whose value is itself. Symbols are commonly used in Ruby to denote "specialness," such as being one of a set of fixed choices like an enumeration. Symbols aren't the same as strings, but they can easily be converted back and forth with the methods **to_s** and **to_string**.

- Ruby statements are separated by newlines, or less commonly, by semicolons.

- Ruby's regular expression facilities are comparable to those of other modern languages, including support for capture groups using parentheses and for match modifiers such as a trailing **i** for "ignore case when matching."

Self-Check 3.1.1 *Which of the following Ruby expressions are equal to each other:*
(a) **:foo** *(b)* **%q{foo}** *(c)* **%Q{foo}** *(d)* **'foo'.to_sym** *(e)* **:foo.to_s**
◇ (a) and (d) are equal to each other; (b), (c), and (e) are equal to each other ∎

Self-Check 3.1.2 *What is captured by* **$1** *when the string* **25 to 1** *is matched against each of the following regexps:*
(a) **/(\d+)$/**
(b) **/^\d+([^0-9]+)/**
◇ (a) the string "**1**" (b) the string " **to** " (including the leading and trailing spaces) ∎

Self-Check 3.1.3 *When is it correct to write*
Fixnum num=3
to initialize the variable **num***: (a) on its first use; (b) on any use, as long as it's the same class* **Fixnum** *each time; (c) never*
◇ Never; variable declarations aren't used in Ruby. ∎

3.2 Everything is an Object

Ruby supports the usual basic types—fixed-point integers (class **Fixnum**), floating-point numbers (class **Float**), strings (class **String**), linear arrays (class **Array**), and associative arrays or hashmaps (class **Hash**). But in contrast to Java, Ruby is ***dynamically typed***: the type of a variable is generally not inferable until runtime. That is, while objects have types, the variables that reference them do not. So **s = 5** can follow **s = "foo"** in the same block of code. Because variables do not have types, an array or hash can consist of elements of all different types, as Figure 3.1 suggests. We speak only of "an array" rather than "an array of Ints" and of "a hash" rather than "a hash with keys of type Foo and values of type Bar."

Ruby's object model descends from Smalltalk, whose design was inspired by ideas in Simula. Everything in Ruby, even a plain integer, is an object that is an instance of some class. All operations, without exception, are performed by calling a method on an object, and every such call (indeed, every Ruby statement) returns a value. The notation **obj.meth()** calls method **meth** on the object **obj**, which is said to be the *receiver* and is hopefully able to *respond to* **meth**. As we will see shortly, parentheses around method arguments are often optional. For example:

http://pastebin.com/Et6NwUfh

```
1  5.class        # => Fixnum
```

(We strongly recommend you start up a Ruby interpreter by typing `irb` in a Terminal window in your VM so you can try these examples as you go.) The above call *sends* the method call **class** to the object **5**. The **class** method happens to return the class that an object belongs to, in this case **Fixnum**.

Every object is an instance of some class. Classes can inherit from superclasses as they do in Java, and all classes ultimately inherit from **Object**, sometimes called the *root class*. Ruby does not support multiple inheritance, so every class has exactly one superclass, except for **Object**, which has no superclass. As with most languages that support inheritance, if an object receives a call for a method not defined in its class, the call will be passed up to the superclass, and so on until the root class is reached. If no class along the way, including the root class, is able to handle the method, an *undefined method* exception is raised.

Try **5.class.superclass** to find out what **Fixnum**'s superclass is; this illustrates *method chaining*, a very common Ruby idiom. Method chaining associates to the left, so this example could be written **(5.class).superclass**, meaning: "Call the **class** method on the receiver **5**, and whatever the result of that is, call the **superclass** method on that receiver."

Object-orientation (OO) and class inheritance are *distinct properties*. Because popular languages such as Java combine both, many people conflate them. Ruby also happens to have both, but the two features do not necessarily interact in all the same ways they would in Java. In particular, compared to Java, reuse through inheritance is much less important, but the implications of object-orientation are much more important. For example, Ruby supports comprehensive *reflection*—the ability to ask objects about themselves. **5.respond_to?('class')** tells you that the object **5** would be able to respond to the method **class** if you asked it to. **5.methods** lists all methods to which the object **5** responds including those defined in its ancestor classes, and **5.methods(false)** lists all methods to which the object **5** responds *excluding* those defined in its ancestor classes. Given that an object responds to a method, how can you tell if the method is defined in the object's class or an ancestor class? **5.method(:+)** reveals that the + method is defined in class **Fixnum**, whereas **5.method(:ceil)** reveals that the **ceil** method is defined in **Integer**, an ancestor class of **Fixnum**. Determining which class's methods will handle a method call is called *looking up a method* on a receiver, and is analogous to virtual method dispatch in Java.

Kristen Nygaard (left, 1926–2002) and Ole-Johan Dahl (right, 1931–2002) shared the 2001 Turing Award for inventing fundamental OO concepts including objects, classes, and inheritance, and demonstrating them in Simula, the ancestor of every OO language.

Even a class in Ruby is itself an object—it's an instance of **Class**, which is a class whose instances are classes (a *metaclass*).

Summary

- The notation **a.b** means "call method **b** on object **a**." Object **a** is said to be the *receiver*, and if it cannot handle the method call, it will pass the call to its superclass. This process is called *looking up a method* on a receiver.

- Ruby has comprehensive *reflection*, allowing you to ask objects about themselves.

■ *Elaboration: Looking up a method*

Previously we said that if method lookup fails in the receiver's class, the call is passed up to the ancestor (superclass). The truth is a bit more subtle: mix-ins and **method_missing**, both of which we'll describe shortly, can be used to handle an undefined-method call *before* punting up to the superclass.

Self-Check 3.2.1 *Why does* **5.superclass** *result in an "undefined method" error? (Hint: consider the difference between calling* **superclass** *on 5 itself vs. calling it on the object returned by* **5.class**.)

◇ **superclass** is a method defined on classes. The object **5** is not itself a class, so you can't call **superclass** on it. ■

3.3 Every Operation is a Method Call

To cement the concept that every operation is a method call, note that even basic math operations such as $+, *, ==$ (equality comparison) are *syntactic sugar* for method calls: the operators are actually method calls on their receivers. The same is true for array dereferences such as **x[0]** and array assignment such as **x[0]="foo"**.

The table in Figure 3.3 shows the de-sugared versions of these expressions and of the regex syntax introduced in Section 3.1, as well as showing how Ruby's core method **send** can be used to send any method call to any object. Many Ruby methods including **send** accept either a symbol or a string argument, so the first example in the table could also be written **10.send('modulo',3)**.

A critical implication of "everything is a method" is that concepts such as *type casting* rarely apply in Ruby. In Java, if we write **f+i** where **f** is a float and **i** is an integer, the type casting rules state that **i** will be converted internally to a float so it can be added to **f**. If we wrote **i+s** where **s** is a **String**, a compile-time error would result.

In contrast, in Ruby $+$ is just like any other method that can be defined differently by each class, so its behavior depends entirely on the receiver's implementation of the method. Since **f+i** is syntactic sugar for **f.+(i)**, it's entirely up to the + method (presumably defined in **f**'s class or one of its ancestor classes) to decide how to handle different types of values for **i**. Thus, both **3+2** and **"foo"+"bar"** are legal Ruby expressions, evaluating to **5** and **"foobar"** respectively, but the first one is calling + as defined in **Numeric** (the ancestor class of **Fixnum**) whereas the second is calling + as defined in **String**. As above, you can verify that **"foobar".method(:+)** and **5.method(:+)** refer to distinct methods. Although this might resemble operator overloading in other languages, it's more general: since only the method's name matters for dispatching, we'll see in Section 3.7 how this feature enables a powerful reuse mechanism called a mix-in.

Sugared	De-sugared	Explicit send
10 % 3	10.modulo(3)	10.send(:modulo, 3)
5+3	5.+(3)	5.send(:+, 3)
x == y	x.==(y)	x.send(:==, y)
a * x + y	a.*(x).+(y)	a.send(:*, x).send(:+, y)
a + x * y	a.+(x.*(y))	a.send(:+, x.send(:*, y)) *(operator precedence preserved)*
x[3]	x.[](3)	x.send(:[], 3)
x[3] = 'a'	x.[]=(3,'a')	x.send(:[]=, 3, 'a')
/abc/, %r{abc}	Regexp.new("abc")	Regexp.send(:new, 'abc')
str =˜ regex regex =˜ str	str.match(regex) regex.match(str)	str.send(:match, regex) regex.send(:match, str)
$1... $n (regex capture)	Regexp.last_match(n)	Regexp.send(:last_match,n)

Figure 3.3: **The first column is Ruby's syntactic sugar for common operations, the second column shows the explicit method call, and the third column shows how to perform the same method call using Ruby's send, which accepts either a string or a symbol (more idiomatic) for the method name.**

In Ruby the notation **ClassName#method** is used to indicate the instance method **method** in **ClassName**, whereas **ClassName.method** indicates the class (static) method **method** in **ClassName**. Using this notation, we can say that the expression **3+2** results in calling **Fixnum#+** on the receiver **3**, whereas the expression **"foo"+"bar"** results in calling **String#+** on the receiver **"foo"**.

Similarly, in Java it's common to see explicit casts of a variable to a superclass, such as **Foo x = (Foo)y** where **y** is an instance of a superclass of **Foo**. In Ruby this is meaningless because variables don't have types, and it doesn't matter whether the responding method is in the receiver's class or one of its ancestors.

A method is defined with **def method_name(arg1,arg2)** and ends with **end**; all statements in between are the method definition. Every expression in Ruby has a value—for example, the value of an assignment is its right-hand side, so the value of **x=5** is 5—and if a method doesn't include an explicit **return(blah)**, the value of the last expression in the method is returned. Hence the following trivial method returns 5:

http://pastebin.com/eWP5FDmF

```
1  def trivial_method    # no arguments; can also use trivial_method()
2    x = 5
3  end
```

The variable **x** in the example is a local variable; its scope is limited to the block in which it's defined, in this case the method, and is undefined outside that method. In other words, Ruby uses *lexical scoping* for local variables. When we talk about classes in Ruby, we'll see how class and instance variables are alternatives to local variables.

An important Ruby idiom is *poetry mode*: the ability to omit parentheses and curly braces when the parsing is unambiguous. Most commonly, Ruby programmers may omit parentheses around arguments to a method call, and omit curly braces when the *last* argument to a method call is a hash. Hence the following two method calls are equivalent, given a method **link_to** (which we'll meet in Section 3.12) that takes one string argument and one hash argument:

http://pastebin.com/ScDU84MV

```
1  link_to('Edit', {:controller => 'students', :action => 'edit'})
2  link_to 'Edit', :controller => 'students', :action => 'edit'
```

Poetry mode is exceedingly common among experienced Rubyists, is used pervasively in Rails, and provides a welcome elimination of clutter once you get used to it.

Summary

- Everything in Ruby is an object, even primitive types like integers.

- Ruby objects have types, but the variables that refer to them don't.

- Ruby uses lexical scoping for local variables: a variable is defined in the scope in which it's first assigned and in all scopes enclosed inside that one, but reusing the same local variable name in an inner scope temporarily "shadows" the name from the enclosing scope.

- Poetry mode reduces clutter by allowing you to omit parentheses around method arguments and curly braces surrounding a hash, as long as the resulting code is syntactically unambiguous.

■ *Elaboration: Number of arguments*

Although parentheses around method arguments are optional both in the method's definition and when calling the method, the *number* of arguments does matter, and an exception is raised if a method is called with the wrong number of arguments. The following code snippet shows two idioms you can use when you need more flexibility. The first is to make the last argument a hash and give it a default value of {} (the empty hash). The second is to use a splat (*), which collects any extra arguments into an array. As with so many Rubyisms, the right choice is whichever results in the most readable code.

http://pastebin.com/fwKku0js

```
1  # using 'keyword style' arguments
2  def mymethod(required_arg, args={})
3    do_fancy_stuff if args[:fancy]
4  end
5
6  mymethod "foo",:fancy => true # => args={:fancy => true}
7  mymethod "foo"               # => args={}
8
9  # using * (splat) arguments
10 def mymethod(required_arg, *args)
11   # args is an array of extra args, maybe empty
12 end
13
14 mymethod "foo","bar",:fancy => true # => args=["bar",{:fancy=>true}]
15 mymethod "foo"                      # => args=[]
```

Self-Check 3.3.1 *What is the de-sugared equivalent of each of the following expressions:* a<b, a==b, x[0], x[0]='foo'.

◇ a.send(:<,b), a.send(:==,b), x.send(:[],0), x.send(:[]=,0,'foo') ■

Self-Check 3.3.2 *Suppose method* **foo** *takes two hash arguments. Explain why we can't use poetry mode to write*
foo :a => 1, :b => 2

http://pastebin.com/HwUiVaMC

```
1   class Movie
2     def initialize(title, year)
3       @title = title
4       @year = year
5     end
6     def title
7       @title
8     end
9     def title=(new_title)
10      @title = new_title
11    end
12    def year ; @year ; end
13    def year=(new_year) ; @year = new_year ; end
14    # How to display movie info
15    @@include_year = false
16    def Movie.include_year=(new_value)
17      @@include_year = new_value
18    end
19    def full_title
20      if @@include_year
21        "#{self.title} (#{self.year})"
22      else
23        self.title
24      end
25    end
26  end
27
28  # Example use of the Movie class
29
30  beautiful = Movie.new('Life is Beautiful', '1997')
31
32  # What's the movie's name?
33  puts "I'm seeing #{beautiful.full_title}"
34
35  # And with the year
36  Movie.include_year = true
37  puts "I'm seeing #{beautiful.full_title}"
38
39  # Change the title
40  beautiful.title = 'La vita e bella'
41  puts "Ecco, ora si chiama '#{beautiful.title}!'"
```

Figure 3.4: A simple class definition in Ruby. Lines 12 and 13 remind us that it's idiomatic to combine short statements on a single line using semicolons; most Rubyists take advantage of Ruby's conciseness to introduce spaces around the semicolons for readability.

◇ Without curly braces, there's no way to tell whether this call is trying to pass a hash with two keys or two hashes of one key each. Therefore poetry mode can only be used when there's a single hash argument and it's the last argument. ∎

3.4   Classes, Methods, and Inheritance

The excerpt of a class definition for a **Movie** in Figure 3.4 illustrates some basic concepts of defining a class in Ruby. Let's step through it line by line.

Line 1 opens the **Movie** class. As we'll see, unlike in Java, **class Movie** is *not* a declaration but actually a method call that creates an object representing a new class and assigns this object to the constant **Movie**. The subsequent method definitions will occur in the context of this newly-created class.

Line 2 defines the default constructor for the class (the one called when you say **Movie.new**), which *must* be named **initialize**. The inconsistency of naming a method

initialize but calling it as **new** is an unfortunate idiosyncrasy you'll just have to get used to. As in Java, you can define other constructors as well. This constructor expects two arguments, and in **lines 3–4**, it sets the *instance variables* of the new **Movie** object to those values. The instance variables, such as **@title**, are associated with each instance of an object. The local variables **title** and **year** passed in as arguments are out of scope (undefined) outside the constructor, so if we care about those values we must capture them in instance variables.

Lines 6–8 define a *getter method* or *accessor method* for the **@title** instance variable. You might wonder why, if **beautiful** were an instance of **Movie**, we couldn't just write **beautiful.@title**. It's because in Ruby, **a.b** always means "Call method **b** on receiver **a**", and **@title** is not the name of any method in the **Movie** class. In fact, it is not a legal name for a method at all, since only instance variable names and class variable names may begin with **@**. In this case, the **title** getter is an instance method of the **Movie** class. That means that any object that is an instance of **Movie** (or of one of **Movie**'s subclasses, if there were any) could respond to this method.

Lines 9–11 define the instance method **title=**, which is distinct from the **title** instance method. Methods whose names end in = are *setter* or *mutator* methods, and just as with the getter, we need this method because we cannot write **beautiful.@title = 'La vita e bella'**. However, as line 40 shows, we *can* write **beautiful.title = 'La vita e bella'**. Beware! If you're used to Java or Python, it's very easy to think of this syntax as *assignment to an attribute*, but it is really just a method call like any other, and in fact could be written as **beautiful.send(:title=, 'La vita e bella')**. And since it is a method call, it has a return value: in the absence of an explicit **return** statement, the value returned by a method is just the value of the last expression evaluated in that method. Since in this case the last expression in the method is the assignment **@title=new_title** and the value of any assignment is its right-hand side, the method happens to return the value of **new_title** that was passed to it.

Unlike Java, which allows attributes as well as getters and setters, Ruby's data hiding or *encapsulation* is total: the *only* access to an instance variables or class variables from outside the class is via method calls. This restriction is one reason that Ruby is considered a more "pure" OO language than Java. But since poetry mode allows us to omit parentheses and write **movie.title** instead of **movie.title()**, conciseness need not be sacrificed to achieve this stronger encapsulation.

Lines 12–13 define the getter and setter for **year**, showing that you can use semicolons as well as newlines to separate Ruby statements if you think it looks less cluttered. As we'll soon see, though, Ruby provides a much more concise way to define getters and setters using metaprogramming.

Line 14 is a comment, which in Ruby begins with # and extends to the end of the line.

Line 15 defines a *class variable*, or what Java calls a *static variable*, that defines whether a movie's year of release is included when its name is printed. Analogously to the setter for **title**, we need one for **include_year=** (**lines 16–18**), but the presence of **Movie** in the name of the method (**Movie.include_year=**) tells us it's a class method. Notice we haven't defined a getter for the class variable; that means the value of this class variable cannot be inspected at all from outside the class.

Lines 19–25 define the instance method **full_title**, which uses the value of **@@include_year** to decide how to display a movie's full title. Line 21 shows that the syntax #{} can be used to interpolate (substitute) the value of an expression into a double-quoted string, as with #{**self.title**} and #{**self.year**}. More precisely, #{} evaluates the ex-

Java	Ruby
class MyString extends String	class MyString < String
class MyCollection extends Array implements Enumerable	class MyCollection < Array include Enumerable
Static variable: static int anInt = 3	Class variable: @@an_int = 3
Instance variable: this.foo = 1	Instance variable: @foo = 1
Static method: public static int foo(...)	Class method: def self.foo ... end
Instance method: public int foo(...)	Instance method: def foo ... end

Figure 3.5: A summary of some features that translate directly between Ruby and Java.

pression enclosed in the braces and calls **to_s** on the result, asking it to convert itself into a string that can be inserted into the enclosing string. The root class **Object** defines a default **to_s**, but most classes override it to produce a prettier representation of themselves.

Summary: Figure 3.5 compares basic OO constructs in Ruby and Java:

- **class Foo** opens a class (new or existing) in order to add or change methods in it. Unlike Java, it is not a declaration but actual code executed immediately, creating a new **Class** object and assigning it to the constant **Foo**.

- **@x** specifies an instance variable and **@@x** specifies a class (static) variable. The namespaces are distinct, so **@x** and **@@x** are different variables.

- A class's instance variables and class variables can be accessed only from within the class. Any access from the "outside world" requires a method call to either a getter or a setter.

- A class method in class **Foo** can be defined using either **def Foo.some_method** or **def self.some_method**.

■ *Elaboration: Using self to define a class method.*

As we'll soon see, the class method definition **def Movie.include_year** can actually appear *anywhere*, even outside the **Movie** class definition, since Ruby allows adding and modifying methods in classes after they've been defined. However, another way to define the class method **include_year** inside the class definition would be **def self.include_year=(...)**. This is because, as we mentioned above, **class Movie** in line 1 is not a declaration but actual code that is executed when this file is loaded, and inside the code block enclosed by **class Movie...end** (lines 2–25), the value of **self** is the new class object created by the **class** keyword. (In fact, **Movie** itself is just a plain old Ruby constant that refers to this class object, as you can verify by doing **c = Movie** and then **c.new('Inception',2010)**.)

■ *Elaboration: Why* self.title *in* Movie#full_title?

In lines 19–25, why do we call **self.title** and **self.year** rather than just referring directly to **@title** and **@year**, which would be perfectly legal inside an instance method? The reason is that in the future, we might want to change the way the getters work. For example, when we introduce Rails and ActiveRecord in Section 3.11, we'll see that getters for basic Rails models work by retrieving information from the database, rather than tracking the information using instance variables. Encapsulating instance and class variables using getters and setters hides the implementation of those attributes from the code that uses them, and there's no advantage to be gained by violating that encapsulation inside an instance method, even though it's legal to do so.

Self-Check 3.4.1 *Why is* **movie.@year=1998** *not a substitute for* **movie.year=1998**?
◇ The notation **a.b** always means "call method **b** on receiver **a**", but **@year** is the name of an instance variable, whereas **year=** is the name of an instance method. ■

Self-Check 3.4.2 *Suppose we delete line 12 from Figure 3.4. What would be the result of executing* **Movie.new('Inception',2011).year**?
◇ Ruby would complain that the **year** method is undefined. ■

3.5 All Programming is Metaprogramming

Since defining simple getters and setters for instance variables is so common, we can make the example more Ruby-like by replacing lines 6–11 with the single line **attr_accessor :title** and lines 12–13 with **attr_accessor :year**. **attr_accessor** is not part of the Ruby language—it's a regular method call that defines the getters and setters on the fly. That is, **attr_accessor :foo** defines instance methods **foo** and **foo=** that get and set the value of instance variable **@foo**. The related method **attr_reader** defines only a getter but no setter, and vice versa for **attr_writer**.

This is an example of *metaprogramming*—creating code at runtime that defines new methods. In fact, in a sense *all* Ruby programming is metaprogramming, since even a class definition is not a declaration as it is in Java but actually code that is executed at runtime. Given that this is true, you might wonder whether you can *modify* a class at runtime. In fact you can, by adding or changing instance methods or class methods, even for Ruby's built-in classes. For example, here is a way to do time arithmetic that takes advantage of the **now** method in the **Time** class in the standard Ruby library, which returns the number of seconds since 1/1/1970.

http://pastebin.com/T0wDR4h3

```
1  # Note: Time.now returns current time as seconds since epoch
2  class Fixnum
3    def seconds  ; self ; end
4    def minutes  ; self * 60 ; end
5    def hours    ; self * 60 * 60 ; end
6    def ago      ; Time.now - self ; end
7    def from_now ; Time.now + self ; end
8  end
9  Time.now
10 # => Mon Nov 07 10:18:10 -0800 2011
11 5.minutes.ago
12 # => Mon Nov 07 10:13:15 -0800 2011
13 5.minutes - 4.minutes
14 # => 60
15 3.hours.from_now
16 # => Mon Nov 07 13:18:15 -0800 2011
```

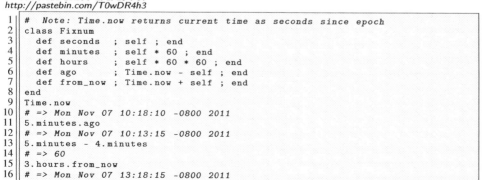

Unix was invented in 1970, so its designers chose to represent time as the number of seconds since midnight (GMT) 1/1/1970, sometimes called the beginning of the *epoch*. For convenience, a Ruby **Time** object responds to arithmetic operator methods by operating on this representation if possible, though internally Ruby can represent any time past or future.

In this example, we *reopened* the **Fixnum** class, a core class that we met earlier, and added six new instance methods to it. Since each of the new methods also returns a fixnum, they can be nicely "chained" to write expressions like **5.minutes.ago**. In fact, Rails includes a more complete version of this feature that does comprehensive time calculations.

Of course, we cannot write **1.minute.ago** since we only defined a method called **minutes**, not **minute**. We could define additional methods with singular names that duplicate the functionality of the methods we already have, but that's not very DRY. Instead, we can take advantage of Ruby's heavy-duty metaprogramming construct **method_missing**. If a method call cannot be found in the receiver's class, *before* trying the ancestor classes, Ruby will try to call **method_missing** on the receiver, passing it the name and arguments of the nonexistent method. The default implementation of **method_missing** just punts up to the superclass, but we can override it to implement "singular" versions of the time-calculation methods above:

http://pastebin.com/4zScNFr4

```
1  class Fixnum
2    def method_missing(method_id, *args)
3      name = method_id.to_s
4      if name =~ /^second|minute|hour$/
5        self.send(name + 's')
6      else
7        super # pass the buck to superclass
8      end
9    end
10 end
```

We convert the method ID (which is passed as a symbol) into a string, and use a regular expression to see if the string matches any of the words *hour, minute, second*. If so, we pluralize the name, and send the pluralized method name to **self**, that is, to the object that received the original call. If it doesn't match, what should we do? You might think we should signal an error, but because Ruby has inheritance, we must allow for the possibility that one of our ancestor classes might be able to handle the method call. Calling **super** with no arguments passes the original method call and its original arguments intact up the inheritance chain.

Try augmenting this example with a **days** method so that you can write **2.days.ago** and **1.day.ago**. Later in the chapter we'll see **method_missing** in action for constructing XML documents and for enhancing the power of the **find** method in the ActiveRecord part of the Rails framework.

Summary

- **attr_accessor** is an example of metaprogramming: it creates new code at runtime, in this case getters and setters for an instance variable. This style of metaprogramming is extremely common in Ruby.

- When a receiver cannot handle a method call, **method_missing** is called on the receiver *before* passing the call up the inheritance chain. **method_missing** can inspect the name of the nonexistent method and its arguments, and can either take action to handle the call or just pass the call to the ancestor, as the default implementation of **method_missing** does.

Self-Check 3.5.1 *In the* **method_missing** *example above, why are* ^ *and* $ *necessary in* *the regular expression match in line 4? (Hint: consider what happens if you omit them and call* **5.minutes***)*

◇ Without **$**, a call like **5.minutes** would match the regular expression and lead to infinite recursion as **method_missing** tries to call **5.minutess**; we want to match only the singular. Without **^**, a call like **5.millisecond** would match, which will cause an error when **method_missing** tries to redispatch the call as **5.milliseconds**; we want to match only the whole word. ■

■*Elaboration: Pitfalls of dynamic language features*

If your **Bar** class has actually been using an instance variable **@fox** but you accidentally write **attr_accessor :foo** (instead of **attr_accessor :fox**), you will get an error when you write **mybar.fox**. Since Ruby doesn't require you to declare instance variables, **attr_accessor** cannot check whether the named instance variable exists. Therefore, as with all dynamic language features, we must employ care in using it, and cannot "lean on the compiler" as we would in Java. As we will see in Chapter 5, test-driven development (TDD) helps avoid such errors. Furthermore, to the extent that your app is part of a larger Service-Oriented Architecture ecosystem, you *always* have to worry about runtime errors in other services that your app depends on, as we'll see in Chapters 6 and 10.

■*Elaboration: Variable length argument lists*

A call such as **1.minute** doesn't have any arguments—the only thing that matters is the receiver, **1**. So when the call is redispatched in line 5 of **method_missing**, we don't need to pass any of the arguments that were collected in ***args**. The asterisk is how Ruby deals with argument lists that have zero or more arguments: ***args** will be an array of any arguments passed to the original method, and if no arguments were passed it will be an empty array. It would be correct in any case for line 5 to read **self.send(name+'s', *args)** if we weren't sure what the length of the argument list was.

Self-Check 3.5.2 *Why should* **method_missing** *always call* **super** *if it can't handle the missing method call itself?*

◇ It's possible that one of your ancestor classes intends to handle the call, but you must explicitly "pass the method call up the chain" with **super** to give the ancestor classes a chance to do so. ■

Self-Check 3.5.3 *In the example above, is* **Time.now** *a class method, an instance method, or a constant?*

◇ It can't be a constant, since the current time is constantly changing. The fact that its receiver is a class name (**Time**) tells us it's a class method. ■

3.6 Blocks: Iterators, Functional Idioms, and Closures

Ruby uses the term ***block*** somewhat differently than other languages do. In Ruby, a block is just a method without a name, or an ***anonymous lambda expression*** in programming-language terminology. Like a regular named method, it has arguments and can use local variables. Here is a simple example assuming **movies** is an array of **Movie** objects as we defined in the previous examples:

http://pastebin.com/fdj7wkjj

```
1 | movies.each do |m|
2 |   puts "#{m.title} is rated #{m.rating}"
3 | end
```

The method **each** is an *iterator* available in all Ruby classes that are collection-like. **each** takes one argument—a block—and passes each element of the collection to the block in turn. As you can see, a block is bracketed by **do** and **end**; if the block takes arguments, the argument list is enclosed in |pipe symbols| after the **do**. The block in this example takes one argument: each time through the block, **m** is set to the next element of **movies**.

Unlike named methods, a block can also access any variable accessible to the scope in which the block appears. For example:

http://pastebin.com/NsVvfaeD

```
1 | separator = '=>'
2 | movies.each do |m|
3 |   puts "#{m.title} #{separator} #{m.rating}"
4 | end
```

In the above code, the value of **separator** is visible inside the block, even though the variable was created and assigned *outside* the block. In contrast, the following would *not* work, because **separator** is not visible within **print_movies**, and therefore not visible to the **each** block:

http://pastebin.com/UFBAkQMf

```
1 | separator = '=>'
2 | print_movies(movies)
3 | #
4 | def print_movies(movie_list)
5 |   movie_list.each do |m|
6 |     puts "#{m.title} #{separator} #{m.rating}"   # === FAILS!! ===
7 |   end
8 | end
```

In programming-language parlance, a Ruby block is a ***closure***: whenever the block executes, it can "see" the entire lexical scope available at the place where the block appears in the program text. In other words, it's as if the presence of the block creates an instant snapshot of the scope, which can be reconstituted later whenever the block executes. This fact is exploited by many Rails features that improve DRYness, including view rendering (which we'll see later in this chapter) and model validations and controller filters (Chapter 6), because they allow separating the definition of *what* is to occur from *when* in time and *where* in the structure of the application it occurs.

The fact that blocks are closures should help explain the following apparent anomaly. If the *first* reference to a local variable is inside a block, that variable is "captured" by the block's scope and is *undefined* after the block exits. So, for example, the following will *not* work, assuming line 2 is the *first* reference to **separator** within this scope:

http://pastebin.com/TBRgkU2W

```
1 | movies.each do |m|
2 |   separator = '=>'   # first assignment is inside a block!
3 |   puts "#{m.title} #{separator} #{m.rating}"   # OK
4 | end
5 | puts "Separator is #{separator}"        # === FAILS!! ===
```

In a lexically-scoped language such as Ruby, variables are visible to the scope within which they're created and to all scopes enclosed by that scope. Because in the above snippet **separator** is *created* within the block's scope, its visibility is limited to that scope.

In summary, **each** is just an instance method on a collection that takes a single argument (a block) and provides elements to that block one at a time. A related use of blocks is

operations on collections, a common idiom Ruby borrows from ***functional programming***.
For example, to double every element in a collection, we could write:

http://pastebin.com/iVZQ6HB8

```
1  new_collection = collection.map do |elt|
2      2 * elt
3  end
```

If the parsing is unambiguous, it is idiomatic to use curly braces to delineate a short
(one-line) block rather than **do...end**:

http://pastebin.com/XMZmTSRL

```
1  new_collection = collection.map { |elt| 2 * elt }
```

Ruby has a wide variety of such collection operators; Figure 3.6 lists some of the most
useful. With some practice, you will automatically start to express operations on collections
in terms of these functional idioms rather than in terms of imperative loops. For example,
to return a list of all the words in some file (that is, tokens consisting entirely of word
characters and separated by non-word characters) that begin with a vowel, are sorted, and
without duplicates:

> **So, no for-loops?**
> Although Ruby allows **for i in collection**, **each** allows us to take better advantage of ***duck typing***, which we'll see shortly, to improve code reuse.

http://pastebin.com/QEBi12kk

```
1  # downcase and split are defined in String class
2  words = IO.read("file").
3      split(/\W+/).
4      select { |s|  s =~ /^[aeiou]/i }.
5      map { |s|  s.downcase }.
6      uniq.
7      sort
```

(Recall that Ruby allows breaking a single statement across lines for readability as long
as it's not ambiguous where the statement ends. The periods at the end of each line make
it clear that the statement continues, since a period must be followed by a method call.)
In general, if you find yourself writing explicit loops in Ruby, you should reexamine your
code to see if these collection idioms wouldn't make it more concise and readable.

Summary

- Ruby includes aspects of ***functional programming*** such as the ability to operate
  on entire collections with methods such as **map** and **sort**. It is highly idiomatic to
  use such methods to manipulate collections rather than iterating over them using
  for-loops.

- The **each** collection method returns one element of the collection at a time and
  passes it to a ***block***. Blocks in Ruby can only occur as arguments to methods like
  each that expect a block.

- Blocks are closures: all variables visible to the block's code at the place where
  the block is defined will also be visible whenever the block executes.

- Most methods that appear to modify a collection, such as **reject**, actually return
  a new copy with the modifications made. Some have destructive versions whose
  name ends in **!**, as in **reject!**.

Method	#Args	Returns a *new* collection containing...
c.map	1	elements obtained by applying block to each element of **c**
c.select	1	Subset of **c** for which block evaluates to true
c.reject	1	Subset of **c** obtained by removing elements for which block evaluates to true
c.uniq		all elements of **c** with duplicates removed
c.reverse		elements of **c** in reverse order
c.compact		all non-**nil** elements of **c**
c.flatten		elements of **c** and any of its sub-arrays, recursively flattened to contain only non-array elements
c.partition	1	Two collections, the first containing elements of **c** for which the block evaluates to true, and the second containing those for which it evaluates to false
c.sort	2	Elements of **c** sorted according to a block that takes 2 arguments and returns -1 if the first element should be sorted earlier, +1 if the second element should be sorted earlier, and 0 if the two elements can be sorted in either order.
The following methods require the *collection elements* to respond to $<=>$; see Section 3.7.		
c.sort		If **sort** is called *without* a block, the elements are sorted according to how they respond to $<=>$.
c.sort_by	1	Applies the block to each element of **c** and sorts the result using $<=>$. For example, **movies.sort_by { |m| m.title }** sorts **Movie** objects according to how their titles respond to $<=>$.
c.max, c.min		Largest or smallest element in the collection

Figure 3.6: **Some common Ruby methods on collections. For those that expect a block, we show the number of arguments expected by the block; if blank, the method doesn't expect a block. For example, a call to sort, whose block expects 2 arguments, might look like: c.sort { |a,b| a $<=>$ b }. These methods all return a new object rather than modifying the receiver. Some methods also have a *destructive* variant ending in !, for example sort!, that modify their argument in place (and also return the new value). Use destructive methods with extreme care.**

■ *Elaboration: Blocks and metaprogramming in XML Builder*

An elegant example of combining blocks and metaprogramming is the XML Builder[4] class. (As we mentioned briefly in Section 2.3, HTML is a subset of XML.) In the following example, the XML markup shown in lines 1–8 was generated by the Ruby code in lines 9–18. The method calls **name, phone, address**, and so on all use **method_missing** to turn each method call into an XML tag, and blocks are used to indicate tag nesting.

http://pastebin.com/5bZvPUZZ

```
1  <person type="faculty">
2    <name>Barbara Liskov</name>
3    <contact>
4      <phone location="office">617-253-2008</phone>
5      <email>liskov@csail.mit.edu</email>
6    </contact>
7  </person>
8
9  # Code that generates the above markup:
10 require 'builder'
11 b = Builder::XmlMarkup.new(:indent => 2)
12 b.person(:type => 'faculty') do
13   b.name "Barbara Liskov"
14   b.contact do
15     b.phone(:location => 'office') "617-253-2008"
16     b.email "liskov@csail.mit.edu"
17   end
18 end
```

Self-Check 3.6.1 *Write one line of Ruby that checks whether a string* **s** *is a palindrome, that is, it reads the same backwards as forwards.* **Hint:** *Use the methods in Figure 3.6, and don't forget that upper vs. lowercase shouldn't matter:* ℛ𝑒𝒟𝒾𝓋𝒾𝒹𝑒𝓇 *is a palindrome.*
◇ **s.downcase == s.downcase.reverse**
You might think you could say **s.reverse=~Regexp.new(s)**, but that would fail if **s** happens to contain regexp metacharacters such as **$**. ∎

3.7 Mix-ins and Duck Typing

You may be surprised to learn that the collection methods summarized in Figure 3.6 (and several others not in the figure) aren't part of Ruby's **Array** class. In fact, they aren't even part of some superclass from which **Array** and other collection types inherit. Instead, they take advantage of an even more powerful mechanism for reuse, called ***mix-ins***.

A mix-in is a collection of related behaviors that can be added to any class, although in some cases the class may have to fulfill a "contract" in order to use the mix-in. This may sound similar to an Interface in Java, but there are two differences. First, a mix-in is easier to reuse: the "contract," if any, is specified in the mix-in's documentation rather than being formally declared as a Java interface would be. Second, unlike a Java interface, which says nothing about *how* a class implements an interface, a mix-in is all about making it easy to reuse an implementation.

> If you use the Emacs editor, you can think of Emacs minor modes (auto-fill, abbreviation support, and so on) as mix-ins that rely on contracts provided by the major mode and use Lisp's dynamic typing to allow mixing them into any major mode.

A *module* is Ruby's method for packaging together a group of methods as a mix-in. (Modules have other uses too, but mix-ins are the most important.) When a module is included into a class with **include ModuleName**, the instance methods, class methods, and variables in the module become available in the class.

The collection methods in Figure 3.6 are part of a module called **Enumerable** that is part of Ruby's standard library; to mix **Enumerable** into your own class, just say **include Enumerable** inside the class definition.

As its documentation[5] states, **Enumerable** requires the class mixing it in to provide an **each** method, since **Enumerable**'s collection methods are implemented in terms of **each**. Unlike a Java interface, this simple contract is the *only* requirement for mixing in the module; it doesn't matter what class you mix it into as long as that class defines the **each** instance method, and neither the class nor the mix-in have to declare their intentions in advance. For example, the **each** method in Ruby's **Array** class iterates over the array elements, whereas the **each** method in the **IO** class iterates over the lines of a file or other I/O stream. Mix-ins thereby allow reusing whole collections of behaviors across classes that are otherwise unrelated.

> **Watch out!** Because Ruby allows adding and defining methods at runtime, **include** cannot check whether the module's contract is fulfilled by the class.

The term "duck typing" is a popular description of this capability, because "if something looks like a duck and quacks like a duck, it might as well be a duck." That is, from **Enumerable**'s point of view, if a class has an **each** method, it might as well be a collection, thus allowing **Enumerable** to provide other methods implemented in terms of **each**. Unlike Java's **Interface**, no formal declaration is required for mix-ins; if we invented a new mixin that relied on (say) a class implementing the dereference operator **[]**, we could then mix it into any such class without otherwise modifying the classes themselves. When Ruby programmers say that some class "quacks like an **Array**," they usually mean that it's not necessarily an **Array** nor a descendant of **Array**, but it responds to most of the same methods as **Array** and can therefore be used wherever an **Array** would be used.

Because **Enumerable** can deliver all the methods in Figure 3.6 (and some others) to any class that implements **each**, all Ruby classes that "quack like a collection" mix in

Enumerable for convenience. The methods **sort** (with no block), **max**, and **min** also require that the *elements* of the collection (not the collection itself) respond to the $<=>$ method, which returns -1, 0, or 1 depending on whether its first argument is less than, equal to, or greater than its second argument. You can still mix in **Enumerable** even if the collection elements don't respond to $<=>$; you just can't use **sort**, **max**, or **min**. In contrast, in Java every collection class that implemented the **Enumerable** interface would have to ensure that its elements could be compared, whether that functionality was required or not.

$<=>$ is sometimes called the *spaceship operator* since some people think it looks like a flying saucer.

In Chapter 5 we will see how the combination of mix-ins, open classes, and **method_missing** allows you to write eminently readable unit tests using the RSpec tool.

Summary

- A *mix-in* is a set of related behaviors that can be added to any class that satisfies the mix-in's contract. For example, **Enumerable** is a set of behaviors on enumerable collections that requires the including class to define the **each** iterator.

- Ruby uses modules to group mix-ins. A module is mixed into a class by putting **include ModuleName** after the **class ClassName** statement.

- A class that implements some set of behaviors characteristic of another class, possibly by using mix-ins, is sometimes said to "quack like" the class it resembles. Ruby's scheme for allowing mix-ins without static type checking is therefore sometimes called *duck typing*.

- Unlike interfaces in Java, mix-ins require no formal declaration. But because Ruby doesn't have static types, it's your responsibility to ensure that the class including the mix-in satisfies the conditions stated in the mix-in's documentation, or you will get a runtime error.

■ *Elaboration: Duck typing in the Time class*

Ruby can represent times arbitrarily far in the past or future, can use timezones, and can handle non-Gregorian calendrical systems. Yet as we saw in Section 3.5, when a **Time** object receives a method call like + that expects an arithmetic argument, it attempts to return a representation of itself compatible with the Unix representation (seconds since the epoch). In other words, a **Time** object is not just a simple integer, but when necessary, it quacks like one.

Self-Check 3.7.1 *Suppose you mix* **Enumerable** *into a class* **Foo** *that does not provide the* **each** *method. What error will be raised when you call* **Foo.new.map { |elt| puts elt }**?
◇ The **map** method in **Enumerable** will attempt to call **each** on its receiver, but since the new **Foo** object doesn't define **each**, Ruby will raise an Undefined Method error. ■

Self-Check 3.7.2 *Which statement is correct and why: (a)* **include 'enumerable'** *(b)* **include Enumerable**
◇ (b) is correct, since **include** expects the name of a module, which (like a class name) is a constant rather than a string. ■

http://pastebin.com/tbAWcZE9

```
1   # return every n'th element in an enumerable
2   def every_nth(count)
3     index = 0
4     self.each do |elt|
5       yield elt if index % count == 0
6       index += 1
7     end
8   end
9
10  list = (1..10).to_a # make an array from a range
11  list.every_nth(3) { |s| print "#{s}, " }
12  # => 1, 4, 7, 10
13  list.every_nth(2) { |s| print "#{s}, " }
14  # => 1, 3, 5, 7, 9
```

Figure 3.7: An example of using Ruby's yield, which is based on a construct introduced in the language CLU.

3.8 Make Your Own Iterators Using Yield

The **each** iterator isn't part of the Ruby language: it is just a method that uses a Ruby language feature called **yield**, which first appeared in the CLU language invented by Barbara Liskov. **yield** lets you construct methods like **each** that take a block, and in so doing, provides a new kind of reuse.

Figure 3.7 shows how this unusual construct works. When a method containing **yield** is called, it starts executing until **yield** is reached; at that point, control is transferred to the block that was passed to the method. If **yield** had any arguments, those arguments become the arguments to the block.

A common use of **yield** is implementing iterators like **each** and **every_nth**. Unlike Java, in which you have to create an iterator by passing it a collection of some type and then repeatedly call **while (iter.hasNext())** and **iter.getNext()**, Ruby iterators allow turning the control structure "inside-out" and letting data structures manage *their own* iteration.

yield also enables reuse in situations where you need to "sandwich" some custom functionality inside of some common functionality. For example, consider an app that creates HTML pages and uses a standard HTML template for most pages that looks like this, where the only difference between different pages is captured by line 8:

Barbara Liskov (1939–) received the 2008 Turing Award for foundational innovations in programming language design. Her inventions include abstract data types and iterators, both of which are central to Ruby.

http://pastebin.com/49uSasCn

```
1   <!DOCTYPE html>
2   <html>
3     <head>
4     <title>Report</title>
5     </head>
6     <body>
7       <div id="main">
8         ...user-generated content here...
9       </div>
10    </body>
11  </html>
```

Don't confuse this use of the term *yield* with the unrelated usage from operating systems, in which one thread or process is said to *yield* to another by giving up the CPU.

In most languages, we could encapsulate the code that generates the boilerplate in lines 1–7 and 9–11 in methods called **make_header** and **make_footer**, and then require each method that wants to generate a page to do this:

http://pastebin.com/WUDZauuP

```
 1  def one_page
 2     page = ''
 3     page << make_header()
 4     page << "Hello"
 5     page << make_footer()
 6  end
 7  def another_page
 8     page = ''
 9     page << make_header()
10     page << "World"
11     page << make_footer()
12  end
```

Since this code looks repetitive, we might instead wrap up both calls in a single method:

http://pastebin.com/eTNQRyNc

```
 1  def make_page(contents)
 2     page = ''
 3     page << make_header()
 4     page << contents
 5     page << make_footer()
 6  end
 7  #
 8  def one_page
 9     make_page("Hello")
10  end
11  def another_page
12     make_page("World")
13  end
```

But in Chapter 2 we learned that useful design patterns arise from the desire to *separate the things that change from those that stay the same.* **yield** provides a better way to encapsulate the common part—the boilerplate "around" the user content—in its own method:

http://pastebin.com/ZziARCHG

```
 1  def make_page
 2     page = ''
 3     page << make_header()
 4     page << yield
 5     page << make_footer()
 6  end
 7  def one_page
 8     make_page do
 9        "Hello"
10     end
11  end
12  def another_page
13     make_page do
14        "World"
15     end
16  end
```

In this example, when **one_page** calls **make_page**, the **yield** at line 4 returns control to the block at line 9. The block executes, and its return value (in this case, **"Hello"**) is returned to line 4 as the result of the **yield**, and gets appended to **page** (using the **«** operator), after which **make_page** continues.

We can exploit Ruby's idiom for single-line blocks to boil this down to:

http://pastebin.com/wRLaf8Bg

```
1  def make_page
2    make_header << yield << make_footer
3  end
4
5  def one_page
6    make_page { "Hello" }
7  end
8  def another_page
9    make_page { "World" }
10 end
```

As we'll see, **yield** is actually how Rails implements HTML template rendering for views: the common HTML code that goes at the beginning and end of each page is rendered, and then **yield** is used to render the page-specific content in between. In Chapter 9, we'll see how the combination of blocks and the Factory design pattern gives an exceptional degree of conciseness and code beauty in separating the things that change from those that stay the same.

With this brief introduction to Ruby's most distinctive features, we're ready to meet the Rails framework.

Summary

- In the body of a method that takes a block as a parameter, **yield** transfers control to the block and optionally passes it an argument.

- Because the block is a closure, its scope is the one that was in effect when the block was defined, even though the method yielding to the block is executing in a completely different scope.

- Yielding is the general mechanism behind iterators: an iterator is simply a method that traverses some data structure and uses **yield** to pass one element at a time to the iterator's receiver.

Self-Check 3.8.1 *Referring to Figure 3.7, observe that* **every_nth** *uses* **elt** *as an instance variable name in lines 5 and 6. Suppose that in line 11 we used* **elt** *instead of* **s** *as the name of the local variable in our block. What would be the effect of this change, if any, and why?*
◇ There would be no effect. **every_nth** and the block we pass to it execute in different scopes, so there is no "collision" of the local variable name **elt**. ∎

Self-Check 3.8.2 *Referring to Figure 3.7, what would be the effect of changing line 11 as follows:*
list.every_nth(3) { print "Rah" }

◇ A "wrong number of arguments" error would be raised, since line 5 suggests that the block passed to **every_nth** expects 1 argument to be passed, but the block **{ print "Rah" }** is a block of zero arguments. ∎

3.9 Rails Basics: From Zero to CRUD

As we saw in Chapter 2, Rails is a SaaS application framework that defines a particular structure for organizing your application's code and provides an interface to a Rails application server such as Rack. The app server waits for a Web browser to contact your app and maps every incoming request (URI and HTTP method) to a particular action in one of your app's controllers. Rails consists of both the framework itself and a new command `rails` that is used to set up and manipulate Rails apps. Three main modules make up the heart of Rails' support for MVC: ActiveRecord for creating models, ActionView for creating views, and ActionController for creating controllers.

Using the explanation of Model–View–Controller in Chapter 2 as a reference framework, we will start from zero and create the Rotten Potatoes app described in Chapter 2 for maintaining a simple database of movie information. We will briefly visit each of the "moving parts" of a basic Rails application with a single model, in the following order:

1. Creating the skeleton of a new app

2. Routing

3. The database and migrations

4. Models and Active Record

5. Controllers, views, forms, and CRUD

Begin by logging into the bookware VM, changing to a convenient directory such as Documents (`cd Documents`), and creating a new, empty Rails app with `rails new` `myrottenpotatoes -T`. If all goes well, you'll see several messages about files being created, ending with "Your bundle is complete." You can now `cd` to the newly-created `myrottenpotatoes` directory, called the ***app root*** directory for your new app. From now on, unless we say otherwise, all file names will be relative to the app root. Before going further, spend a few minutes examining the contents of the new app directory `myrottenpotatoes`, as described in Figure 3.8, to familiarize yourself with the directory structure common to all Rails apps.

-T omits directories for tests that use Ruby's `Test::Unit` framework, since in Chapter 5 we will use the RSpec testing framework instead. `rails -help` shows more options for creating a new app.

The message "Your bundle is complete" refers to the `Gemfile` that was automatically created for your app. While the Ruby standard library includes a vast collection of useful classes[6], Rubygems is a system for managing external user-contributed Ruby libraries or ***gems***. Bundler, a gem preinstalled with the bookware, looks for a `Gemfile` in the app's root directory that specifies not only what gems your app depends on, but what versions of those gems. It might surprise you that there are already gem names in this file even though you haven't written any app code, but that's because Rails itself is a gem and also depends on several other gems. For example, if you open the `Gemfile` in an editor, you can see that `sqlite3` is listed, because the default Rails development environment expects to use the SQLite3 database.

We will make two changes to `Gemfile`. Add the line **gem 'haml'** to use the Haml templating system rather than the built-in `erb`, and uncomment the line beginning `#gem 'ruby-debug19'` to enable using the Ruby interactive debugger. Now run `bundle install`, which checks if any gems specified in our `Gemfile` need to be installed. In this case no installation should be needed, since we've preloaded most gems you need in the bookware VM. `bundle install` should report that "Your bundle is complete"— just as it did before. As the margin icon suggests, Bundler is the first of many examples we'll encounter of *automation for repeatability:* rather than manually installing the gems your app needs, listing them in the `Gemfile` and letting Bundler install them automatically ensures that the task can be repeated consistently in a variety of environments, eliminating

Gemfile	list of Ruby gems (libraries) this app uses (Chapter 3)
Rakefile	commands to automate maintenance and deployment (Chapter 10)
app	your application
app/models	model code
app/controllers	controller code
app/views	view templates
app/views/layouts	page templates used by all views in the app (see text)
app/helpers	helper methods to streamline view templates
app/assets	static assets (JavaScript, images, stylesheets)
config	basic configuration information
config/environments	settings for running in development vs. production
config/database.yml	database configuration for development vs. production
config/routes.rb	mappings of URIs to controller actions
db	files describing the database schema
db/development.sqlite3	Data storage for SQLite development database
db/test.sqlite3	Database used for running tests
db/migrate/	Migrations (descriptions of changes to database schema)
doc	generated documentation
lib	additional app code shared among M, V, C
log	log files
public	error pages served by Web server
script	development tools, not part of app
tmp	temporary data maintained at runtime

Figure 3.8: The standard directory structure of a Rails project includes an app **directory for the actual application logic with subdirectories for the app's models, views, and controllers, showing how Rails exposes the MVC architectural choice even in the arrangement of project files.**

mistakes in doing such tasks as a possible source of app errors. is important because when
you deploy your app, the information is used to make the deployment environment match
your development environment.

Start the app with `rails server` and point a browser to `http://localhost:3000`.
Recall from Chapter 2 that a URI that specifies only the hostname and port will fetch
the home page. Most Web servers implement the convention that unless the app specifies
otherwise, the home page is `index.html`, and indeed the welcome page you should be
looking at is stored at `public/index.html`—the generic welcome page for new Rails
apps.

If you now visit `http://localhost:3000/movies`, you should get a Routing Error
from Rails. Indeed, you should verify that *anything* you add to the URI results in this
error, and it's because we haven't specified any **routes** mapping URIs to app methods. Try
`rake routes` and verify that unlike the result in Chapter 2, it prints nothing since there
are no routes in our brand-new app. (You may want to open multiple Terminal windows
so that the app can keep running while you try other commands.) More importantly, use
an editor to open the file `log/development.log` and observe that the error message is
logged there; this is where you look to find detailed error information when something
goes wrong. We'll show other problem-finding and debugging techniques in Section 3.13.

To fix this error we need to add some routes. Since our initial goal is to store movie
information in a database, we can take advantage of a Rails shortcut that creates RESTful
routes for the four basic CRUD actions (Create, Read, Update, Delete) on a model. (Recall
that RESTful routes specify self-contained requests of what operation to perform and what
entity, or resource, to perform it on.) Edit `config/routes.rb`, which was auto-generated
by the `rails new` command and is heavily commented. Around line 14 you should see
a line containing **resources :products** and a comment explaining that this shortcut is a
sample resource route that maps HTTP verbs to controller actions automatically. The line
is inside a `routes.draw do` block that begins at line 1 and continues until the end of the
file. Uncomment that line and change it to **resources :movies**. Save the file and run
`rake routes` again, and observe that because of our change to `routes.rb`, the first line
of output says that the URI `GET /movies` will try to call the `index` action of the `movies`
controller.

Using convention over configuration, Rails will expect this controller's actions to be defined in the class **MoviesController**, and if that class isn't defined at application start time,
Rails will try to load it from the file app/controllers/movies_controller.rb. Sure
enough, if you now reload the page `http://localhost:3000/movies` in your browser,
you should see a different error: `uninitialized constant MoviesController`. This
is good news: a Ruby class name is just a constant that refers to the class object, so Rails is
essentially complaining that it can't find the **MoviesController** class, indicating that our
route is working correctly! As before, this error message and additional information are
captured in the log file `log/development.log`.

Having covered the first two steps in the list—setting up the app skeleton and creating
some initial routes—we can move on to setting up the database that will store the models,
the "M" of MVC.

**Address already in
use?** If you see this error,
you already have an app
server listening on the default
port of 3000, so find the
terminal window where you
started it and type Control-C
to stop it if necessary.

Symbol or string?As
with many Rails methods,
resources 'movies'
would also work, but
idiomatically, a symbol
indicates that the value is one
of a fixed set of choices
rather than an arbitrary string.

Summary: You used the following commands to set up a new Rails app:

- `rails new` sets up the new app; the `rails` command also has subcommands to run the app locally with WEBrick (`rails server`) and other management tasks.

- Rails and the other gems your app depends on (we added the Haml templating system and the Ruby debugger) are listed in the app's `Gemfile`, which Bundler uses to automate the process of creating a consistent environment for your app whether in development or production mode.

- To add routes in `config/routes.rb`, the one-line `resources` method provided by the Rails routing system allowed us to set up a group of related routes for CRUD actions on a RESTful resource.

- The log files in the `log` directory collect error information when something goes wrong.

■ *Elaboration: Automatically reloading the app*

You may have noticed that after changing `routes.rb`, you didn't have to stop and restart the app in order for the changes to take effect. In development mode, Rails reloads all of the app's classes on every new request, so that your changes take effect immediately. In production this would cause serious performance problems, so Rails provides ways to change various app behaviors between development and production mode, as we'll see in Section 3.10.

■ *Elaboration: Non-resource-based routes*

The shortcut **resources :movies** creates RESTful routes for CRUD, but any nontrivial app will have many additional controller actions beyond CRUD. The Rails Routing from the Outside In guide[7] has much more detail, but one way to set up routes is to map components of the URI directly to controller and action names. As the table shows, the "wildcard" tokens **:controller** and **:action**, if present, determine the controller and action that will be invoked, and any other tokens beginning with : plus any additional parameters encoded in the URI will be made available in the **params** hash.

Route	Example URI and behaviors
match ':controller/:action/:id' or **match** 'photos/preview/:id'	/photos/preview/3 method: **PhotosController#preview** params[]: {:id=>3}
match 'photos/preview/:id'	/photos/look/3?color=true Error: no route will match (`look` doesn't match **preview**)
match 'photos/:action/:id'	/photos/look/3?color=true method: **PhotosController#look** (`look` matches **:action**) params[]: {:id=>3, :color=>'true'}
match ':controller/:action/:vol/:num'	/magazines/buy/3/5?newuser=true&discount=2 method: **MagazinesController#buy** params[]: {:vol=>3, :num=>5, :newuser=>'true', :discount=>'2'

Self-Check 3.9.1 *Recall the generic Rails welcome page you saw when you first created the app. In the `development.log` file, what is happening when the line `Started GET`*

"assets/rails.png" *is printed? (Hint: recall the steps needed to render a page containing embedded assets, as described in Section 2.3.)*
◇ The browser is requesting the embedded image of the Rails logo for the welcome page.
■

Self-Check 3.9.2 *What are the two steps you must take to have your app use a particular Ruby gem?*
◇ You must a line to your Gemfile and re-run bundle install. ■

3.10 Databases and Migrations

The persistence tier of a Rails app (see Figure 2.7) uses a relational database (RDBMS) by default, for the reasons we discussed in Chapter 2. Amazingly, you don't need to know much about RDBMSs to use Rails, though as your apps become more sophisticated it definitely helps. Just as we use the "lite" Web server WEBrick for development, Rails apps are configured by default to use SQLite3, a "lite" RDBMS, for development. In production you'd use a production-ready database such as MySQL, PostgreSQL or Oracle.

But more important than the "lightweight" aspect is that you wouldn't want to develop or test your app against the production database, as bugs in your code might accidentally damage valuable customer data. So Rails defines three *environments*—production, development, and test—each of which manages its own separate copy of the database, as specified in config/database.yml. The test database is entirely managed by the testing tools and should never be modified manually: it is wiped clean and repopulated at the beginning of every testing run, as we'll see in Chapter 5.

An empty database was created for us by the rails new command in the file db/development.sqlite3, as specified in **config/database.yml**. We need to create a table for movie information. We could use the sqlite3 command-line tool or a SQLite GUI tool to do this manually, but how would we later create the table in our production database when we deploy? Typing the same commands a second time isn't DRY, and the exact commands might be hard to remember. Further, if the production database is something other than SQLite3 (as is almost certainly the case), the specific commands might be different. And in the future, if we add more tables or make other changes to the database, we'll face the same problem.

A better alternative is a ***migration***—a portable script for changing the database schema (layout of tables and columns) in a consistent and repeatable way, just as Bundler uses the Gemfile to identify and install necessary gems (libraries) in a consistent and repeatable way. Changing the schema using migrations is a three-step process:

1. Create a migration describing what changes to make. As with rails new, Rails provides a migration ***generator*** that gives you the boilerplate code, plus various helper methods to describe the migration.

2. Apply the migration to the development database. Rails defines a rake task for this.

3. Test your code, and if all is well, apply the migration to the production database. The process for doing this depends on the deployment environment; Chapter 8 covers how to do it using Heroku, the cloud computing deployment environment used for the examples in this book.

http://pastebin.com/VYwbc5fq

```
 1  class CreateMovies < ActiveRecord::Migration
 2    def up
 3      create_table 'movies' do |t|
 4        t.string 'title'
 5        t.string 'rating'
 6        t.text 'description'
 7        t.datetime 'release_date'
 8        # Add fields that let Rails automatically keep track
 9        # of when movies are added or modified:
10        t.timestamps
11      end
12    end
13
14    def down
15      drop_table 'movies' # deletes the whole table and all its data!
16    end
17  end
```

Figure 3.9: A migration that creates a new Movies table, specifying the desired fields and their types. The documentation for the ActiveRecord::Migration class (from which all migrations inherit) is part of the Rails documentation[9], and gives more details and other migration options.

We'll use this 3-step process to add a new table that stores each movie's title, rating, description, and release date, to match Chapter 2. Each migration needs a name, and since this migration will create the movies table, we choose the name CreateMovies. Run the command `rails generate migration create_movies`, and if successful, you will find a new file under `db/migrate` whose name begins with the creation time and date and ends with the name you supplied, for example, `20111201180638_create-_movies.rb`. (This naming scheme lets Rails apply migrations in the order they were created, since the file names will sort in date order.) Edit this file to make it look like Figure 3.9. As you can see, migrations illustrate an idiomatic use of blocks: the **ActiveRecord::Migration#create_table** method takes a block of 1 argument and yields to that block an object representing the table being created. The methods **string**, **datetime**, and so on are provided by this table object, and calling them results in creating columns in the newly-created database table; for example, **t.string 'title'** creates a column named `title` that can hold a string, which for most databases means up to 255 characters.

Save the file and type `rake db:migrate` to actually apply the migration and create this table. Note that this housekeeping task also stores the migration number itself in the database, and by default it only applies migrations that haven't already been applied. (Type `rake db:migrate` again to verify that it does nothing the second time.) `rake db:rollback` will "undo" the last migration by running its **down** method. (Try it.) However, some migrations, such as those that delete data, can't be "undone"; in these cases, the **down** method should raise an **ActiveRecord::IrreversibleMigration** exception.

Summary

- Rails defines three environments—development, production and test—each with its own copy of the database.

- A migration is a script describing a specific set of changes to the database. As apps evolve and add features, migrations are added to express the database changes required to support those new features.

- Changing a database using a migration takes three steps: create the migration, apply the migration to your development database, and (if applicable) after testing your code apply the migration to your production database.

- The `rails generate migration` generator fills in the boilerplate for a new migration, and the **ActiveRecord::Migration** class contains helpful methods for defining it.

- `rake db:migrate` applies only those migrations not already applied to the development database. The method for applying migrations to a production database depends on the deployment environment.

■ Elaboration: Environments

Different environments can also override specific app behaviors. For example, production mode might specify optimizations that give better performance but complicate debugging if used in development mode. Test mode may "stub out" external interactions, for example, saving outgoing emails to a file rather than actually sending them. The file `config/environment.rb` specifies general startup instructions for the app, but `config/environments/production.rb` allows setting specific options used only in production mode, and similarly `development.rb` and `test.rb` in the same directory.

Self-Check 3.10.1 *In line 3 of Figure 3.9, how many arguments are we passing to* **create_table**, *and of what types?*
◇ Two arguments: the first is a symbol and the second is a block. We used poetry mode, allowing us to omit parentheses. ■

Self-Check 3.10.2 *In Figure 3.9, the _____ method yields _____ to the block.*
◇ **create_table**; the variable **t** ■

3.11 Models: Active Record Basics

With our **Movies** table ready to go, we've completed the first three steps—app creation, routing, and initial migration—so it's time to write some app code. The database stores the model objects, but as we said in Chapter 2, Rails uses the Active Record design pattern to "connect" models to the database, so that's what we will explore next. Create a file `app/models/movie.rb` containing just these two lines:

http://pastebin.com/HPTPVfig

```
1  class Movie < ActiveRecord::Base
2  end
```

http://pastebin.com/PS1eJQCa

```
1   ####  Create
2   starwars = Movie.create!(:title => 'Star Wars',
3     :release_date => '25/4/1977', :rating => 'PG')
4   # note that numerical dates follow European format: dd/mm/yyyy
5   requiem =  Movie.create!(:title => 'Requiem for a Dream',
6     :release_date => 'Oct 27, 2000', :rating => 'R')
7   #  Creation using separate 'save' method, used when updating existing
         records
8   field = Movie.new(:title => 'Field of Dreams',
9     :release_date => '21-Apr-89', :rating => 'PG')
10  field.save!
11  field.title = 'New Field of Dreams'
12  ####  Read
13  pg_movies = Movie.where("rating = 'PG'")
14  ancient_movies = Movie.where('release_date < :cutoff and rating = :rating',
15    :cutoff => 'Jan 1, 2000', :rating => 'PG')
16  pg_movies_2 = Movie.find_by_rating('PG')
17  Movie.find(3)   # exception if key not found; find_by_id returns nil instead
18  ####  Update
19  starwars.update_attributes(:description => 'The best space western EVER',
20    :release_date => '25/5/1977')
21  requiem.rating = 'NC-17'
22  requiem.save!
23  ####  Delete
24  requiem.destroy
25  Movie.where('title = "Requiem for a Dream"')
26  ####  Find returns an enumerable
27  Movie.find_all_by_rating('PG').each do |mov|
28    mov.destroy
29  end
```

Figure 3.10: **Although Model behaviors in MVC are usually called from the controller, these simple examples will help familiarize you with ActiveRecord's basic features before writing the controller.**

Thanks to convention over configuration, those two lines `movie.rb` enable a great deal of behavior. To explore some of it, stop the running application with Control-C and instead run `rails console`, which gives you an interactive Ruby prompt like `irb(main):001.0>` with the Rails framework and all of your application's classes already loaded. Figure 3.10 illustrates some basic ActiveRecord features by creating some movies in our database, searching for them, changing them, and deleting them (CRUD). As we describe the role of each set of lines, you should copy and paste them into the console to execute the code. The URI accompanying the code example will take you to a copy-and-pastable version of the code on Pastebin.

Lines 1–6 (Create) create new movies in the database. **create!** is a method of **ActiveRecord::Base**, from which **Movie** inherits, as do nearly all models in Rails apps. ActiveRecord uses convention over configuration in three ways. First, it uses the name of the class (**Movie**) to determine the name of the database table corresponding to the class (`movies`). Second, it queries the database to find out what columns are in that table (the ones we created in our migration), so that methods like **create!** know which attributes are legal to specify and what types they should be. Third, it gives every **Movie** object attribute getters and setters similar to **attr_accessor**, except that these getters and setters do more than just modify an instance variable. To demonstrate that the getters and setters really are based on the database schema, try **Movie.create(:chunky=>'bacon')**. The error message you get looks discouragingly long, but the first line should tell you that the actual error was that you specified an unknown attribute; the rest is Ruby's way of giving you more context, as we'll discuss further in Section 3.13. Before going on, type **Movie.all**, which returns a collection of all the objects in the table associated with the **Movie** class.

For the purposes of demonstration, we specified the release date in line 6 using a different format than in line 3. Because Active Record knows from the database schema that **release_date** is a `datetime` column (recall the migration file in Figure 3.9), it will helpfully try to convert whatever value we pass for that attribute into a date.

Recall from Figure 3.1 that methods whose names end in **!** are "dangerous." **create!** is dangerous in that if anything goes wrong in creating the object and saving it to the database, an exception will be raised. The non-dangerous version, **create**, returns the newly-created object if all goes well or **nil** if something goes wrong. For interactive use, we prefer **create!** so we don't have to check the return value each time, but in an application it's much more common to use **create** and check the return value.

Lines 7–11 (Create) show that Active Record model objects in memory are independent of the copies in the database, which must be updated explicitly. For example, lines 8–9 create a new **Movie** object *in memory* without saving it to the database. (You can tell by trying **Movie.all** after executing lines 8–9. You won't see *Field of Dreams* among the movies listed.) Line 10 actually persists the object to the database. The distinction is critical: line 11 changes the value of the movie's **title** field, but *only on the in-memory copy*—do **Movie.all** again and you'll see that the database copy hasn't been changed. **save** and **create** both cause the object to be written to the database, but simply changing the attribute values doesn't.

Lines 12–15 (Read) show one way to look up objects in the database. The **where** method is named for the `WHERE` keyword in SQL, the Structured Query Language used by most RDBMSs including SQLite3. You can specify a constraint directly as a string as in line 13, or use keyword substitution as in lines 14–15. Keyword substitution is always preferred because, as we will see in Chapter 10, it allows Rails to thwart *SQL injection attacks* against your app. As with **create!**, the time was correctly converted from a string to a **Time** object and thence to the database's internal representation of time. Since the conditions specified might match multiple objects, **where** always returns an **Enumerable** on which you can call any of **Enumerable**'s methods, such as those in Figure 3.6.

Line 16 (Read) shows another way to look up objects that uses **method_missing**. If you make a method call on a model class of the form **find_by_***attribute* where *attribute* matches one of the model's attributes, ActiveRecord overrides **method_missing** (just as we did in Section 3.5) to intercept that call, turning line 16 into something like **find.where("rating='PG'")**. You could even say **find_by_release_date_and_-rating** and pass two arguments. These methods return *one* such object found (and you shouldn't rely on which one); if you instead say **find_all_by_***attribute*, you get back an **Enumerable** of all matching elements.

Line 17 (Read) shows the most primitive way of looking up objects, which is to return a single object corresponding to a given primary key. Recall from Figure 2.11 that every object stored in an RDBMS is assigned a primary key that is devoid of semantics but guaranteed to be unique within that table. When we created our table in the migration, Rails included a numeric primary key by default. Since the primary key for an object is permanent and unique, it often identifies the object in RESTful URIs, as we saw in Section 2.7.

Lines 18–22 (Update) show how to Update an object. As with **create** vs. **save**, we have two choices: use **update_attributes** to update the database immediately, or change the attribute values on the in-memory object and then persist it with **save!** (which, like **create!**, has a "safe" counterpart **save** that returns **nil** rather than raising an exception if something goes wrong).

Lines 23–25 (Delete) show how to **D**elete an object. The **destroy** method (line 24) deletes the object from the database permanently. You can still inspect the in-memory copy of the object, but trying to modify it, or to call any method on it that would cause a database access, will raise an exception. (After doing the **destroy**, try **requiem.update_attributes(...)** or even **requiem.rating='R'** to prove this.)

Lines 26–29 show that the result of **find_all_by_***attribute* does indeed quack like a collection—we can use **each** to iterate over it and delete each movie in turn.

This whirlwind overview of Active Record barely scratches the surface, but it should clarify how the methods provided by **ActiveRecord::Base** support the basic CRUD actions.

Summary

- Active Record uses convention over configuration to infer database table names from the names of model classes, and to infer the names and types of the columns (attributes) associated with a given kind of model.

- Basic Active Record support focuses on the CRUD actions: create, read, update, delete.

- Model instances can be **C**reated either by calling **new** followed by **save** or by calling **create**, which combines the two.

- Every model saved in the database receives an ID number unique within its table called the primary key, whose attribute name (and therefore column name in the table) is **id** and which is never "recycled" (even if the corresponding row is deleted). The combination of table name and **id** uniquely identifies a model stored in the database, and is therefore how objects are usually referenced in RESTful routes.

- Models can be **R**ead (looked up) by using **where** to express the matching conditions or **find** to look up the primary key (ID) directly, as might occur if processing a RESTful URI that embeds an object ID.

- Model instances can be **U**pdated with **update_attributes**.

- Model instances can be **D**eleted with **destroy**, after which the in-memory copy can still be read but not modified or asked to access the database.

■ *Elaboration: It quacks like a collection, but it isn't one*

The object returned by ActiveRecord's **all**, **where** and **find**-based methods certainly quacks like a collection, but as we will see in Chapter 9, it's actually a *proxy object* that doesn't even do the query until you force the issue by asking for one of the collection's elements, allowing you to build up complex queries with multiple **where**s without paying the cost of doing the query each time.

■ *Elaboration: Overriding convention over configuration*

Convention over configuration is great, but there are times you may need to override it. For example, if you're trying to integrate your Rails app with a non-Rails legacy app, the database tables may already have names that don't match the names of your models, or you may want friendlier attribute names than those given by taking the names of the table's columns. All of these defaults can be overridden at the expense of more code, as the ActiveRecord documentation describes. In this book we choose to reap the benefits of conciseness by sticking to the conventions.

Self-Check 3.11.1 *Why are* **where** *and* **find** *class methods rather than instance methods?*
◇ Instance methods operate on one instance of the class, but until we look up one or more objects, we have no instance to operate on. ■

Self-Check 3.11.2 *Do Rails models acquire the methods* **where** *and* **find** *via (a) inheritance or (b) mix-in? (Hint: check the* `movie.rb` *file.)*
◇ (a) they inherit from **ActiveRecord::Base**. ■

3.12 Controllers and Views

We'll complete our tour by creating some views to support the CRUD actions we just learned about. The RESTful routes we defined previously (`rake routes` to remind yourself what they are) expect the controller to provide actions for **index**, **show**, **new/create** (recall from Chapter 2 that creating an object requires two interactions with the user), **edit/update** (similarly), and **destroy**. Starting with the two easiest actions, **index** should display a list of all movies, allowing us to click on each one, and **show** should display details for the movie we click on.

For the **index** action, we know from the walk-through examples in Section 3.11 that **Movie.all** returns a collection of all the movies in the Movies table. Thus we need a controller method that sets up this collection and an HTML view that displays it. By convention over configuration, Rails expects the following for a method implementing the Show RESTful action on a Movie resource (note the uses of singular vs. plural and of CamelCase vs. snake_case):

- The model code is in class **Movie**, which inherits from **ActiveRecord::Base** and is defined in `app/models/movie.rb`

- The controller code is in class **MoviesController**, which inherits from **ActionController** and is defined in `app/controllers/movies_controller.rb` (note that the model's class name is pluralized to form the controller file name.)

- Each instance method of the controller is named using **snake_lower_case** according to the action it handles, so the **show** method would handle the Show action

- The Show view template is in `app/views/movies/show.html.haml`, with the `.haml` extension indicating use of the Haml renderer. Other extensions include `.xml` for a file containing XML Builder code (as we saw in Section 3.6, `.erb` (which we'll meet shortly) for Rails' built-in Embedded Ruby renderer, and many others.

http://pastebin.com/A3aj5W42

```
1  # This file is app/controllers/movies_controller.rb
2  def index
3    @movies = Movie.all
4  end
```

http://pastebin.com/CegypDvc

```
1  -# This file is app/views/movies/index.html.haml
2  %h2 All Movies
3
4  %table#movies
5    %thead
6      %tr
7        %th Movie Title
8        %th Rating
9        %th Release Date
10       %th More Info
11   %tbody
12     - @movies.each do |movie|
13       %tr
14         %td= movie.title
15         %td= movie.rating
16         %td= movie.release_date
17         %td= link_to "More about #{movie.title}", movie_path(movie)
```

Figure 3.11: The controller code and template markup to support the Index RESTful action.

The Rails module that choreographs how views are handled is **ActionView::Base**. Since we've been using the Haml markup for our views (recall we added the Haml gem to our `Gemfile` dependencies), our view files will have names ending in `.html.haml`. Therefore, to implement the Index RESTful action, we must define an **index** action in `app/controllers/movies_controller.rb` and a view template in `app/views/movies/index.html.haml`. Create these two files using Figure 3.11 (you will need to create the intermediate directory `app/views/movies/`).

The controller method just retrieves all the movies in the Movies table using the **all** method introduced in the previous section, and assigns it to the **@movies** instance variable. Recall from the tour of a Rails app in Chapter 2 that instance variables defined in controller actions are available to views; line 12 of `index.html.haml` iterates over the collection **@movies** using **each**. There are three things to notice about this simple template.

First, the columns in the table header (`th`) just have static text describing the table columns, but the columns in the table body (`td`) use Haml's = syntax to indicate that the tag content should be evaluated as Ruby code, with the result substituted into the HTML document. In this case, we are using the attribute getters on **Movie** objects supplied by **ActiveRecord**.

Second, we've given the table of movies the HTML ID `movies`. We will use this later for visually styling the page using CSS, as we learned about in Chapter 2.

Third is the call in line 17 to **link_to**, one of many helper methods provided by **ActionView** for creating views. As its documentation[11] states, the first argument is a string that will appear as a link (clickable text) on the page and the second argument is used to create the URI that will become the actual link target. This argument can take several forms; the form we've used takes advantage of the URI helper **movie_path()** (as shown by `rake routes` for the **show** action), which takes as its argument an instance of a RESTful resource (in this case an instance of **Movie**) and generates the RESTful URI for the Show RESTful route for that object. As `rake routes` reminds you, the Show ac-

Sanitization Haml's = syntax sanitizes[10] the result of evaluating the Ruby code before inserting it into the HTML output, to help thwart cross-site scripting and similar attacks described in Chapter 10.

Helper method	URI returned	RESTful Route and action	
movies_path	/movies	GET /movies	index
movies_path	/movies	POST /movies	create
new_movie_path	/movies/new	GET /movies/new	new
edit_movie_path(m)	/movies/1/edit	GET /movies/:id/edit	edit
movie_path(m)	/movies/1	GET /movies/:id	show
movie_path(m)	/movies/1	PUT /movies/:id	update
movie_path(m)	/movies/1	DELETE /movies/:id	destroy

Figure 3.12: As described in the documentation for the ActionView::Helpers class, Rails uses metaprogramming to create route helpers based on the name of your ActiveRecord class. m is assumed to be an ActiveRecord Movie object. The RESTful routes are as displayed by the output of rake routes; recall that different routes may have the same URI but different HTTP methods, for example create vs. index.

tion for a movie is expressed by a URI /movies/:id where :id is the movie's primary key in the Movies table, so that's what the link target created by **link_to** will look like. To verify this, restart the application (rails server in the app's root directory) and visit http://localhost:3000/movies/, the URI corresponding to the index action. If all is well, you should see a list of any movies in the database. If you use your browser's View Source option to look at the generated source, you can see that the links generated by **link_to** have URIs corresponding to the **show** action of each of the movies. (Go ahead and click one, but expect an error since we haven't yet created the controller's **show** method.)

The resources :movies line that we added in Section 3.9 actually creates a whole variety of helper methods for RESTful URIs, summarized in Figure 3.12. As you may have guessed, convention over configuration determines the names of the helper methods, and metaprogramming is used to define them on the fly as the result of calling resources :movies. The creation and use of such helper methods may seem gratuitous until you realize that it is possible to define much more complex and irregular routes beyond the standard RESTful ones we've been using so far, or that you might decide during the development of your application that a different routing scheme makes more sense. The helper methods insulate the views from such changes and let them focus on *what* to display rather than including code for *how* to display it.

■ *Elaboration: Reflection and metaprogramming for conciseness*

More concisely, if **link_to**'s second argument is an ActiveRecord model of class **Movie**, **link_to** will implicitly call **movie_path** on it so you don't have to. So the **link_to** call could have been written as
link_to "More about #movie.title", movie.

There's one last thing to notice about these views. If you View Source in your browser, you'll see it includes HTML markup that doesn't appear in our Haml template, such as a head element containing links to the application.css stylesheet and a title tag. This markup comes from the application template, which "wraps" all views by default. The default file app/views/layouts/application.html.erb created by the rails new command uses Rails' erb templating system, but since we like Haml's conciseness, we recommend deleting that file and replacing it with Figure 3.13, then watch Screencast 3.12.1 to understand how the "wrapping" process works.

http://pastebin.com/VCgyH4u8

```
 1   !!! 5
 2   %html
 3     %head
 4       %title Rotten Potatoes!
 5       = stylesheet_link_tag 'application'
 6       = javascript_include_tag 'application'
 7       = csrf_meta_tags
 8
 9     %body
10       = yield
```

Figure 3.13: Save this file as `app/views/layouts/application.html.haml` **and delete the existing**
`application.html.erb` **in that directory; this file is its Haml equivalent. Line 6 loads some basic JavaScript support;
while we won't discuss JavaScript programming until Chapter 6, some of Rails' built-in helpers use it transparently. Line
7 introduces protection against** *cross-site request forgery* **attacks described in Chapter 10. We also made the** title
element a bit more human-friendly.

http://pastebin.com/yMujWkYv

```
 1   # in app/controllers/movies_controller.rb
 2
 3   def show
 4     id = params[:id] # retrieve movie ID from URI route
 5     @movie = Movie.find(id) # look up movie by unique ID
 6     # will render app/views/movies/show.html.haml by default
 7   end
```

**Figure 3.14: An example implementation of the controller method for the Show action. A more robust implementation
would use find_by_id and check the result, as we warned in Section 3.11. We'll show how to handle such cases in
Chapter 6.**

Screencast 3.12.1: The Application layout.
`http://vimeo.com/34754667`
The screencast shows that the `app/views/layouts/application` template is used to
"wrap" action views by default, using **yield** much like the example in Section 3.8.

On your own, try creating the controller action and view for **show** using a similar
process:

1. Use `rake routes` to remind yourself what name you should give to the controller
   method and what parameters will be passed in the URI

2. In the controller method, use the appropriate ActiveRecord method introduced in
   Section 3.11 to retrieve the appropriate **Movie** object from the database and assign
   it to an instance variable

3. Create a view template in the right location in the `app/views` hierarchy and use
   Haml markup to show the various attributes of the **Movie** object you set up in the
   controller method

4. Exercise your method and view by clicking on one of the movie links on the `index`
   view

Once you're done, you can check yourself against the sample controller method in
Figure 3.14 and the sample view in Figure 3.15. Experiment with other values for the
arguments to **link_to** and **strftime** to get a sense of how they work.

http://pastebin.com/ALAf1fwb

```
1  -# in app/views/movies/show.html.haml
2
3  %h2 Details about #{@movie.title}
4
5  %ul#details
6    %li
7      Rating:
8      = @movie.rating
9    %li
10     Released on:
11     = @movie.release_date.strftime("%B %d, %Y")
12
13 %h3 Description:
14
15 %p#description= @movie.description
16
17 = link_to 'Back to movie list', movies_path
```

Figure 3.15: An example view to go with Figure 3.14. For future CSS styling, we gave unique ID's to the bullet-list of details (ul) and the one-paragraph description (p). We used the strftime library function[13] to format the date more attractively, and the link_to method with the RESTful helper movies_path (Figure 3.12) to provide a convenient link back to the listings page. In general, you can append _path to any of the RESTful resource helpers in the leftmost column of the rake routes output to call a method that will generate the corresponding RESTful URI.

Since the current "bare-bones" views are ugly, as long as we're going to keep working on this app we might as well have something more attractive to look at. Copy the simple CSS styling below into app/assets/stylesheets/application.css, which is already included by line 5 of the application.html.haml template.

http://pastebin.com/PBLKpPyk

```
1  /* Simple CSS styling for RottenPotatoes app */
2  /* Add these lines to app/assets/stylesheets/application.css */
3
4
5  html {
6    font-family: Verdana,Helvetica,sans-serif;
7    color: navy;
8  }
9
10 body {
11   background-color: silver;
12 }
13
14 h1, h2 {
15   background-color: #ddd;
16   margin: 0;
17 }
18 form label {
19   display: block;
20   color: #333;
21   font-style: italic;
22         padding-top: 1ex;
23         padding-left: 1ex;
24 }
```

Summary:

- The Haml templating language allows you to intersperse HTML tags with Ruby code for your views. The result of evaluating Ruby code can either be discarded or interpolated into the HTML page.

- For conciseness, Haml relies on indentation to reveal HTML element nesting.

- Convention over configuration is used to determine the file names for controllers and views corresponding to a given model. If the RESTful route helpers are used, as in **resources :movies**, convention over configuration also maps RESTful action names to controller action (method) names.

- Rails provides various helper methods that take advantage of the RESTful route URIs, including **link_to** for generating HTML links whose URIs refer to RESTful actions.

Self-Check 3.12.1 *What is the role of indentation in Figure 3.11?*

◇ When one HTML element encloses other elements, indentation tells Haml the structure of the nesting so that it can generate closing tags such as `</tr>` in the proper places. ∎

Self-Check 3.12.2 *In Figure 3.11, Why does line 12 of* `index.html.haml` *begin with - while the tag contents in lines 14–17 begin with* =?

◇ - evaluates code *without* inserting the result into the template, which is appropriate for the **each** block. = evaluates code *and also* inserts the result into the template, which is appropriate for displaying information about each **Movie** object. ∎

Self-Check 3.12.3 *In Figure 3.11, why is there no* **end** *corresponding to the* **do** *in line 12?*

◇ Unlike Ruby itself, Haml relies on indentation to indicate nesting, so the **end** is supplied by Haml when executing the Ruby code in the **do**. ∎

3.13 Debugging: When Things Go Wrong

The amazing sophistication of today's software stacks makes it possible to be highly productive, but with so many "moving parts," it also means that things inevitably go wrong, especially when learning new languages and tools. Errors might happen because you mistyped something, because of a change in your environment or configuration, or any number of other reasons. Although we take steps in this book to minimize the pain, such as using Test-Driven Development (Chapter 5) to avoid many problems and providing a VM image with a consistent environment, errors *will* occur. You can react most productively by remembering the acronym **RASP**: Read, Ask, Search, Post.

Read the error message. Ruby's error messages can look disconcertingly long, but a long error message is often your friend because it gives the ***backtrace*** showing not only the method where the error occurred, but also its caller, its caller's caller, and so on. Don't throw up your hands when you see a long error message; use the information to understand both the proximate cause of the error (the problem that "stopped the show") and the possible paths towards the root cause of the error. This will require some understanding of the syntax of the erroneous code, which you might lack if you blindly cut-and-pasted someone else's code with no understanding of how it works or what assumptions it makes. Of course, a syntax error due to cut-and-paste is just as likely to occur when reusing your own code as someone else's, but at least you understand your own code (right?).

An amusing perspective on the perils of blind "shotgun problem solving" is the Jargon File's hacker koan "Tom Knight and the Lisp Machine."[14]

A particularly common proximate cause of Ruby errors is "Undefined method **foobar** for **nil:NilClass**", which means "You tried to call method **foobar** on an object whose value is **nil** and whose class is **NilClass**, which doesn't define **foobar**." (**NilClass** is a special class whose only instance is the constant **nil**.) This often occurs when some computation fails returns **nil** instead of the object you expected, but you forgot to check for this error and subsequently tried to call a method on what you assumed was a valid object. But if the computation occurred in another method "upstream," the backtrace can help you figure out where.

In SaaS apps using Rails, this confusion can be compounded if the failed computation happens in the controller action but the invalid object is passed as an instance variable and then dereferenced in the view, as in the following excerpts from a controller and view:

http://pastebin.com/Rz2DTTMP

```
1  # in controller action:
2  def show
3    @movie = Movie.find_by_id(params[:id]) # what if this movie not in DB?
4    # BUG: we should check @movie for validity here!
5  end
6
7  -# ...later, in the Haml view:
8
9  %h1= @movie.title
10 -# will give "undefined method 'title' for nil:NilClass" if @movie is nil
```

Ask a coworker. If you are programming in pairs, two brains are better than one. If you're in an "open seating" configuration, or have instant messaging enabled, put the message out there.

Search for the error message. You'd be amazed at how often experienced developers deal with an error by using a search engine such as Google to look up key words or key phrases in the error message. You can also search sites like StackOverflow[15] and Server-Fault[16], which specialize in helping out developers and allow you to vote for the most helpful answers to particular questions so that they eventually percolate to the top of the answer list.

Post a question on one of those sites if all else fails. Be as specific as possible about what went wrong, what your environment is, and how to reproduce the problem:

- **Vague:** "The sinatra gem doesn't work on my system." There's not enough information here for anyone to help you.

- **Better, but annoying:** "The sinatra gem doesn't work on my system. Attached is the 85-line error message." Other developers are just as busy as you and probably won't take the time to extract relevant facts from a long trace.

- **Best:** Look at the actual transcript[17] of this question on StackOverflow. At 6:02pm, the developer provided specific information, such as the name and version of her operating system, the specific commands she successfully ran, and the unexpected error that resulted. Other helpful voices chimed in asking for specific additional information, by 7:10pm, two of the answers had identified the problem.

While it's impressive that she got her answer in just over an hour, it means she also lost an hour of coding time, which is why you should post a question only after you've exhausted the other alternatives. How can you make progress on debugging problems on your own? There are two kinds of problems. In the first kind, an error or exception of some kind stops the app in its tracks. Since Ruby is an interpreted language, syntax errors can cause this (unlike Java, which won't even compile if there are syntax errors). Here are some things to try if the app stops in its tracks.

- Exploit automatic indentation and syntax highlighting. If your text editor insists on indenting a line farther than you want it to be indented, you may have forgotten to close a parenthesis, brace, or **do. . . end** block somewhere upstream, or you may have forgotten to "escape" a special character (for example, a single-quote inside a single-quoted string). If your editor isn't so equipped, you can either write your code on stone tablets, or switch to one of the more productive modern editors suggested in Appendix A.

- Look in the log file, usually `log/development.log`, for complete error information including the backtrace. In production apps, this is often your only alternative, as Rails apps are usually configured to display a more user-friendly error page in production mode, rather than the error backtrace you'd see if the error occurred in development mode.

In the second kind of problem, the app runs but produces an incorrect result or behavior. Most developers use a combination of two approaches to debug such problems. The first is to insert *instrumentation*—extra statements to record values of important variables at various points during program execution. There are various places we can instrument a Rails SaaS app—try each of the below to get a feel for how they work:

printf debugging is an old name for this technique, from the C library function that prints a string on the terminal.

- Display a detailed description of an object in a view. For example, try inserting = **debug(@movie)** or = **@movie.inspect** in any view (where the leading = tells Haml to execute the code and insert the result into the view).

- "Stop the show" inside a controller method by raising an exception whose message is a representation of the value you want to inspect, for example, **raise params.inspect** to see the detailed value of the **params** hash inside a controller method. Rails will display the exception message as the Web page resulting from the request.

- Use **logger.debug(** *message***)** to print *message* to the log. **logger** is available in models and controllers and can record messages with a variety of urgencies; compare `config/environments/production.rb` with `development.rb` to see how the default logging level differs in production vs. development environments.

The second way to debug correctness problems is with an interactive debugger. We already installed the `ruby-debug19` gem via our Gemfile; to use the debugger in a Rails app, start the app server using `rails server --debugger`, and insert the statement **debugger** at the point in your code where you want to stop the program. When you hit that statement, the terminal window where you started the server will give you a debugger prompt. In Section 3.14, we'll show how to use the debugger to shed some light on Rails internals.

To debug non-Rails Ruby apps, insert the line require 'ruby-debug' at the beginning of the program.

Summary

- Use a language-aware editor with syntax highlighting and automatic indentation to help find syntax errors.

- Instrument your app by inserting the output of **debug** or **inspect** into views, or by making them the argument of **raise**, which will cause a runtime exception that will display *message* as a Web page.

- To debug using the interactive debugger, make sure your app's Gemfile includes `ruby-debug19`, start the app server with `rails server --debugger`, and place the statement **debugger** at the point in your code where you want to break.

Self-Check 3.13.1 *Why can't you just use* **print** *or* **puts** *to display messages to help debug your SaaS app?*

◇ Unlike command-line apps, SaaS apps aren't attached to a terminal window, so there's no obvious place for the output of a print statement to go. ■

Self-Check 3.13.2 *Of the three debugging methods described in this section, which ones are appropriate for collecting instrumentation or diagnostic information once your app is deployed and in production?*

◇ Only the **logger** method is appropriate, since the other two methods ("stopping the show" in a controller or inserting diagnostic information into views) would interfere with the usage of real customers if used on a production app. ■

3.14 Form Submission: New and Create

Our last look at views will deal with a slightly more complex situation: that of submitting a form, such as for creating a new movie or updating an existing one. There are three problems we need to address:

1. How do we display a fill-in form to the user?

2. How is the information filled in by the user actually made available to the controller action, so that it can be used in a **create** or **update** ActiveRecord call?

3. What resource should be returned and displayed as the result of a RESTful request to create or update an item? Unlike when we ask for a list of movies or details about a movie, it's not obvious what to display as the result of a create or update.

Of course, before we go further, we need to give the user a way to get to the fill-in form we're about to create. Since the form will be for creating a new movie, it will correspond to the RESTful action **new**, and we will follow convention by placing the form in `app/views/movies/new.html.haml`. We can therefore take advantage of the automatically- provided RESTful URI helper **new_movie_path** to create a link to the form. Do this by adding a single line to the end of `index.html.haml`:

http://pastebin.com/8QZpp64c

```
1  -# add to end of index.html.haml
2
3  = link_to 'Add new movie', new_movie_path
```

http://pastebin.com/RzrDPA3r

```
1   %h2 Create New Movie
2
3   = form_tag movies_path , :method => :post do
4
5     = label :movie, :title, 'Title'
6     = text_field :movie, :title
7
8     = label :movie, :rating, 'Rating'
9     = select :movie, :rating, ['G','PG','PG-13','R','NC-17']
10
11    = label :movie, :release_date, 'Released On'
12    = date_select :movie, :release_date
13
14    = submit_tag 'Save Changes'
```

Figure 3.16: The form the user sees for creating and adding a new movie to Rotten Potatoes.

What controller action will be triggered if the user clicks on this link? Since we used the URI helper **new_movie_path**, it will be the **new** controller action. We haven't defined this action yet, but for the moment, since the user is creating a brand-new movie entry, the only thing the action needs to do is cause the corresponding view for the new action to be rendered. Recall that by default, every controller method automatically tries to render a template with the corresponding name (in this case new.html.haml), so you can just add the following trivial **new** method to movies_controller.rb:

http://pastebin.com/YgSUci2K

```
1   def new
2     # default: render 'new' template
3   end
```

Rails makes it easy to describe a fill-in form in using form tag helpers[18] available to all views. Put the code in Figure 3.16 into app/views/movies/new.html.haml and watch Screencast 3.14.1 for a description of what's going on in it.

Screencast 3.14.1: Views with fill-in forms.

http://vimeo.com/34754683

The **form_tag** method for generating a form requires a route to which the form should be submitted—that is, a URI and an HTTP verb. We use the RESTful URI helper and HTTP POST method to generate a route to the **create** action, as rake routes reminds us.

As the screencast mentions, not all input field types are supported by the form tag helpers (in this case, the date fields aren't supported), and in some cases you need to generate forms whose fields don't necessarily correspond to the attributes of some ActiveRecord object. A separate collection of helpers, ActionView::Helpers::FormTagHelper[19], facilitates this task.

To recap where we are, we created the **new** controller method that will render a view giving the user a form to fill in, placed that view in new.html.haml, and arranged to have the form submitted to the **create** controller method. All that remains is to use the information in **params** (the form field values) to actually create the new movie in the database.

Summary

- Rails provides form helpers to generate a fill-in form whose fields are related to the attributes of a particular type of ActiveRecord object.

- When creating a form, you specify the controller action that will receive the form submission by passing **form_tag** the appropriate RESTful URI and HTTP method (as displayed by `rake routes`).

- When the form is submitted, the controller action can inspect **params[]**, which will contain a key for each form field whose value is the user-supplied contents of that field.

Self-Check 3.14.1 *In line 3 of Figure 3.16, what would be the effect of changing* **:method=>:post** *to* **:method=>:get** *and why?*

◇ The form submission would result in listing all movies rather than creating a new movie. The reason is that a route requires both a URI and a method. As Figure 3.12 shows, the **movies_path** helper with the GET method would route to the **index** action, whereas the **movies_path** helper with the POST method routes to the **create** action. ∎

Self-Check 3.14.2 *Given that submitting the form shown in Figure 3.16 will create a new movie, why is the view called* `new.html.haml` *rather than* `create.html.haml`*?*

◇ A RESTful route and its view should name the resource being requested. In this case, the resource requested when the user *loads* this form is the form itself, that is, the ability to create a new movie; hence `new` is an appropriate name for this resource. The resource requested when the user *submits* the form, named by the route specified for form submission on line 3 of the figure, is the actual creation of the new movie. ∎

3.15 Redirection and the Flash

Recall from the examples in Section 3.11 that the **Movie.create!** call takes a hash of attribute names and values to create a new object. As Screencast 3.15.1 shows, the form field names created by the form tag helpers all have names of the form **params['movie']['title']**, **params['movie']['rating']**, and so on. As a result, the value of **params[:movie]** is exactly a hash of movie attribute names and values, which we can pass along directly using **Movie.create!(params[:movie])**. The screencast also shows the helpful technique of using debug breakpoints to provide a detailed look "under the hood" during execution of a controller action.

Screencast 3.15.1: The Create action.
`http://vimeo.com/34754699`
Inside the **create** controller action, we placed a debug breakpoint to inspect what's going on, and used a subset of the debugger commands in Figure 3.17 to inspect the **params** hash. In particular, because our form's field names all looked like **movie[...]**, **params['movie']** is itself a hash with the various movie fields, ready for assigning to a new **Movie** object. Like many Rails methods, **params[]** can take either a symbol or a string—in fact **params** is not a regular hash at all, but a **HashWithIndifferentAccess**, a Rails class that quacks like a hash but allows its keys to be accessed as either symbols or strings.

n	execute next line
s	execute next statement
f	finish current method call and return
p *expr*	print *expr*, which can be anything that's in scope within the current stack frame
eval *expr*	evaluate *expr*; can be used to set variables that are in scope, as in **eval x=5**
up	go up the call stack, to caller's stack frame
down	go down the call stack, to callee's stack frame
where	display where you are in the call stack
b *file:num*	set a breakpoint at line *num* of *file* (current file if *file:* omitted)
b *method*	set a breakpoint when *method* called
c	continue execution until next breakpoint
q	quit program

Figure 3.17: **Command summary of the interactive Ruby debugger.**

That brings us to the third question posed at the beginning of Section 3.14: what view should we display when the **create** action completes? To be consistent with other actions like **show**, we could create a view app/views/movies/create.html.haml containing a nice message informing the user of success, but it seems gratuitous to have a separate view just to do that. What most web apps do instead is return the user to a more useful page—say, the home page, or the list of all movies—but they display a success message as an added element on that page to let the user know that their changes were successfully saved.

Rails makes it easy to implement this behavior. To send the user to a different page, **redirect_to** causes a controller action to end not by rendering a view, but by restarting a whole new request to a different action. Thus, **redirect_to movies_path** is just as if the user suddenly requested the RESTful Index action GET movies (that is, the action corresponding to the helper **movies_path**): the **index** action will run to completion and render its view as usual. In other words, a controller action must finish by either rendering a view or redirecting to another action. Remove the debug breakpoint from the controller action and modify it to look like the listing below; then test out this behavior by reloading the movie listing page, clicking Add New Movie, and submitting the form.

http://pastebin.com/mbC68hhx

```
1 | # in movies_controller.rb
2 | def create
3 |   @movie = Movie.create!(params[:movie])
4 |   redirect_to movies_path
5 | end
```

Of course, to be user-friendly, we would like to display a message acknowledging that creating a movie succeeded. (We'll soon deal with the case where it fails.) The hitch is that when we call **redirect_to**, it starts a whole new HTTP request; and since HTTP is stateless, all of the variables associated with the **create** request are gone.

To address this common scenario, the **flash[]** is a special method that quacks like a hash, but persists from the current request to the next. (In a moment we'll explore how Rails accomplishes this.) In other words, if we put something into **flash[]** during the current controller action, we can access it during the *subsequent* action. The entire hash is persisted, but by convention, **flash[:notice]** is used for informational messages and **flash[:warning]**

http://pastebin.com/7TwiY5My

```
1   -# this goes just inside %body
2
3   - if flash[:notice]
4     #notice.message
5       %p= flash[:notice]
6   - elsif flash[:warning]
7     #notice.warning
8       %p= flash[:warning]
```

Figure 3.18: Note the use of CSS for styling the flash messages: each type of message is displayed in a div whose unique ID is either notice or warning depending on the message's type, but that share the common class message. This gives us the freedom in our CSS file to either style the two types of messages the same by referring to their class, or style them differently by referring to their IDs. Remarkably, Haml's conciseness allows expressing each div's class and ID attributes *and* the message text to be displayed all on a single line.

is used for messages about things going wrong. Modify the controller action to store a useful message in the **flash**, and try it out:

http://pastebin.com/av9Auxck

```
1   # in movies_controller.rb
2   def create
3     @movie = Movie.create!(params[:movie])
4     flash[:notice] = "#{@movie.title} was successfully created."
5     redirect_to movies_path
6   end
```

What happened? Even though creating a new movie appears to work (the new movie shows up in the list of all movies), there's no sign of the helpful message we just created. As you've probably guessed, that's because we didn't actually modify any of the views to display that message!

But which view should we modify? In this example, we chose to redirect the user to the movies listing, so perhaps we should add code to the Index view to display the message. But in the future we might decide to redirect the user someplace else instead, and in any case, the idea of displaying a confirmation message or warning message is so common that it makes sense to factor it out rather than putting it into one specific view.

Recall that app/views/layouts/application.html.haml is the template used to "wrap" all views by default. This is a good candidate for displaying flash messages since any pending messages will be displayed no matter what view is rendered. Make application.html.haml look like Figure 3.18—this requires adding four lines of code between **%body** and **=yield** to display any pending flash messages at the beginning of the page body.

Try styling all **flash** messages to be printed in red text and centered. You'll need to add the appropriate CSS selector(s) in app/assets/stylesheets/application.css to match the HTML elements that display the **flash** in the Application page template. The CSS properties color: red and text-align: center will get these effects, but feel free to experiment with other visual styles, colors, borders, and so on.

If you do any nontrivial CSS work, you'll want to use a dedicated CSS editor, such as the open-source and cross-platform Amaya[20] or one of many commercial products.

Summary

- Although the most common way to finish a controller action is to render the view corresponding to that action, for some actions such as **create** it's more helpful to send the user back to a different view. Using **redirect_to** replaces the default view rendering with a redirection to a different action.

- Although redirection triggers the browser to start a brand-new HTTP request, the **flash** can be used to save a small amount of information that will be made available to that new request, for example, to display useful information to the user regarding the redirect.

- You can DRY out your views by putting markup to display **flash** messages in one of the application's templates, rather than having to replicate it in every view that might need to display such messages.

Self-Check 3.15.1 *Why must every controller action either render a view or perform a redirect?*

◇ HTTP is a request-reply protocol, so every action must generate a reply. One kind of reply is a view (Web page) but another kind is a redirect, which instructs the browser to issue a new request to a different URI. ∎

Self-Check 3.15.2 *In Figure 3.18, why does line 5 begin with* **%p=** *rather than just* **%p**?

◇ = directs Haml to evaluate the Ruby expression—that is, to get the value of **flash[:notice]**—and substitute it into the view. Without =, the view would display the actual text "`flash[:notice]`". ∎

3.16 Finishing CRUD: Edit/Update and Destroy

We can now follow a similar process to add the code for the **update** functionality. Like **create**, this requires two actions—one to display the form with editable information (**edit**) and a second to accept the form submission and apply the updated information (**update**). Of course, we first need to give the user a way to specify the Edit action, so before going further, modify the show.html.haml view so its last two lines match the code below, where line 2 uses the helper **edit_movie_path** to generate a RESTful URI that will trigger the **edit** action for **@movie**.

http://pastebin.com/TL1vrUur

```
1  -# modify last 2 lines of app/views/movies/show.html.haml to:
2  = link_to 'Edit info', edit_movie_path(@movie)
3  = link_to 'Back to movie list', movies_path
```

In fact, as Figure 3.19 shows, the new/create and edit/update action pairs are similar in many respects.

Use Figure 3.19 to create the edit.html.haml view, which is almost identical new view (Figure 3.16)—the only difference is line 3, which specifies the RESTful route for form submission. As rake routes tells us, the **new** action requires an HTTP POST to the URI /movies, so Figure 3.16 uses **:method=>:post** and the URI helper **movies_path** in the form action. In contrast, the **update** action requires an HTTP PUT to /movies/:id

Shouldn't we DRY out similar things? In Chapter 6 we'll show a way to take advantage of this similarity to DRY out the views, but for now we'll tolerate a little duplication in order to finish the example.)

	Create	Update
Parameters passed to view	none	existing instance of **Movie**
Default form field values	blank	existing movie attributes
Submit button label	"Create Movie" (or "Save Changes")	"Update Movie" (or "Save Changes")
Controller actions	**new** serves form, **create** receives form and modifies database	**edit** serves form, **update** receives form and modifies database
params[]	Attribute values for new movie	Updated attribute values for existing movie

http://pastebin.com/25WV7TwQ

```
1   %h2 Edit Movie
2
3   = form_tag edit_movie_path(@movie), :method => :put do
4
5     = label :movie, :title, 'Title'
6     = text_field :movie, 'title'
7
8     = label :movie, :rating, 'Rating'
9     = select :movie, :rating, ['G','PG','PG-13','R','NC-17']
10
11    = label :movie, :release_date, 'Released On'
12    = date_select :movie, :release_date
13
14    = submit_tag 'Save Changes'
```

Figure 3.19: The edit/update action pair is very similar to the new/create action pair we've already implemented (top); in fact, The Haml markup for the edit view differs from the new view only in line 3 (bottom). In Chapter 6 we will discover ways to DRY out the common parts.

where :id is the primary key of the resource to be updated, so line 3 of Figure 3.19 specifies **:method=>:put** and uses the URI helper **movie_path(@movie)** to construct the URI for editing this specific movie. We could have constructed the URIs manually, using **form_tag "/movies"** in new.html.haml and **form_tag "/movies/#{@movie.id}"** in edit.html.haml, but the URI helpers are more concise, convey intent more clearly, and are independent of the actual URI strings, should those have a reason to change. As we'll see, when your app introduces relationships among different kinds of resources, such as a moviegoer having favorite movies, the RESTful URIs become more complicated and the helpers become correspondingly more concise and easy to read.

Below are the actual controller methods you'll need to add to movies_controller.rb to try out this feature, so go ahead and add them.

http://pastebin.com/TCucUHVc

```
1   # in movies_controller.rb
2
3   def edit
4     @movie = Movie.find params[:id]
5   end
6
7   def update
8     @movie = Movie.find params[:id]
9     @movie.update_attributes!(params[:movie])
10    flash[:notice] = "#{@movie.title} was successfully updated."
11    redirect_to movie_path(@movie)
12  end
```

Try clicking on the Edit link you inserted above to edit an existing movie. Observe that when updating an existing movie, the default filled-in values of the form fields correspond to the movie's current attributes. This is because helpers such as **text_field** in line 6 of the `new` or `edit` templates will by default look for an instance variable whose name matches their first argument—in this case, the first argument is **:movie** so the **text_field** helper will look for a variable **@movie**. If it exists and corresponds to an ActiveRecord model, the helper assumes that this form is for editing an existing object, and **@movie**'s current attribute values will be used to populate the form fields. If it doesn't exist or doesn't respond to the attribute method in the second argument (**'title'**), the form fields will be blank. This behavior is a good reason to name your instance variable **@movie** rather than (say) **@my_movie**: you can still get the extra functionality from the helpers, but you'll have to pass extra arguments to them.

The last CRUD action is Delete, which Figure 3.10 shows can be accomplished by calling **destroy** on an ActiveRecord model. As with the Update action, it's common practice to respond to a Delete by destroying the object and then returning the user to some other useful page (such as the Index view) and displaying a confirmation message that the item was deleted, so we already know how to write the controller method—add the following lines to `movies_controller.rb`:

http://pastebin.com/vgqGSge2

```
1  def destroy
2    @movie = Movie.find(params[:id])
3    @movie.destroy
4    flash[:notice] = "Movie '#{@movie.title}' deleted."
5    redirect_to movies_path
6  end
```

(Recall from the explanation accompanying Figure 3.10 that even after destroying an object in the database, the in-memory copy can still be queried for its attributes as long as we don't try to modify it or ask it to persist itself.)

As we did with Edit, we'll provide access to the Delete action from each movie's Show page. What kind of HTML element should we use? `rake routes` tells us the Delete action requires the URI `/movies/:id` with the HTTP verb DELETE. This seems similar to Edit, whose URI is similar but uses the GET method. Since we've been using the URI helpers to generate routes, you might think that you could construct a clickable link for the Delete action similar to the one we used for Edit:

http://pastebin.com/GiRQQbcd

```
1  -# Our Edit link from previous example:
2  = link_to 'Edit info', edit_movie_path(@movie)
3  -# You might think to try this for Delete, but it won't work:
4  = link_to 'Delete', movie_path(@movie), :method => :delete
```

The reason this won't work has to do with the way Web browsers handle links: clicking on a link *always* uses the GET action, and trying to override this with **:method=>:delete** simply doesn't work.

On the other hand, clicking on a form submission *button* generates a POST, and in those cases, Rails "decorates" the URI of the submitted form so that any **:method=>** overrides are correctly "seen" by the routing subsystem and controller action. (We took advantage of this in Figure 3.19 by specifying PUT as the form submission action; in reality the form is delivered using POST, but before the controller action is called, the HTTP verb is internally changed to PUT because of the `:method=>:put` in line 3.)

So do we really to set up a whole HTTP form just to delete a movie? Yes and no. We will indeed use the HTML form submission mechanism, but we can take advantage of a Rails shortcut provided for just this purpose. Add the following line to the end of the Show view to provide access to the Delete action:

http://pastebin.com/YRCvW2JZ

```
1  = button_to 'Delete', movie_path(@movie), :method => :delete, :confirm => '
     Are you sure?'
```

button_to appears very similar to **link_to**, but what it generates is quite different, as the Screencast 3.16.1 shows.

Screencast 3.16.1: The button_to helper.
`http://vimeo.com/34754731`
The **button_to** helper takes three arguments: the button's textual name, an options hash specifying the route *or* a URI encoding the route, and another hash of optional HTML options. In our usage, the second argument is supplied by the **movie_path** helper, and we provide keys in the HTML options to specify the HTTP submission method and to display a confirmation dialog for the user. The result is a form with only a single user-visible control, namely the button itself, that uses some JavaScript tricks we'll learn in Chapter 6 to supply the confirmation dialog.

■ *Elaboration: GET vs. POST*

Long before RESTfulness became a prominent SaaS concept, there was already a general guideline that SaaS app requests that used GET should always be "safe"—they should not cause any side effects such as deleting an item or purchasing something, and should be safely repeatable. In the language of computer science, GETs should be *idempotent*—doing it many times has the same effect as doing it once. Your browser reflects this guideline: you can always reload or refresh a page that was fetched via GET, but if you try to reload a page that resulted from a POST operation, most browsers will display a warning asking if you really want to resubmit a form. The "GETs should be safe" guideline became particularly important when search engines became widespread, since they crawl (explore the Web) by following links. It would be bad if Google triggered millions of spurious purchases every time it crawled an e-commerce site. So in this sense, Rails' helpers are just providing convenient shortcuts that implement existing best practice.

Try modifying the index view (list of all movies) so that each table row displaying a movie title also includes an Edit link that brings up the edit form for that movie and a Destroy button that deletes that movie with a confirmation dialog.

Self-Check 3.16.1 *Why does the form in* new.html.haml *submit to the* **create** *method rather than the* **new** *method?*
◇ As we saw in Chapter 2, creating a new record requires two interactions. The first one, **new**, loads the form. The second one, **create**, submits the form and causes the actual creation of the new record. ■

Self-Check 3.16.2 *Why does it make no sense to have both a render and a redirect (or two renders, or two redirects) along the same code path in a controller action?*
◇ Render and redirect are two different ways to reply to a request. Each request needs exactly one reply. ■

Summary

- Rails provides various helpers for creating HTML forms that refer to ActiveRecord models. In the controller method that receives the form submission, the keys in the **params** hash are the form fields' name attributes and the corresponding values are the user-selected choices for those fields.

- Creating and updating an object are resources whose visible representation is just the success or failure status of the request. For user friendliness, rather than displaying a web page with just success or failure and requiring the user to click to continue, we can instead **redirect_to** a more useful page such as **index**. Redirection is an alternative way for a controller action to finish, rather than rendering a view.

- For user friendliness, it's typical to modify the application layout to display messages stored in **flash[:notice]** or **flash[:warning]**, which persist until the next request so they can be used with **redirect_to**.

- To specify the URIs required by both form submissions and redirections, we can use RESTFUL URI helpers like **movies_path** and **edit_movie_path** rather than creating the URIs manually.

3.17 Fallacies and Pitfalls

 Pitfall: **Writing Java in Ruby.**

It takes some mileage to learn a new language's idioms and how it fundamentally differs from other languages. Common examples for Java programmers new to Ruby include:

- Thinking in terms of casting rather than method calls: **100.0 * 3** doesn't cast 3 to a Float, but calls **Float#***.

- Reading **a.b** as "attribute **b** of object **a**" rather than "call method **b** on object **a**."

- Thinking in terms of classes and traditional static types, rather than duck typing. When calling a method on an object, or doing a mix-in, all that matters is whether the object responds to the method. The object's type or class are irrelevant.

- Writing explicit for-loops rather than using an iterator such as **each** and the collection methods that exploit it via mix-ins such as **Enumerable**. Use functional idioms like **select**, **map**, **any?**, **all?**, and so on.

- Thinking of **attr_accessor** as a declaration of attributes. This shortcut and related ones save you work *if* you want to make an attribute publicly readable or writable. But you don't need to "declare" an attribute in any way at all (the existence of the instance variable is sufficient) and in all likelihood some attributes *shouldn't* be publicly visible. Resist the temptation to use **attr_accessor** as if you were writing attribute declarations in Java.

Pitfall: **Thinking of symbols and strings as interchangeable.**

While many Rails methods are explicitly constructed to accept either a string or a symbol, the two are not in general interchangeable. A method expecting a string may throw an error if given a symbol, or depending on the method, it may simply fail. For example, **['foo','bar'].include?('foo')** is true, whereas **['foo','bar'].include?(:foo)** is legal but false.

 Pitfall: **Naming a local variable when you meant a local method.**

Suppose class **C** defines a method **x=**. In an instance method of **C**, writing **x=3** will not have the desired effect of calling the **x=** method with the argument 3; rather, it will set a local variable **x** to 3, which is probably not what you wanted. To get the desired effect, write **self.x=3**, which makes the method call explicit.

 Pitfall: **Confusing require with include.**

require loads an arbitrary Ruby file (typically the main file for some gem), whereas **include** mixes in a module. In both cases, Ruby has its own rules for locating the files containing the code; the Ruby documentation describes the use of **$LOAD_PATH**, but you should rarely if ever need to manipulate it directly if you use Rails as your framework and Bundler to manage your gems.

 Pitfall: **Modifying the database manually rather than using migrations, or managing gems manually rather than using Bundler.**

Especially if you've come from other SaaS frameworks, it may be tempting to use the SQLite3 command line or a GUI database console to manually add or change database tables or to install libraries. But if you do this, you'll have no consistent way to reproduce these steps in the future (for example at deployment time) and no way to roll back the changes in an orderly way. Also, since migrations and Gemfiles are just files that become part of your project, you can keep them under version control and see the entire history of your changes.

 Pitfall: **Fat controllers and fat views.**

Because controller actions are the first place in your app's code that are called when a user request arrives, it's remarkably easy for the actions' methods to get fat—putting all kinds of logic in the controller that really belongs in the model. Similarly, it's easy for code to creep into views—most commonly, a view may find itself calling a model method such as **Movie.all**, rather than having the controller method set up a variable such as **@all=Movie.all** and having the view just use **@all**. Besides violating MVC, coupling views to models can interfere with caching, which we'll explore in Chapter 6. The view should focus on displaying content and facilitating user input, and the controller should focus on mediating between the view and the model and set up any necessary variables to keep code from leaking into the view.

3.18 Concluding Remarks: Designing for SOA

The introduction to Rails in this chapter may seem to introduce a lot of very general machinery to handle a fairly simple and specific task: implementing a Web-based UI to CRUD actions. However, we will see in Chapter 6 that this solid groundwork will position us to appreciate the more advanced mechanisms that will let you truly DRY out and beautify your Rails apps.

One simple example we can show immediately relates to Service-Oriented Architecture, an important concept introduced in Chapter 1 and to which we'll return often. If we intended Rotten Potatoes to be used in an SOA, its RESTful actions might be performed either by a human who expects to see a Web page as a result of the action or by another service that expects (for example) an XML response. To simplify the task of making your app work with SOA, you can return different formats for the same resource using the **respond_to**[21] method of **ActionController** (not to be confused with Ruby's built-in **respond_to?** introduced in Section 3.2). **ActionController::MimeResponds#respond_to** yields an object that can be used to select the format in which to render a response. Here's how the **create** action can be immediately converted into an SOA-friendly RESTful API that returns an XML representation of the created object, while preserving the existing user interface for human users:

http://pastebin.com/bT16LhJ4

```
1  def create
2    @movie = Movie.find params[:id]
3    @movie.update_attributes!(params[:movie])
4    respond_to do |client_wants|
5      client_wants.html {  redirect_to movie_path(@movie)  } # as before
6      client_wants.xml  {  render :xml => @movie.to_xml     }
7    end
8  end
```

Similarly, the only reason **new** requires its own controller action is that the human user needs an opportunity to fill in the values that will be used for **create**. Another *service* would never call the **new** action at all. Nor would it make sense to redirect back to the list of movies after a **create** action: the **create** method could just return an XML representation of the created object, or even just a the created object's ID.

Thus, as with many tools we will use in this book, the initial learning curve to do a simple task may seem a bit steep, but you will quickly reap the rewards by using this strong foundation to add new functionality and features quickly and concisely.

3.19 To Learn More

- The online documentation for Ruby[22] and Rails[23] gives details on the language, its classes, and the Rails framework.

- It's worth spending some time skimming the documentation for the Ruby standard library[24]. A few of the most useful classes include **IO** (file and network I/O, including CSV files), **Set** (collection operations such as set difference, set intersection, and so on), and **Time** (the standard class for representing times, which we recommend over **Date** even if you're representing only dates without times).

- Programming Ruby[25] and The Ruby Programming Language (Flanagan and Matsumoto 2008), co-authored by Ruby inventor Yukihiro "Matz" Matsumoto, are definitive references for Ruby.

- The Ruby Way (Fulton 2006) and The Rails 3 Way (Fernandez 2010) go into great depth on Ruby and Rails advanced features and wizardry.

- PeepCode[26] publishes high-quality screencasts covering almost every tool and technique in the Rails ecosystem for a very reasonable price (in the authors' opinion). The two-part Meet Rails 3[27] screencast is a particularly good complement to the information in this chapter.

- Before writing new code for any functionality that isn't specific to your app, check `rubygems`[28] and `rubyforge`[29] (at least) to see if someone has created a gem that does most of what you need. As we saw in this chapter, using a gem is as easy as adding a line to your `Gemfile` and re-running `bundle install`.

O. Fernandez. *Rails 3 Way, The (2nd Edition) (Addison-Wesley Professional Ruby Series)*. Addison-Wesley Professional, 2010. ISBN 0321601661. URL `http://www.amazon.com/Rails-Way-Addison-Wesley-Professional-Ruby/dp/0321601661`.

D. Flanagan and Y. Matsumoto. *The Ruby Programming Language*. O'Reilly Media, 2008. ISBN 0596516177. URL `http://www.amazon.com/Ruby-Programming-Language-David-Flanagan/dp/0596516177`.

H. Fulton. *The Ruby Way, Second Edition: Solutions and Techniques in Ruby Programming (2nd Edition)*. Addison-Wesley Professional, 2006. ISBN 0672328844. URL `http://www.amazon.com/Ruby-Way-Second-Techniques-Programming/dp/0672328844`.

Notes

[1] `http://validator.w3.org`
[2] `http://code.google.com/apis/searchappliance/documentation/50/xml_reference.html#request_parameters`
[3] `http://pastebin.com`
[4] `http://builder.rubyforge.org/`
[5] `http://ruby-doc.org/core-1.9.3/Enumerable.html`
[6] `http://ruby-doc.org/core-1.9.3/`
[7] `http://edgeguides.rubyonrails.org/routing.html`
[8] `http://api.rubyonrails.org/`
[9] `http://api.rubyonrails.org/`
[10] `http://en.wikipedia.org/wiki/HTML_sanitization`
[11] `http://api.rubyonrails.org/classes/ActionView/Helpers/UrlHelper.html#method-i-link_to`
[12] `http://ruby-doc.org/core-1.9.3/Time.html#method-i-strftime`
[13] `http://ruby-doc.org/core-1.9.3/Time.html#method-i-strftime`
[14] `http://catb.org/jargon/html/koans.html`
[15] `http://stackoverflow.com`
[16] `http://serverfault.com`
[17] `http://stackoverflow.com/questions/2945228/i-see-gem-in-gem-list-but-have-no-such-file-to-load`
[18] `http://api.rubyonrails.org/classes/ActionView/Helpers/FormTagHelper.html`
[19] `http://api.rubyonrails.org/classes/ActionView/Helpers/FormTagHelper.html`
[20] `http://www.w3.org/Amaya`
[21] `http://api.rubyonrails.org/classes/ActionController/MimeResponds.html#method-i-respond_to`
[22] `http://ruby-doc.org/core-1.9.3/`
[23] `http://api.rubyonrails.org/`

[24]http://ruby-doc.org
[25]http://ruby-doc.org/docs/ProgrammingRuby
[26]http://peepcode.com
[27]https://peepcode.com/products/meet-rails-3-i
[28]http://rubygems.org
[29]http://rubyforge.org

3.20 Exercises

OO and Classes

Exercise 3.1 *How many class ancestors does the object* **5** *have? (Hint: use method chaining to follow the superclass chain all the way up to* **Object***)*

Exercise 3.2 *Given that* **superclass** *returns* **nil** *when called on* **Object** *but a non-***nil** *value otherwise, write a Ruby method that, if passed any object, will print the object's class and its ancestor classes all the way up to* **Object***.*

http://pastebin.com/0WHkGSbS

```
1  def print_ancestors(obj)
2    klass = obj.class
3    until klass.nil? do
4      puts klass
5      klass = klass.superclass
6    end
7  end
```

Metaprogramming

Exercise 3.3 *Building on the example in Section 3.5, take advantage of* **Time***'s duck typing to define a method* **at_beginning_of_year** *that lets you write:*

http://pastebin.com/Gydkd9K9

```
1  Time.now.at_beginning_of_year + 1.day
2  # => 2011-01-02 00:00:00 -0800
```

Hint 1: The **Time** *documentation[1] will tell you that the* **local** *class method can be used to create a new* **Time** *object with a specified year, month and day.*

Hint 2: The receiver of **at_beginning_of_year** *in the above code is* **now***, just as it was in the example in Section 3.5. But unlike that example, think carefully about how you'd like* **now** *to quack.*

Exercise 3.4 *Define a method* **attr_accessor_with_history** *that provides the same functionality as* **attr_accessor** *but also tracks every value the attribute has ever had:*

http://pastebin.com/Qy75meTC

```
1   class Foo ; attr_accessor_with_history :bar ;   end
2   => nil
3   f = Foo.new
4   => #<Foo:0x127e678>
5   f.bar = 3
6   => 3
7   f.bar = :wowzo
8   => :wowzo
9   f.bar = 'boo!'
10  => 'boo!'
11  f.history(:bar)
12  >> [3, :wowzo, 'boo!']
```

Mix-ins and Iterators

Exercise 3.5 *Recall that the first two integers in the Fibonacci sequence are 1 and 1, and each successive Fibonacci number is the sum of the previous two. Create a class that returns an iterator for the first n Fibonacci numbers. You should be able to use the class as follows:*

http://pastebin.com/FSt1KC5x

```
1  # Fibonacci iterator should be callable like this:
2  f = FibSequence.new(6) # just the first 6 Fibonacci numbers
3  f.each { |s| print(s,':') }  # => 1:1:2:3:5:8:
4  f.reject { |s| s.odd? }      # => [2, 8]
5  f.reject(&:odd?)             # => [2, 8] (a shortcut!)
6  f.map { |x| 2*x }            # => [2, 2, 4, 6, 10, 16]
```

HINT: as long as objects of your class implement **each**, *you can mix in* **Enumerable** *to get* **reject**, **map**, *and so on.*

http://pastebin.com/mhX9JydS

```
1  # Each instance of FibSequence remembers how many Fibonacci numbers are
2  #   desired using the @limit instance variable.
3  # FibSequence#each is just  an instance method that yields the
4  #   first @limit Fibonacci numbers one at a time.
5  class FibSequence
6    include Enumerable
7    def initialize(limit) ; @limit = limit ; end
8    def each
9      case @limit
10     when 0 then return
11     when 1 then yield 1
12     else
13       yield 1
14       yield 1
15       lastfib,nextfib = 1,2
16       @limit.downto(3) do
17         yield nextfib
18         lastfib, nextfib = nextfib, nextfib+lastfib
19       end
20     end
21   end
22 end
```

■

Exercise 3.6 *Referring to the solution for Exercise 3.5, observe that* **each** *uses* **lastfib** *as a local variable (line 11). What will the following code do, and why?*

http://pastebin.com/CE2idL3p

```
1  lastfib = "Surprise!"
2  FibSequence.new(3) do |f|
3    print lastfib
4  end
```

◇ "Surprise!" will be printed, because the **lastfib** in line 1 of the excerpt is in a different scope than the **lastfib** in line 11 of Exercise 3.5. ■

Exercise 3.7 *Referring again to Exercise 3.5, what will the following code do, and why?*

http://pastebin.com/QGPGEsKi

```
1  FibSequence.new(3) do
2    print "Rah"
3  end
```

◇ A "wrong number of arguments" exception will be raised: **yield** will try to pass our block 1 argument, but our block is written to take 0 arguments. ■

Exercise 3.8 *Implement an iterator* **each_with_flattening** *that behaves as follows:*
http://pastebin.com/6g44WBas

```
1  [1, [2, 3], 4, [[5, 6], 7]].each_with_flattening { |s| print "\#\{s\}," }
2  >> 1, 2, 3, 4, 5, 6, 7
```

What assumption(s) must your iterator make about its receiver? What assumption(s) must it make about the elements of its receiver?
http://pastebin.com/wxP4HyDC

```
1  def each_with_flattening
2    self.each do |elt|
3      if elt.respond_to?(:each)
4        elt.each_with_flattening { |s| yield s }
⋄  5      else
6        yield elt
7      end
8    end
9  end
```

■

Exercise 3.9 *An ordered binary tree is one in which every node has an element value and up to 2 children, each of which is itself an ordered binary tree, and all elements in the left subtree of some node are less than any element in the right subtree of that node.*

Define a **BinaryTree** *collection class that provides the instance methods* << *(insert element),* **empty?** *(returns true if tree has no elements), and* **each** *(the standard iterator that yields each element in turn, in any order you desire).*

Exercise 3.10 *Augment your ordered binary tree class so that it also provides the following methods, each of which takes a block:* **include?(elt)** *(true if tree includes elt),* **all?** *(true if the given block is true for all elements),* **any?** *(true if the given block is true for any element),* **sort** *(sorts the elements according to a block of two arguments that returns -1, 0 or 1 depending on whether the first argument is less than, equal to, or greater than the second).* **HINT:** *A single line of code suffices to do all this.*
⋄ Add **include Enumerable** just after opening the class. ■

Exercise 3.11 *Similar to the* **days.ago** *example in Section 3.5, define the appropriate conversions between Euros, US Dollars, and Yen so that you can type the following conversions:*
http://pastebin.com/0SHapuVe

```
1  # assumes 1 Euro=1.3 US dollars, 1 Yen=0.012 US dollars
2  5.dollars.in(:euros)  # => 6.5
3  (1.euro - 50.yen).in(:dollars)  # => 0.700
```

Exercise 3.12 *Which of these methods actually cause mutations to happen the way you expect?*

http://pastebin.com/sNhjFaDJ

```
 1   def my_swap(a,b)
 2     b,a = a,b
 3   end
 4
 5   class Foo
 6   attr_accessor :a, :b
 7     def my_swap_2()
 8       @b,@a = @a,@b
 9     end
10   end
11
12   def my_string_replace_1(s)
13     s.gsub( /Hi/, 'Hello')
14   end
15
16   def my_string_replace_2(s)
17     s.gsub!( /Hi/, 'Hello')
18   end
```

Exercise 3.13 *Extend the* **Time** *class with a* **humanize** *method that prints out an informative phrase describing the time of day to the nearest fifteen-minute division, in twelve-hour mode, and making a special case for midnight:*

http://pastebin.com/9niERnaY

```
 1   >>  Time.parse("10:47 pm").humanize
 2   # => "About a quarter til eleven"
 3   >>  Time.parse("10:31 pm").humanize
 4   # => "About half past ten"
 5   >>  Time.parse("10:07 pm").humanize
 6   # => "About ten"
 7   >>  Time.parse("23:58").humanize
 8   # => "About midnight"
 9   >>  Time.parse("00:29").humanize
10   # => "About 12:30"
```

http://pastebin.com/wuXJkN3U

```
 1   require 'time'
 2   class Time
 3     private
 4       def hour_to_words(hr)
 5         puts self
 6         case hr
 7         when 12 then "noon"
 8         when 0,24 then "midnight"
 9         else ['zero','one','two','three','four','five','six','seven',
10             'eight','nine','ten','eleven'][hr % 12]
11         end
12       end
13     public
14     def humanize
15       "About " +
16         case self.min # what minute is it?
17         when 0..7   then "#{hour_to_words(hour)}"
18         when 8..22  then "a quarter after #{hour_to_words(hour)}"
19         when 23..37 then "half past #{hour_to_words(hour)}"
20         when 38..52 then "a quarter til #{hour_to_words(hour+1)}"
21         when 53..59 then "#{hour_to_words(hour+1)}"
22         end
23     end
24   end
```

■

Rails Basics: Unless otherwise indicated, these exercises are based on the myrottenpotatoes app you created in this chapter.

Exercise 3.14 *Modify the app's routes so that visiting* http://localhost:3000 *takes* you to the list of movies, rather than the generic Rails welcome page. (Hint: consult the ActionDispatch::Routing[2] documentation.)

Exercise 3.15   *1. Add a default banner to the main application layout that will appear on every page of Rotten Potatoes. It should display "Rotten Potatoes" in large red letters, but no visual styling information should go into the template itself. (Hint: pick an element type that reflects the role of this banner, assign it a unique ID, and modify the CSS style file to style the element.)*

2. *Make it so that clicking on the banner always takes you to RP homepage.*

Exercise 3.16 *Instead of redirecting to the Index action after a successful* **create**, *redirect to the* **show** *action for the new movie that was just created. Hint: you can use the* **movie_path** *URI helper but you'll need to supply an argument identifying which movie. To obtain the this argument, recall that* **Movie.create** *if successful returns the newly-created object in addition to creating it.*

Exercise 3.17 *Modify the listing of movies as follows. Each modification task will require making a change at a different layer of abstraction:*

1. *Modify the Index view to include a row number for each row in the movies table. HINT: look up the documentation of the* each_with_index *function used in line 11 of the view template.*

2. *Modify the Index view so that hovering a mouse over a row in the movies table causes the row to temporarily assume a yellow background. HINT: look up the* hover pseudo-class *supported by CSS.*

3. *Modify the Index controller action to return the movies ordered alphabetically by title, rather than by release date. HINT: Don't try to sort the result of the controller's call to the database. RDBMS's provide ways to specify the order in which a list of results is delivered, and because of Active Record's tight coupling to the underlying RDBMS, the Rails* ActiveRecord *library's* find *and* all *methods provide a way to ask the underlying RDBMS to do this.*

4. *Pretend you didn't have the tight coupling of Active Record, and so you could not assume the underlying storage system can return collection items in any particular order. Modify the Index controller action to return the movies ordered alphabetically by title. HINT: Look up the* sort *method in Ruby's* Enumerable *module.*

Exercise 3.18 *What if the user changes his mind before submitting a Create or Update form and decides not to proceed after all? Add a "Cancel" link to the form that just takes the user back to the list of movies.*

Exercise 3.19 *Modify the "Cancel" link so that if it's clicked as part of a Create flow, the user is taken back to the list of movies, but if clicked as part of an Update flow, the user is taken back to the Show template (view) for the movie he began to edit. Hint: the instance method* **ActiveRecord::Base#new_record?** *returns true if its receiver is a new model object, that is, one that has never been saved in the database. Such objects won't have ID's.*

Exercise 3.20 *The dropdown menus for Release Date don't allow adding movies released earlier than 2006. Modify it to allow movies as early as 1930. (Hint: check the documentation[3] for the* **date_select** *helper used in the form.)*

Exercise 3.21 *The* **description** *field of a movie was created as part of the initial migration, but so far isn't displayed and cannot be edited. Make the necessary changes so that the description is visible in the Show view and editable in the New and Edit views. Hint: you should only need to change two files.*

Exercise 3.22 *Our current controller methods aren't very robust: if the user manually enters a URI to Show a movie that doesn't exist (for example* /movies/99999*), she will see an ugly exception message. Modify the* **show** *method in the controller so that if the requested movie doesn't exist, the user is redirected to the Index view with a friendly message explaining that no movie with the given ID could be found. (Hint: you can either use* **find_by_id** *and check the result, or you can continue to use* **find** *but place it in a* **begin...rescue...end** *and rescue from* **ActiveRecord::RecordNotFound***. Opinions differ as to which is more idiomatic; normally, exceptions are used to indicate unexpected events, but it's not obvious whether such an event is truly unexpected or simply rare.)*

Putting it all together

Exercise 3.23 *Putting it all together exercise: Write and deploy a Rails app that scrapes some information from a Web page using Nokogiri's XPath features, and turns it into an RSS feed using Builder. Verify that you can subscribe to the RSS feed in your browser or RSS news reader.*

4 Validating Software Requirements: Behavior-Driven Design and User Stories

One of the most important lessons, perhaps, is the fact that SOFTWARE IS HARD. ... During the past decade I was surprised to learn that the writing of programs for T_EX and METAFONT proved to be much more difficult than all the other things I had done (like proving theorems or writing books). The creation of good software demands a significantly higher standard of accuracy than those other things do, and it requires a longer attention span than other intellectual tasks. —Donald Knuth, Keynote address to 11th World Computer Congress, 1989

The first step in the Agile cycle, and often the most difficult, is a dialogue with each of the stakeholders to understand the requirements. We first derive **user stories**, *which are short narratives each describing a specific interaction between some stakeholder and the application. The* **Cucumber** *tool turns these stylized but informal English narratives into acceptance and integration tests. As SaaS usually involves end-users, we also need a user interface. We do this with* **low-fidelity (Lo-Fi)** *drawings of the Web pages and combine them into* **storyboards** *before creating the UI in HTML.*

Donald Knuth (1938–) one of the most illustrious computer scientists, received the Turing Award in 1974 for major contributions to the analysis of algorithms and the design of programming languages, and in particular for his contributions to his multi-volume *The Art of Computer Programming.* Many consider this series the definitive reference on analysis of algorithms; "bounty checks" from Knuth for finding errors in his books are among the most prized trophies among computer scientists. Knuth also invented the widely-used T_EX typesetting system, with which this book was prepared.

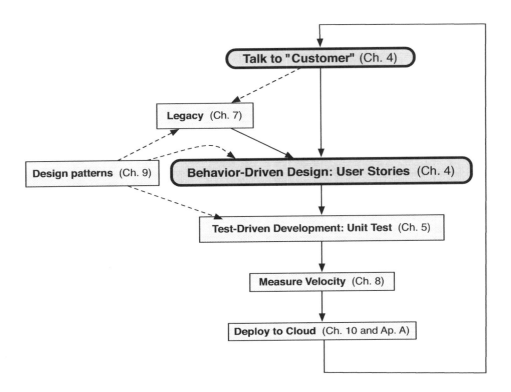

Figure 4.1: An iteration of the Agile software lifecycle and its relationship to the chapters in this book. This chapter emphasizes talking to customers as part of Behavior-Driven Design.

4.1   Introduction to Behavior-Driven Design and User Stories

> *Behavior-Driven Design is Test-Driven Development done correctly.*   —
> Anonymous

Software projects fail because they don't do what customers want; or because they are late; or because they are over budget; or because they are hard to maintain and evolve; or all of the above.

The Agile lifecycle was invented to attack these problems for many common types of software. Figure 4.1 shows one iteration of the Agile lifecycle from Chapter 1, highlighting the portion covered in this chapter. As we saw in Chapter 1, the Agile lifecycle involves:

> **Agile stakeholders** include users, customers, developers, maintenance programmers, operators, project management, ...

- Working closely and continuously with stakeholders to develop requirements and tests.

- Maintaining a working prototype while deploying new features typically every two weeks—called an ***iteration***—and checking in with stakeholders to decide what to add next and to validate that the current system is what they really want. Having a working prototype and prioritizing features reduces the chances of a project being late or over budget, or perhaps increasing the likelihood that the stakeholders are satisfied with the current system once the budget is exhausted!

Unlike a Big Design Up Front (BDUF) lifecycle in Chapter 1, Agile development does not switch phases (and people) over time from development mode to maintenance mode. With Agile you are basically in maintenance mode as soon as you've implemented the first set of features. This approach helps make the project easier to maintain and evolve.

We start the Agile lifecycle with **Behavior-Driven Design (BDD)**. BDD asks questions about the behavior of an application *before and during development* so that stakeholders and developers are less likely to miscommunicate. Requirements are written down as in BDUF, but unlike BDUF, requirements are continuously refined to ensure the resulting software meets the stakeholders' desires. That is, using the terms from Chapter 1, the goal of BDD requirements is **validation** (build the right thing), not just **verification** (build the thing right).

The BDD version of requirements is **user stories**, which describe how the application is expected to be used. They are lightweight versions of requirements that are better suited to Agile. User stories help stakeholders plan and prioritize development. Thus, like BDUF, you start with requirements, but in BDD user stories take the place of design documents in BDUF.

By concentrating on the *behavior* of the application versus the *implementation* of application, it is easier to reduce misunderstandings between stakeholders. As we shall see in the next chapter, BDD is closely tied to Test-Driven Development (TDD), which *does* test implementation. In practice they work together hand-in-hand, but for pedagogical reasons we introduce them sequentially.

User stories came from the Human Computer Interface (HCI) community. They developed them using 3-inch by 5-inch (76 mm by 127 mm) index cards, known as "3-by-5 cards." (We'll see other examples of paper and pencil technology from the HCI community shortly.) These cards contain one to three sentences written in everyday nontechnical language written jointly by the customers and developers. The rationale is that paper cards are nonthreatening and easy to rearrange, thereby enhancing brainstorming and prioritizing. The general guidelines for the user stories themselves is that they must be testable, be small enough to implement in one iteration, and have business value. Section 4.2 gives more detailed guidance for good user stories.

Note that individual developers working by themselves without customer interaction don't need these 3-by-5 cards, but this "lone wolf" developer doesn't match the Agile philosophy of working closely and continuously with the customer.

We will use the Rotten Potatoes app from Chapters 2 and 3 as the running example in this chapter and the next one. We start with the stakeholders, which are simple for this simple app:

- The operators of Rotten Potatoes, and

- The movie fans who are end-users of Rotten Potatoes.

We'll introduce a new feature in Section 4.6, but to help understand all the moving parts, we'll start with a user story for an existing feature of Rotten Potatoes so that we can understand the relationship of all the components in a simpler setting. The user story we picked is to add movies to the Rotten Potatoes database:

http://pastebin.com/G1P1U44z

```
1  Feature: Add a movie to Rotten Potatoes
2    As a movie fan
3    So that I can share a movie with other movie fans
4    I want to add a movie to Rotten Potatoes database
```

This user story format was developed by the startup company Connextra and is named after them; sadly, this startup is no longer with us. The format is:

http://pastebin.com/ha3sDEtV

```
1   Feature name
2     As a [kind of stakeholder],
3     So that [I can achieve some goal],
4     I want to [do some task]
```

This format identifies the stakeholder since different stakeholders may describe the desired behavior differently. For example, users may want to link to information sources to make it easier to find the information while operators may want links to trailers so that they can get an income stream from the advertisers. All three clauses have to be present in the Connextra format, but they are not always in this order.

Summary of BDD and User Stories

- BDD emphasizes working with stakeholders to define the behavior of the system being developed. Stakeholders include nearly everyone: customers, developers, managers, operators, ...

- *User stories*, a device borrowed from the HCI community, make it easy for non-technical stakeholders to help create requirements.

- *3x5 cards*, each with a user story of one to three sentences, are an easy and non-threatening technology that lets *all* stakeholders brainstorm and prioritize features.

- The Connextra format of user stories captures the stakeholder, the stakeholder's goal for the user story, and the task at hand.

Self-Check 4.1.1 *True or False: User stores on 3x5 cards in BDD play the same role as design requirements in BDUF.*

◇ True. ∎

■ *Elaboration: User Stories and Case Analysis*

User stories represent a lightweight approach to *use case analysis*, a term traditionally used in software engineering to describe a similar process. A full use case analysis would include the use case name; actor(s); goals of the action; summary of the use case; preconditions (state of the world before the action); steps occurring in the scenario (both the actions performed by the user and the system's responses); related use cases; and postconditions (state of the world after the action). A *use case diagram* is a UML-like diagram (see Chapter 9) with stick figures standing in for the actors, and can be used to generalize or extend use cases or to include a use case by reference. For example, if we have a use case for "user logs in" and another use case for "logged-in user views her account summary", the latter could include the former by reference, since a precondition to the second use case is that the user has logged in.

4.2 SMART User Stories

What makes a good user story versus a bad one? The SMART acronym offers concrete and (hopefully) memorable guidelines: Specific, Measurable, Achievable, Relevant, and Timeboxed.

- *Specific.* Here are examples of a vague feature paired with a specific version:

  http://pastebin.com/9xTtZWak

  ```
  1  Feature: User can search for a movie (vague)
  2  Feature: User can search for a movie by title (specific)
  ```

- *Measurable.* Adding Measurable to Specific means that each story should be testable, which implies that there are known expected results for some good inputs. An example of a pair of an unmeasurable versus measurable feature is

  http://pastebin.com/XumgjTFJ

  ```
  1  Feature:  Rotten Potatoes should have good response time (unmeasurable)
  2  Feature:  When adding a movie, 99% of Add Movie pages
  3            should appear within 3 seconds (measurable)
  ```

  Only the second case can be tested to see if the system fulfills the requirement.

- *Achievable.* Ideally, you implement the user story in one Agile iteration. If you are getting less than one story per iteration, then they are too big and you need to subdivide these stories into smaller ones. Chapter 8 describes the tool ***Pivotal Tracker*** that measures ***velocity***, which is the rate of completing stories of varying difficulty.

- *Relevant.* A user story must have business value to one or more stakeholders. To drill down to the real business value, one technique is to keep asking "Why." Using as an example a ticket-selling app for a regional theater, suppose the proposal is to add a Facebook linking feature. Here are the "Five Whys" in action with their recursive questions and answers:

  1. Why add the Facebook feature? As box office manager, I think more people will go with friends and enjoy the show more.

  2. Why does it matter if they enjoy the show more? I think we will sell more tickets.

  3. Why do you want to sell more tickets? Because then the theater makes more money.

  4. Why does theater want to make more money? We want to make more money so that we don't go out of business.

  5. Why does it matter that theater is in business next year? If not, I have no job.

  (We're pretty sure the business value is now apparent to at least one stakeholder!)

- *Timeboxed.* Timeboxing means that you stop developing a story once you've exceeded the time budget. Either you give up, divide the user story into smaller ones, or reschedule what is left according to a new estimate. If dividing looks like it won't help, then you go back to the customers to find the highest value part of the story that you can do quickly.

The reason for a time budget per user story is that it extremely easy to underestimate the length of a software project. Without careful accounting of each iteration, the whole project could be late, and thus fail. Learning to budget a software project is a critical skill, and exceeding a story budget and then refactoring it is one way to acquire that skill.

Summary of SMART User Stories

- The *SMART* acronym captures the desirable features of a good user story: Specific, Measurable, Achievable, Relevant, and Timeboxed.

- The *Five Whys* are a technique to help you drill down to uncover the real business relevance of a user story.

Self-Check 4.2.1 *Which SMART guideline(s) does the feature below violate?*
http://pastebin.com/iBwgWT1u

```
1 | Feature: Rotten Potatoes should have a good User Interface
```

⬦ It is not Specific, not Measurable, not Achievable (within 1 iteration), and not Timeboxed. While business Relevant, this feature goes just one for five. ∎

Self-Check 4.2.2 *Rewrite this feature to make it SMART.*
http://pastebin.com/khnvEMLg

```
1 | Feature: I want to see sorted list of movies sold.
```

⬦ Here is one SMART revision of this user story:
http://pastebin.com/VDNkEVSS

```
1 | Feature: As a customer, I want to see the top 10 movies sold, listed by
         price, so that I can buy the cheapest ones first.
```

∎

4.3 Introducing Cucumber and Capybara

Remarkably enough, the tool *Cucumber* automates turning customer-understandable user stories into *acceptance tests*, which ensure the customer is satisfied, and *integration tests*, which ensure that the interfaces between modules have consistent assumptions and communicate correctly. (Chapter 1 describes types of testing). The key is that Cucumber meets halfway between the stakeholder and the developer: user stories don't look like code, so they are clear to the stakeholder and can be used to reach agreement, but they also aren't completely freeform. This section explains how Cucumber accomplishes this minor miracle.

In the Cucumber context we will use the term *user story* to refer a single *feature* with one or more *scenarios* that show different ways a feature is used. The keywords **Feature** and **Scenario** identify the respective components. Each scenario is in turn composed of a sequence of 3 to 8 *steps*.

Figure 4.2 is an example user story, showing a feature with one scenario of adding the movie *Men In Black*; the scenario has eight steps. (We show just a single scenario in this example, but features usually have many scenarios.) Although stilted writing, this format

http://pastebin.com/u/saasbook

```
1  Feature: User can manually add movie
2
3  Scenario: Add a movie
4    Given I am on the RottenPotatoes home page
5    When I follow "Add new movie"
6    Then I should be on the Create New Movie page
7    When I fill in "Title" with "Men In Black"
8    And I select "PG-13" from "Rating"
9    And I press "Save Changes"
10   Then I should be on the RottenPotatoes home page
11   And I should see "Men In Black"
```

Figure 4.2: A Cucumber scenario associated with the adding a movie feature for Rotten Potatoes.

that Cucumber can act upon is still easy for the nontechnical customer to understand and help develop, which is a founding principle of Agile and BDD.

Each step of a scenario starts with its own keyword. Steps that start with **Given** usually set up some preconditions, such as navigating to a page. Steps that start with **When** typically use one of Cucumber's built-in web steps to simulate the user pressing a button, for example. Steps that start with **Then** will usually check to see if some condition is true. The conjunction **And** allows more complicated versions of **Given**, **When**, or **Then** phrases. The only other keyword you see in this format is **But**.

> **Cucumber keywords**
> **Given, When, Then And**, and **But** have different names just for benefit of human readers, but they are all aliases to the same method. Thus, you don't have to remember the syntax for many different keywords.

A separate set of files defines the Ruby code that tests these steps. These are called *step definitions*. Generally, many steps map onto a single step definition.

How does Cucumber match the steps in the scenarios in the *feature* files with *step definitions* that perform these tests? The trick is that Cucumber uses regular expressions or *regexes* (Chapter 3) to match the English phrases in the steps files of the scenarios to the step definitions files of the testing harness.

For example, below is a string from a step definition file in the scenario for Rotten Potatoes:

Given /^(?:|I)am on (.+)$/

This regex can match the text "I am on the Rotten Potatoes home page" on line 4 of Figure 4.2. The regex also captures the string after the phrase "am on " until the end of the line ("the Rotten Potatoes home page"). The body of the step definition contains Ruby code that tests that the step, likely using captured strings such as the one above.

Thus, a way to think of the relationship between step definitions and steps is that step definitions are like method definitions, and the steps of the scenarios are like method calls.

We then need a tool that will act as a user and pretend to use the feature under different scenarios. The part of Cucumber that "pretends to be a user" (taking actions in a web browser like pressing a button) is called *Capybara*. By default, it "simulates" many aspects of a browser—it can interact with the app to receive pages, parse the HTML, and submit forms as a user would.

Summary of Cucumber Introduction

- Cucumber combines a *feature* that you want to add with a set of *scenarios*. We call this combination a *user story*.

- The steps of the scenarios use the keyword **Given** to identify the current state, **When** to identify the action, and **Then** to identify the consequence of the action.

- The scenario steps also use the keywords **And** and **But** to act as conjunctions to make more complex descriptions of state, action, and consequences.

- *Cucumber* matches *steps* to *step definitions* using *regular expressions*.

- *Capybara* puts the SaaS application through its paces by simulating a user and browser performing the steps of the scenarios.

- By storing *features* in files along with different *scenarios* of feature use composed of many *steps*, and storing Ruby code in separate files containing *step definitions* that tests each type of step, the Rails tools *Cucumber* and *Capybara* automatically test the behavior of the SaaS app.

Self-Check 4.3.1 *True or False: Cucumber matches step definitions to scenario steps using regexes and Capybara pretends to be a user that interacts with the SaaS application according to these scenarios.*

◇ True. ■

■ *Elaboration: Stubbing the web*

Alas, Capybara is not smart enough to do JavaScript, which we'll meet in Chapter 6. Fortunately, with appropriate options, Capybara is also able to interface with Webdriver, which actually fires up a REAL browser and "remote controls" it to make it do what the stories say. For this chapter, we won't enable that mode because it is much slower than the "simulated" mode, and the "simulated" mode is appropriate for everything except testing JavaScript.

4.4 Running Cucumber and Capybara

A major benefit of user stories in Cucumber is *Red-Yellow-Green analysis*. Once a user story is written, we can try to run it immediately. In the beginning, steps may initially be highlighted either in Red (for failing) or Yellow (not yet implemented). Our goal is to take each step and go from Yellow or Red to Green (for passing), by incrementally adding what's needed to make it pass. In some cases, this is really easy. In the next chapter we similarly try to go from Red to Green at the level of *unit tests*. Recall that unit tests are for individual methods whereas Cucumber scenarios test entire paths through the app and thus can be acceptance tests or integration tests.

Cucumbers are green
The test-passing green color of the cucumber plant gives this tool its name.

Like other useful tools we've seen, Cucumber is supplied as a Ruby gem, so the first thing we need to do is declare that our app depends on this gem and use Bundler to install it. Building on the `myrottenpotatoes` app you started in Chapter 3, add the following lines to `Gemfile`; we've indicated that Cucumber and its related gems are only needed in the test and development environments and not the production environment (Section 3.10 introduced the three environments in which Rails apps can run).

http://pastebin.com/HnHbnaZD

```
1  # add to end of Gemfile
2  group :test, :development do
3    gem 'cucumber-rails'
4    gem 'cucumber-rails-training-wheels' # some pre-fabbed step definitions
5    gem 'database_cleaner' # to clear Cucumber's test database between runs
6    gem 'capybara'         # lets Cucumber pretend to be a web browser
7    gem 'launchy'          # a useful debugging aid for user stories
8  end
```

Once you've modified Gemfile, run bundle install. If all goes well, you'll eventually see "Your bundle is complete."

We now have to set up the directories and "boilerplate" files that Cucumber and Capybara need. Like Rails itself, Cucumber comes with a *generator* that does this for you. In the app's root directory, run the following two commands (if they ask whether it's OK to overwrite certain files such as cucumber.rake, you can safely say yes):

rails generate cucumber:install capybara
rails generate cucumber_rails_training_wheels:install

The Cucumber generator gives you commonly used step definitions as a starting point, such as interactions with a web browser. For this app, you will find them in myrottenpotatoes/features/step_definitions/web_steps.rb. In addition to these predefined steps, you'll need to create new step definition to match the unique functionality of your app. You will probably want to learn most common predefined step definitions and use them when you write your features so that you can write fewer step definitions.

Before trying to run Cucumber, there's one more step we must take: you must initialize the test database by running rake db:test:prepare. You need to do this before the first time you run tests or whenever the database schema is changed. Section 3.10 in Chapter 3 provides a more detailed description.

At this point you're ready to start using Cucumber. You add the features themselves in the features directory as files with a .feature file extension. Copy the user story in Figure 4.2 and paste it into a file called AddMovie.feature in the directory features. To see how scenarios and the step definitions interact and how they change color like maple trees in New England when the seasons change, type

cucumber features/AddMovie.feature

Watch the screencast to see what to do next.

Screencast 4.4.1: Cucumber Part I.

http://vimeo.com/34754747

The screencast shows how Cucumber checks to see whether the tests work by coloring the step definitions. Failing steps are red, unimplemented steps are yellow, and passing steps are green. The first step on line 4 is red, so Cucumber skips the rest. It fails because there is no path in paths.rb that matches "the Rotten Potatoes home page", as the Cucumber error message explains. The message even suggests how to fix the failure by adding such a path to paths.rb. This new path turns this first step as green as a cucumber, but now the third step on line 6 is red. As error message explains, it fails because no path matches "Create New Movie page", and we fix it again by adding the path to paths.rb. All steps now are as cool as a cucumber, and the AddMovie scenario passes.

Summary: To add features as part of BDD, we need to define acceptance criteria first. Cucumber enables both capturing requirements as user stories and getting integration and acceptance test out of that story. Moreover, we get automatically runnable tests so that we'll have regression tests to help maintain the code as we evolve it further. (We'll see this approach again in Chapter 7 with a much larger application than Rotten Potatoes.)

Self-Check 4.4.1 *Cucumber colors steps green that pass the test. What is the difference between steps colored yellow and red?*

◇ Yellow steps have not yet been implemented while red steps have implemented but fail the test. ∎

4.5 Lo-Fi User Interface Sketches and Storyboards

We usually need to specify a user interface (UI) when adding a new feature since many SaaS applications interact with end users. Thus, part of the BDD task is to often to propose a UI to match the user stories. If a user story says a user needs to login, then we need to have a mockup of a page that has the login. Alas, building software prototypes of UI can intimidate stakeholders from suggesting improvements to the UI. That is, software prototypes have just the opposite characteristics of what we need at this early point of the design.

What we want is the UI equivalent of 3x5 cards; engaging to the nontechnical stakeholder and encouraging trial and error, which means it must be easy to change or even discard. Just as the HCI community advocates 3x5 cards for user stories, they recommend using kindergarten tools for UI mockups: crayons, construction paper, and scissors. They call this low-tech approach to user interfaces *Lo-Fi UI* and the paper prototypes *sketches*. For example, Figure 4.3 shows a Lo-Fi sketch of the UI for adding a movie to Rotten Potatoes.

Ideally, you make sketches for all the user stories that involve a UI. It may seem tedious, but eventually you are going to have to specify all the UI details when using HTML to make the real UI, and it's a lot easier to get it right with pencil and paper than with code.

Lo-Fi sketches show what the UI looks like at one instant of time. However, we also need to show how the sketches work together as a user interacts with a page. Filmmakers face a similar challenge with scenes of a movie. Their solution, which they call *storyboarding*, is to go through the entire film like it was a comic book, with drawings for every scene. Instead of a linear sequence of images like in a movie, the storyboard for a UI is typically a tree or graph of screens driven by different user choices.

For a storyboard, you want to think about all the user interactions with a web app:

- Pages or sections of pages,

- Forms and buttons, and

- Popups.

Figure 4.4 shows a sequence of Lo-Fi sketches with indications of what the user clicks to cause the transitions between sketches.

After drawing the sketches and storyboards, you are ready to write HTML. Chapter 2 showed how Haml markup becomes HTML, and how the **class** and **id** attributes of HTML

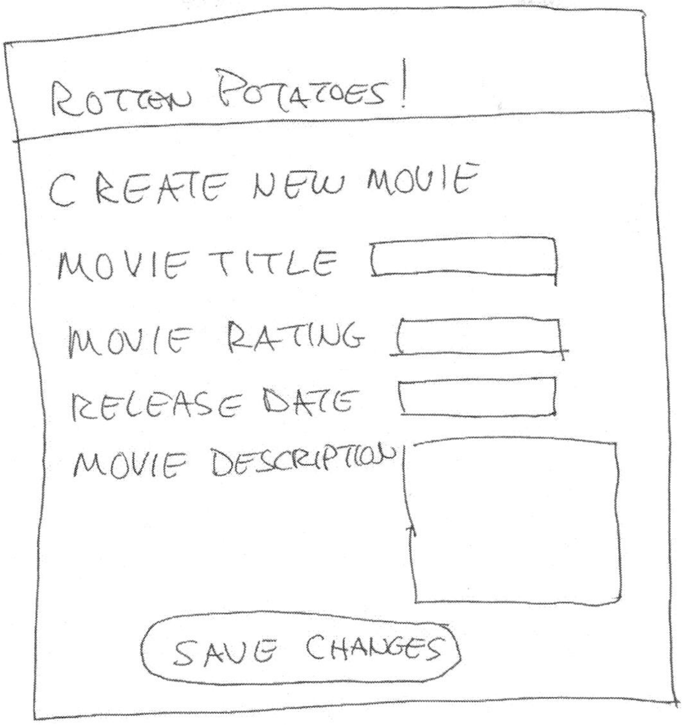

Figure 4.3: Window that appears when adding a movie to Rotten Potatoes.

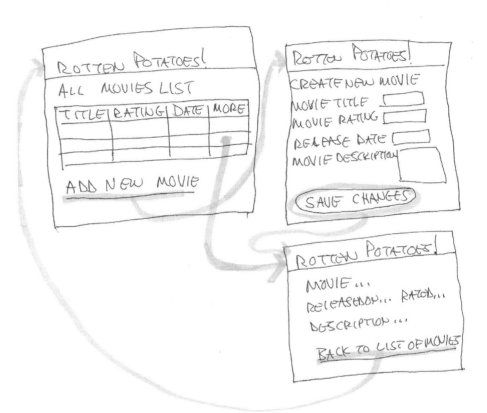

Figure 4.4: Storyboard of images for adding a movie to Rotten Potatoes.

elements can be used to attach styling information to them via Cascading Style Sheets (CSS). The key to the Lo-Fi approach is to get a good overall structure from your sketches, and do minimal CSS (if any) to get the view to look more or less like your sketch. Remember that the common parts of the page layout—banners, structural `divs`, and so on—can go into `views/layouts/application.html.haml`.

Start the process by looking at the Lo-Fi UI sketches and split them into "blocks" of the layout. Use CSS `divs` for obvious layout sections. There is no need to make it pretty until after you have everything working. Adding CSS styling, images, and so on is the fun part, but make it look good *after* it works.

Since the example in Section 4.3 involved existing functionality, there is no need to modify the Haml or CSS. The next section adds a new feature to Rotten Potatoes and thus needs Haml changes.

Summary: Borrowing from the HCI community once again, *Lo-Fi sketches* are low cost ways to explore the user interface of a user story. Paper and pencil makes them easy to change or discard, which once again can involve all stakeholders. *Storyboards* capture the interaction between different pages depending on what the user does. It is much less effort to experiment in this low cost media before using Haml and CSS to create the pages you want in HTML.

Self-Check 4.5.1 *True or False: The purpose of the Lo-Fi UI and storyboards is to debug the UI before you program it.*

◇ True. ∎

4.6 Enhancing Rotten Potatoes

As a second example of user stories and Lo-Fi UIs, suppose we want to search The Open Movie Database (TMDb) to find information about a movie we are interested in adding to Rotten Potatoes. As we'll see in Chapter 5, TMDb has an API (application programming interface) designed to allow its information to be accessed in a Service-Oriented Architecture.

In this chapter, we use Cucumber to develop two scenarios and the corresponding Lo-Fi UI sketches to show how we would like Rotten Potatoes to integrate with TMDb, and we'll get one of the scenarios to go green by temporarily "faking out" some of the code. In Chapter 5, we'll write the code needed to get the other scenario to go green. Getting the first couple of scenarios working can seem tedious, because you usually have to add a lot of infrastructure, but it goes much faster after that, and in fact you will even be able to re-use your step definitions to create higher-level "declarative" steps, as we will see in Section 4.7.

The storyboard in Figure 4.5 shows how we envision the feature working. The home page of Rotten Potatoes, which lists all movies, will be augmented with a search box where we can type some title keywords of a movie and a "Search" button that will search TMDb for a movie whose title contains those keywords. If the search does match—the so-called "happy path" of execution—the first movie that matches will be used to "pre-populate" the fields in the Add New Movie page that we already developed in Chapter 3. (In a real app, you'd want to create a separate page showing all matches and letting the user pick one, but

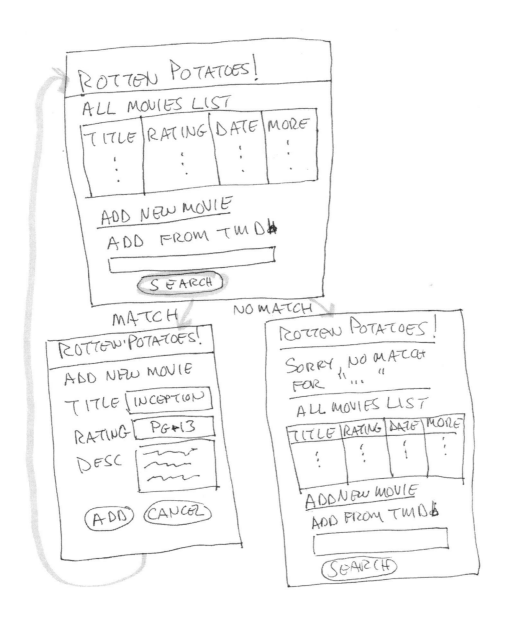

Figure 4.5: Storyboard of UI for searching The Movie Database.

http://pastebin.com/u/saasbook

```
 1  Feature: User can add movie by searching for it in The Movie Database (TMDb)
 2
 3     As a movie fan
 4     So that I can add new movies without manual tedium
 5     I want to add movies by looking up their details in TMDb
 6
 7  Scenario: Try to add nonexistent movie (sad path)
 8
 9     Given I am on the RottenPotatoes home page
10     Then I should see "Search TMDb for a movie"
11     When I fill in "Search Terms" with "Movie That Does Not Exist"
12     And I press "Search TMDb"
13     Then I should be on the RottenPotatoes home page
14     And I should see "'Movie That Does Not Exist' was not found in TMDb."
```

Figure 4.6: A sad path scenario associated with adding a feature to search The Movie Database.

http://pastebin.com/18yYBVbC

```
 1  -# add to end of app/views/movies/index.html.haml:
 2
 3  %h1 Search TMDb for a movie
 4
 5  = form_tag :action => 'search_tmdb' do
 6
 7     %label{:for => 'search_terms'} Search Terms
 8     = text_field_tag 'search_terms'
 9     = submit_tag 'Search TMDb'
```

Figure 4.7: The Haml code for the Search TMDb page.

we're deliberately keeping the example simple.) If the search doesn't match any movies—the "sad path"—we should be returned to the home page with a message informing us of this fact.

Normally you'd complete the happy path first, and when you reach a failing or pending step that requires writing *new* code, you do so via Test Driven Development (TDD). We'll do that in Chapter 5 by writing code that really calls TMDb and integrating it back into this scenario. For now, we'll start with the sad path to illustrate Cucumber features and the BDD process. Figure 4.6 shows the sad path scenario for the new feature; create a file features/search_tmdb.feature containing this code. When we run the feature with cucumber features/search_tmdb.feature, the second step *Then I should see "Search TMDb for a movie"* should fail (red), because we haven't yet added this text to the home page app/views/movies/index.html.haml. So our first task is to get this step to go green by making that change.

Technically, a "pure" BDD approach could be to get this step to pass just by adding the text *Search TMDb for a movie* anywhere in that view, and then re-running the scenario. But of course we know that the very next step *When I fill in "Search Terms" with "Movie That Does Not Exist"* will also fail, because we haven't added a form field called "Search Terms" to the view either. So in the interest of efficiency, modify index.html.haml by adding the lines in Figure 4.7, which we now explain.

Line 3 is the text that allows *Then I should see "Search TMDb for a movie"* to pass. The remaining lines create the fill-in form; we introduced these in Chapter 3, so some of this markup should be familiar. Two things are worth noting. First, as with any user interaction in a view, we need a controller action that will handle that interaction. In this case the interaction is submitting the form with search keywords. Line 5 says that when the form

http://pastebin.com/smwxv70i

```
1 | # add to movies_controller.rb, anywhere inside
2 | #  'class MoviesController < ApplicationController':
3 |
4 | def search_tmdb
5 |   # hardwire to simulate failure
6 |   flash[:warning] = "'#{params[:search_terms]}' was not found in TMDb."
7 |   redirect_to movies_path
8 | end
```

http://pastebin.com/FrfkF6pd

```
1 | # add to routes.rb, just before or just after 'resources :movies' :
2 |
3 | # Route that posts 'Search TMDb' form
4 | post '/movies/search_tmdb'
```

Figure 4.8: (Top) This "fake" controller method always behaves as if no matches were found. It retrieves the keywords typed by the user from the params hash (as we saw in Chapter 3), stores a message in the flash[], and redirects the user back to the list of movies. Recall from Chapter 3 that we added code to app/views/layouts/application.html.haml to display the contents of the flash on every view. (Bottom) A route that triggers this mechanism when a form is POSTed.

is submitted, the controller action **search_tmdb** will receive the form submission. That code doesn't exist yet, so we had to choose a descriptive name for the action.

The second thing to note is the use of the HTML label tag. Figure 2.14 in Chapter 2 tells us that lines 7 and 8 will expand to the following HTML markup:

http://pastebin.com/14AmLnFU

```
1 | <label for='search_terms'>Search Terms</label>
2 | <input id="search_terms" name="search_terms" type="text" />
```

The key is that the for attribute of the label tag matches the id attribute of the input tag, which was determined by the first argument to the **text_field_tag** helper called in line 8 of Figure 4.7. This correspondence allows Cucumber to determine what form field is being referenced by the name "Search Terms" in line of Figure 4.6: *When I fill in "Search Terms"....*

At this point, re-running cucumber features/search_tmdb.feature should show the first three steps passing.   But the step *And I press "Search TMDb"* will fail with an exception: even though we have a button with the name "Search TMDb", the **form_tag** specifies that **MoviesController#search_tmdb** is the controller action that should receive the form, yet no such method exists in movies_controller.rb. Figure 4.1 says that we should now use Test-Driven Development (TDD) techniques to create that method. But since TDD is the topic of the next chapter, we're going to cheat a bit in order to get the scenario running. Since this is the "sad path" scenario where no movies are found, we will temporarily create a controller method that *always* behaves as if nothing was found, so we can finish testing the sad path. Also, as you may recall from Section 3.9, we also have to make sure there is a route to this controller action. The top part of Figure 4.8 shows the code you should add to app/controllers/movies_controller.rb to create the "fake" hardwired **search_tmdb** action. The bottom part of the figure shows the line you must add to config/routes.rb to add a form submission (POST) route to that action.

If you're new to BDD, this step might surprise you. Why would we deliberately create a fake controller method that doesn't actually call TMDb, but just pretends the search failed? In this case, the answer is that it lets us finish the rest of the scenario, making sure that our HTML views match the Lo-Fi sketches and that the sequence of views matches the storyboards. Indeed, once you make the changes in Figure 4.8, the entire sad path should

Doing it over and over? rake cucumber runs all your features, or more precisely, those selected by the *default profile* in Cucumber's configuration file cucumber.yml.[4] In the next chapter we'll meet a tool called autotest that automates re-running tests when you make changes to files.

http://pastebin.com/icQGrYCV

```
1  Feature: User can add movie by searching for it in The Movie Database (TMDb)
2
3    As a movie fan
4    So that I can add new movies without manual tedium
5    I want to add movies by looking up their details in TMDb
6
7  Background: Start from the Search form on the home page
8
9    Given I am on the RottenPotatoes home page
10   Then I should see "Search TMDb for a movie"
11
12 Scenario: Try to add nonexistent movie (sad path)
13
14   When I fill in "Search Terms" with "Movie That Does Not Exist"
15   And I press "Search TMDb"
16   Then I should be on the RottenPotatoes home page
17   And I should see "'Movie That Does Not Exist' was not found in TMDb."
18
19 Scenario: Try to add existing movie (happy path)
20
21   When I fill in "Search Terms" with "Inception"
22   And I press "Search TMDb"
23   Then I should be on the RottenPotatoes home page
24   And I should see "Inception"
25   And I should see "PG-13"
```

Figure 4.9: **DRYing out the common steps between the happy and sad paths using the Background keyword, which groups steps that should be performed before *each* scenario in a feature file.**

pass. Screencast 4.6.1 summarizes what we've done so far.

Screencast 4.6.1: Cucumber Part II.

`http://vimeo.com/34754766`

In this screencast, we do a sad path to illustrate features of Cucumber because it is able to use existing code. The first step on line 5 of Figure 4.6 passes but the step on line 6 fails because we haven't modified `index.html.haml` to include a form for typing in a movie to search for. We fix this by adding this form to `index.html.haml`, using same Rails methods described in Sections 3.12 and 3.14 of Chapter 3. When creating a form, we have to specify which controller action will receive it; we chose the name `search_tmdb` for controller action. (We'll implement this method in the next chapter). Once we have updated `index.html.haml` and named the controller action, Cucumber colors the steps on lines 5 to 7 green. The next step on line 8 fails. Even though we specified name of controller action, there is no route that would match an incoming URI to the name. To keep things simple, we will set up a route just for that action in `config/routes.rb`, again using techniques discussed in Section 3.9 of Chapter 3. However, the step *still* fails since we haven't actually defined the controller action. It will pass once we implement the method `search_tmdb` using Test-Driven Development in the next chapter.

What about the happy path, when we search for an existing movie? Observe that the first two actions on that path—going to the Rotten Potatoes home page and making sure there is a search form there, corresponding to lines 9 and 10 of Figure 4.6—are the same as for the sad path. That should ring a Pavlovian bell in your head asking how you can DRY out the repetition.

Figure 4.9 shows the answer. Modify `features/search_tmdb.feature` to match the figure and once again run `cucumber features/search_tmdb.feature`. Unsurprisingly, the step at line 24 will fail, because we have hardwired the controller method to pre-

tend there is never a match in TMDb. At this point we could change the controller method
to hardwire success and make the happy path green, but besides the fact that this would
cause the sad path to go red, in the next chapter we will see a better way. In particular,
we'll develop the *real* controller action using Test-Driven Development (TDD) techniques
that "cheat" to set up the inputs and the state of the world to test particular conditions in iso-
lation. Once you learn both BDD and TDD, you'll see that you commonly iterate between
these two levels as part of normal software development.

Summary:

- Adding a new feature for a SaaS app normally means you specify a UI for the
  feature, write new step definitions, and perhaps even write new methods before
  Cucumber can successfully color steps green.

- Usually, you'd write and complete scenarios for the happy path(s) first; we began
  with the sad path only because it allowed us to better illustrate some Cucumber
  features.

- The **Background** keyword can be used to DRY out common steps across related
  scenarios in a single feature file.

- Usually, system-level tests such as Cucumber scenarios shouldn't "cheat" by
  hard-wiring fake behavior in methods. BDD and Cucumber are about behavior, not implementation, so we would instead use other techniques such as TDD
  (which the next chapter describes) to write the actual methods to make all scenarios pass.

Self-Check 4.6.1 *True or False: You need to implement all the code being tested before
Cucumber will say that the test passes.*

◇ False. A sad path can pass without having the code written need to make a happy path
pass. ■

4.7 Explicit vs. Implicit and Imperative vs. Declarative Scenarios

Now that we have seen user stories and Cucumber in action, we are ready to cover two
important testing topics that involve contrasting perspectives.

The first is *explicit versus implicit requirements.* A large part of the formal specification in BDUF is requirements, which in BDD are user stories developed by the stakeholders. Using the terminology from Chapter 1, they typically correspond to acceptance tests.
Implicit requirements are the logical consequence of explicit requirements, and typically
correspond to what Chapter 1 calls integration tests. An example of an implicit requirement
in Rotten Potatoes might be that by default movies should be listed in chronological order
by release date. The good news is that you can use Cucumber to kill two birds with one
stone—create acceptances tests *and* integration tests—if you write user stories for both explicit and implicit requirements. (The next chapter shows how to use another tool for unit
testing.)

The second contrasting perspective is ***imperative versus declarative scenarios.*** The example scenario in Figure 4.2 above is imperative, in that you are specifying a logical sequence of user actions: filling in a form, clicking on buttons, and so on. Imperative scenarios tend to complicated have **When** statements with lots of **And** steps. While such scenarios are useful in ensuring that the details of the UI match the customer's expectations, it quickly becomes tedious and non-DRY to write most scenarios this way.

To see why, suppose we want to write a feature that specifies that movies should appear in alphabetical order on the list of movies page. For example, "Zorro" should appear after "Apocalypse Now", even if "Zorro" was added first. It would be the height of tedium to express this scenario naively, because it mostly repeats lines from our existing "add movie" scenario—not very DRY:

http://pastebin.com/uWKRjMjB

```
1   Feature: movies should appear in alphabetical order, not added order
2
3   Scenario: view movie list after adding 2 movies (imperative and non-DRY)
4
5       Given I am on the RottenPotatoes home page
6       When I follow "Add new movie"
7       Then I should be on the Create New Movie page
8       When I fill in "Title" with "Zorro"
9       And I select "PG" from "Rating"
10      And I press "Save Changes"
11      Then I should be on the RottenPotatoes home page
12      When I follow "Add new movie"
13      Then I should be on the Create New Movie page
14      When I fill in "Title" with "Apocalypse Now"
15      And I select "R" from "Rating"
16      And I press "Save Changes"
17      Then I should be on the RottenPotatoes home page
18      And I should see "Apocalypse Now" before "Zorro"
```

Cucumber is supposed to be about *behavior* rather than implementation—focusing on *what* is being done—yet in this poorly-written scenario, only line 18 mentions the behavior of interest! In contrast, declarative scenarios describe the state of the world rather than a sequence of how to get to that state. A declarative version of the above scenario might look like this:

http://pastebin.com/dxqa8634

```
1   Feature: movies when added should appear in movie list
2
3   Scenario: view movie list after adding movie (imperative and non-DRY)
4
5       Given I have added "Zorro" with rating "PG-13"
6       And   I have added "Apocalypse Now" with rating "R"
7       Then I should see "Apocalypse Now" before "Zorro" on the Rotten Potatoes
            home page
```

The declarative version is obviously shorter, easier to understand, and easier to maintain. The good news is that you can *reuse* your existing imperative steps to implement such scenarios. Adding the following code to `app/features/step_definitions/` `movie_steps.rb` allows you to define new scenario steps matching lines 5 (*Given I have added...*) and 6 (*When I search...*) in terms of your existing steps:

http://pastebin.com/iJkGP8ch

```
1   Given /I have added "(.*)" with rating "(.*)"/ do |title, rating|
2      Given %Q{I am on the Create New Movie page}
3      When  %Q{I fill in "Title" with "#{title}"}
4      And   %Q{I select "#{rating}" from "Rating"}
5      And   %Q{I press "Save Changes"}
6   end
7
8   Then /I should see "(.*)" before "(.*)" on (.*)/ do |string1, string2, path|
9      Given %Q{I am on #{path}}
10     regexp = Regexp.new ".*#{string1}.*#{string2}"
11     page.body.should =~ regexp
12  end
```

Recall from Figure 3.1 that **%Q** is an alternative syntax for double-quoting a string, and that **Given**, **When**, **Then** and so on are all synonyms provided for readability only. (We will learn about **should**, which appears in line 10, in the next chapter.)

This is a very powerful form of reuse, and as your app evolves, you will find yourself reusing steps from your first few imperative scenarios to create more concise and descriptive declarative scenarios. Declarative scenarios focus the attention on the feature being described and tested rather than the steps you need to set up the test.

Summary:

- We can use Cucumber for both acceptance and integration testing if we write user stories for both explicit and implicit requirements. Declarative scenarios are simpler, less verbose, and more maintainable than imperative scenarios.

- As you get more experienced, the vast majority of your user stories should be declarative. The exception is for the specific stories where there is business value (customer need) in expressing the details of the user interface.

■ *Elaboration: The BDD ecosystem*

There is enormous momentum, especially in the Ruby community where testable, beautiful and self-documenting code is highly valued, to document and promote best practices for BDD. Good scenarios serve as both documentation of the app designers' intent and executable acceptance and integration tests; they therefore deserve the same attention to beauty as the code itself. For example, this free screencast from RailsCasts[5] describes *scenario outlines*, a way to DRY out a repetitive set of happy or sad paths whose expected outcomes differ based on how a form is filled in, similar to the contrast between our happy and sad paths above. The Cucumber wiki[6] is a good place to start, but as with all programming, you'll learn BDD best by doing it often, making mistakes, and revising and beautifying your code and scenarios as you learn from your mistakes.

Self-Check 4.7.1 *True or False: Explicit requirements are usually defined with imperative scenarios and implicit requirements are usually defined with declarative scenarios.*

◇ False. These are two independent classifications; both requirements can use either type of scenarios. ■

4.8 Fallacies and Pitfalls

 Pitfall: **Adding cool features that do not make the product more successful.**

Agile development was inspired in part by the frustration of software developers building what they thought was cool code but customers dropped. The temptation is strong to add a feature that you think would be great, but it can also be disappointing when your work is discarded. User stories help all stakeholders prioritize development and reduce chances of wasted effort on features that only developers love.

 Pitfall: **Trying to predict what you need before need it.**

Part of the magic of Behavior-Driven Design (and Test-Driven Development in the next chapter) is that you write the tests *before* you write the code you need, and then you write code needed to pass the tests. This top-down approach again makes it more likely for your efforts to be useful, which is harder to do when you're predicting what you think you'll need.

 Pitfall: **Careless use of negative expectations.**

Beware of overusing *Then I should not see. . . .* Because it tests a negative condition, you might not be able to tell if the output is what you intended—you can only tell what the output *isn't*. There are many, many outputs that don't match, so that is not likely to be a good test. Always include positive expectations such as *Then I should see. . .* to check results.

4.9 Concluding Remarks: Pros and Cons of BDD

> *In software, we rarely have meaningful requirements. Even if we do, the only measure of success that matters is whether our solution solves the customer's shifting idea of what their problem is.*
> —Jeff Atwood, *Is Software Development Like Manufacturing?*, 2006

Figure 4.10 shows the relationship of the testing tools introduced in this chapter to the testing tools in the following chapters. Cucumber allows writing user stories as features, scenarios, and steps and matches these steps to step definitions using regular expressions. The step definitions invoke methods in Cucumber and Capybara. We need Capybara because we are writing a SaaS application, and testing requires a tool to act as the user and web browser. If the app was not for SaaS, then we could invoke the methods that test the app directly in Cucumber.

The advantage of user stories and BDD is creating a common language shared by all stakeholders, especially the nontechnical customers. BDD is perfect for projects where the requirements are poorly understood or rapidly changing, which is the often the case. User stories also makes it easy to break projects into small increments or iterations, which makes it easier to estimate how much work remains. The use of 3x5 cards and paper mockups of user interfaces keeps the nontechnical customers involved in the design and prioritization of features, which increases the chances of the software meeting the customer's needs. Iterations drive the refinement of this software development process. Moreover, BDD and

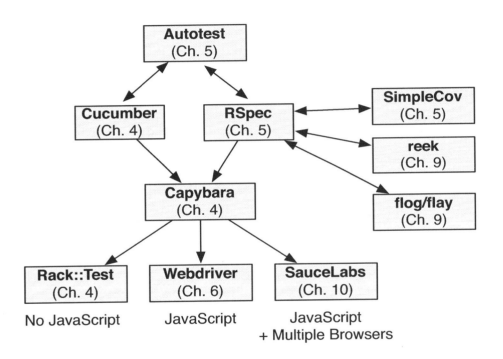

Figure 4.10: The relationship of Cucumber, RSpec, Capybara, and the many other testing tools and services described in this book. This chapter uses Rack::Test, since our application does not yet use JavaScript. If it did, we'd have to use the slower but more complete Webdriver. Chapter 10 shows how we can replace Webdriver with the service from SauceLabs to test your app with many browsers instead of just one.

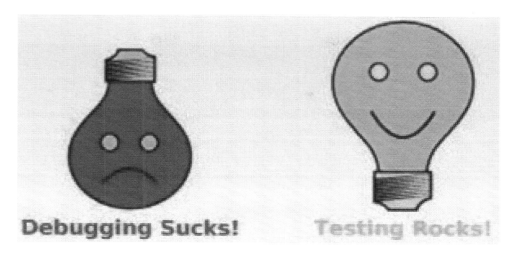

Figure 4.11: Google places these posters inside restrooms to remind developers of the importance of testing.

Cucumber naturally leads to writing tests *before* coding, shifting the validation and development effort from debugging to testing. Figure 4.11 is a poster used at Google that embraces the virtues of testing over debugging.

The downside of user stories and BDD is that it may be difficult or too expensive to have continuous contact with the customer throughout the development process, as some customers may not want to participate. This approach may also not scale to very large software development projects or to safety critical applications. Perhaps BDUF is a better match in both situations.

Another potential downside of BDD is that the project could satisfy customers but not result in a good software architecture, which is an important foundation for maintaining the code. Chapter 9 discusses design patterns, which should be part of your software development toolkit. Recognizing which pattern matches the circumstances and refactoring code when necessary (see Chapter 7) reduces the chances of BDD producing poor software architectures.

All this being said, there is enormous momentum in the Ruby community (which places high value on testable, beautiful and self-documenting code) to document and promote best practices for specifying behavior both as a way to document the intent of the app's developers and to provide executable acceptance tests. The Cucumber wiki[7] is a good place to start.

BDD may not seem initially the natural way to develop software; the strong temptation is to just start hacking code. However, once you have learned BDD and had success at it, for most developers there is no going back. Your authors remind you that good tools, while sometimes intimidating to learn, repay the effort many times over in the long run. Whenever possible in the future, we believe you'll follow the BDD path to writing beautiful code.

4.10 To Learn More

- The Cucumber wiki[8] has links to documentation, tutorials, examples, screencasts, best practices, and lots more on Cucumber.

- Ben Mabey[9] (a core Cucumber developer) and Jonas Nicklas[10], among others, have written eloquently about the benefits of declarative vs. imperative Cucumber scenarios. In fact, the main author of Cucumber, Aslak Hellesøy, deliberately removed[11] **web_steps.rb** (which we met in Section 4.4) from Cucumber in October 2011, which is why we had to separately install the cucumber_rails_training_wheels gem to get it for our examples.

Notes

[1]http://ruby-doc.org/core-1.9.3/Time.html
[2]http://api.rubyonrails.org/classes/ActionDispatch/Routing.html
[3]http://api.rubyonrails.org
[4]https://github.com/cucumber/cucumber/wiki/cucumber.yml
[5]http://railscasts.com/episodes/159-more-on-cucumber
[6]http://cukes.info
[7]http://cukes.info
[8]http://cukes.info
[9]http://benmabey.com/2008/05/19/imperative-vs-declarative-scenarios-in-user-stories.html
[10]http://elabs.se/blog/15-you-re-cuking-it-wrong
[11]http://aslakhellesoy.com/post/11055981222/the-training-wheels-came-off

4.11 Exercises

Exercise 4.1 *Suppose in Rotten Potatoes, instead of dials to pick the rating and pick the release date, the choice was instead fill in the blank form. First, make the appropriate changes to the scenario in Figure 4.2. List the step definitions from* features/cucumber/web_steps.rb *that Cucumber would now invoke in testing these new steps.*

Exercise 4.2 *Add a sad path scenario to the feature in Figure 4.2 of what happens when a user leaves the title field empty.*

5 Software Verification and Testing: Test-Driven Development

There are two ways of constructing a software design: One way is to make it so simple that there are obviously no deficiencies, and the other way is to make it so complicated that there are no obvious deficiencies. The first method is far more difficult... The price of reliability is the pursuit of the utmost simplicity. —Tony Hoare

Charles Antony Richard Hoare (1934–, called "Tony" by almost everyone) received the Turing Award in 1980 for "fundamental contributions to the definition and design of programming languages."

*In test-driven development, you first write failing tests for a small amount of nonexistent code and then fill in the code needed to make them pass, and look for opportunities to refactor (improve the code's structure) before going on to the next test case. This cycle is sometimes called Red–Green–Refactor, since many testing tools print failed test results in red and passing results in green. To keep tests small and isolate them from the behavior of other classes, we introduce mock objects and stubs as examples of **seams**—places where you can change the behavior of your program at testing time without changing the source code itself.*

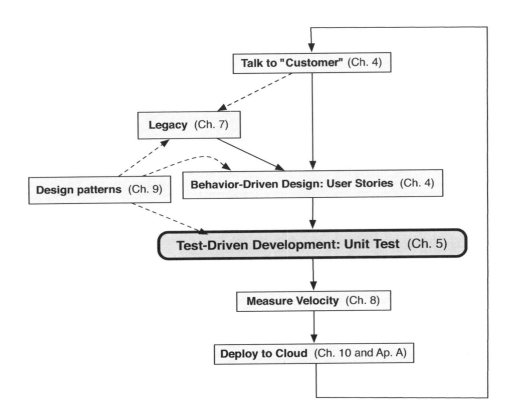

Figure 5.1: The Agile software lifecycle and its relationship to the chapters in this book. This chapter emphasizes unit testing as part of Test-Driven Development.

5.1   Background: A RESTful API and a Ruby Gem

Chapter 1 introduced the Agile lifecycle and distinguished two aspects of software assurance: validation ("Did you build the right thing?") and verification ("Did you build the thing right?"). In this chapter, we focus on verification—building the thing right—via software testing as part of the Agile lifecycle. Figure 4.1 highlights the portion of the Agile lifecycle covered in this chapter.

Although testing is only one technique used for verification, we focus on it because its role is often misunderstood and as a result it doesn't get as much attention as other parts of the software lifecycle. In addition, as we will see, approaching software construction from a test-centric perspective often improves the software's readability and maintainability. In other words, *testable code tends to be good code, and vice versa.*

In Chapter 4 we began working on a new feature for Rotten Potatoes to enable information about a movie to be imported automatically from The Open Movie Database[1]. In this chapter, we'll develop the necessary methods to complete this feature.

Like many SaaS applications, TMDb is designed to be part of a Service-Oriented Architecture: it has an *API* (application programming interface) that allows external applications, not just human Web surfers, to use its functionality. As Screencast 5.1.1 shows, TMDb's API is RESTful, allowing each request made by an external application to be

Method or function?
Following the terminology of OOP (object-oriented programming), we use *method* to mean a named piece of code that implements a behavior associated with a class, whether it's more like a function that returns a value or more like a procedure that causes side effects. Additional historical terms for such a piece of code include *function, routine, subroutine,* and *subprogram.*

entirely self-contained, as described in Chapter 2.

Screencast 5.1.1: Using the TMDb API.

`http://vimeo.com/34754806`

TMDb's API is accessed by constructing a RESTful URI for the appropriate function, such as "search for movies by title" or "retrieve detailed information about a specific movie". To prevent abuse and track each user of the API separately, each developer must first obtain their own **API key** by requesting one via the TMDb website. Request URI's that do not include a valid API key are not honored, returning an error instead. For request URI's containing a valid API key, TMDb returns an XML document containing the result of the request encoded by the URI. This flow—construct a RESTful URI that includes an API key, receive an XML response—is a common pattern for interacting with external services.

Usually, calling such an API from Rotten Potatoes would require us to use the **URI** class in the Ruby standard library to construct the request URI containing our API key, use the **Net::HTTP** class to issue the request to `api.themoviedb.org`, and use an XML parsing library such as **Nokogiri**[2] to parse the reply. But sometimes we can be more productive by standing on the shoulders of others, as we can in this case. The `ruby-tmdb` gem is one of two user-contributed Ruby "wrappers" around TMDb's RESTful API. It's mentioned on the TMDb API documentation pages, but a Google search for `tmdb ruby library` also yields it as a top result. Screencast 5.1.2 shows how to use it.

Screencast 5.1.2: Simplified use of the TMDb API with the `ruby-tmdb` **gem.**

`http://vimeo.com/34754837`

Not every RESTful API has a corresponding Ruby library, but for those that do, such as TMDb, the library can hide the API details behind a few simple Ruby methods. The `ruby-tmdb` gem, which we installed via the Gemfile and Bundler as we learned in Chapter 3, manages URI construction and parses the XML result into Ruby objects such as hashes, strings, dates, and so on.

5.2 FIRST, TDD, and Getting Started With RSpec

The days of developers "tossing their code over the wall" to *Quality Assurance (QA)* are largely over, as are the days of QA engineers manually exercising the software and filing bug reports. Indeed, the idea that quality assurance is the responsibility of a separate group rather than the result of a good process is considered antiquated. Today's developers bear far more responsibility for testing their own code and participating in reviews; the responsibilities of QA have largely shifted to improving the testing tools infrastructure and helping developers make their code more testable.

Testing today is also far more automated. Automated testing doesn't mean that tests are created automatically for you, but that the tests are self-checking: the test code itself can determine whether the code being tested works or not, without requiring a human to manually check test output or interact with the software. A high degree of automation is key to supporting the five principles for creating good tests, which are summarized by the acronym FIRST: **F**ast, **I**ndependent, **R**epeatable, **S**elf-checking, and **T**imely.

- **F**ast: it should be easy and quick to run the subset of test cases relevant to your current coding task, to avoid interfering with your train of thought. We will use a

Ruby tool called Autotest to help with this.

- **Independent:** No test should rely on preconditions created by other tests, so that we can prioritize running only a subset of tests that cover recent code changes.

- **Repeatable:** test behavior should not depend on external factors such as today's date or on "magic constants" that will break the tests if their values change, as occurred with many 1960s programs when the year 2000 arrived[3].

Y2K bug in action This photo was taken on Jan. 3, 2000. (Wikimedia Commons)

- **Self-checking:** each test should be able to determine on its own whether it passed or failed, rather than relying on humans to check its output.

- **Timely:** tests should be created or updated at the same time as the code being tested. As we'll see, with test-driven development the tests are written *immediately before* the code.

Test-driven development (TDD) advocates the use of tests to *drive* the development of code. When TDD is used to create new code, as we do in this chapter, it is sometimes referred to as *test-first development* since the tests come into existence before any of the code being tested. When TDD is used to extend or modify legacy code, as we'll do in Chapter 7, new tests may be created for code that already exists. As we explore TDD in this chapter, we'll show how the Ruby tools support TDD and FIRST. Although TDD may feel strange when you first try it, it tends to result in code that is well tested, more modular, and easier to read than most code developed. While TDD is obviously not the only way to achieve those goals, it is difficult to end up with seriously deficient code if TDD is used correctly.

We will write tests using RSpec, a ***domain-specific language*** (DSL) for testing Ruby code. A DSL is a small programming language designed to ease tackling problems within a single area (domain) at the expense of generality. You've already seen examples of *external* (standalone) DSLs, such as HTML for describing Web pages. RSpec is an *internal* or *embedded* DSL: RSpec code is just Ruby code, but takes advantage of Ruby's features and syntax so as to make up a "mini-language" focused on the job of testing. Regular expressions are another example of an internal DSL embedded in Ruby.

RSpec's facilities help us capture *expectations* of how our code should behave. Such tests are executable specifications or "specs" written in Ruby, hence the name RSpec. How can we capture expectations in tests before there is any code to be tested? The surprising answer is that we write a test that exercises the *code we wish we had*, which forces us to think not only about what the code will do, but how it will be used by its callers and collaborators (other pieces of code that have to work with it). We did this in Chapter 4 in the Cucumber scenario step *And I click "Search TMDb"*: when we modified the List Movies view (`views/movies/index.html.haml`) to include a "Search TMDb" button, we picked the name **search_tmdb** for the not-yet-existing controller method that would respond to the click. Of course, since no method **MoviesController#search_tmdb** existed, the Cucumber step failed (showing red) when you tried to actually run the scenario. In the rest of this chapter we will use TDD to develop the **search_tmdb** method.

In the MVC architecture, the controller's job is to respond to a user interaction, call the appropriate model method(s) to retrieve or manipulate any necessary data, and generate an appropriate view. We might therefore describe the *desired* behavior of our as-yet-nonexistent controller method as follows:

RSpec can also be used for integration tests, but we prefer Cucumber since it facilitates dialogue with the customer and automates acceptance as well as integration tests.

Bar#foo is idiomatic Ruby notation denoting the *instance* method **foo** of class **Bar**. The notation **Bar.foo** denotes the *class* method **foo**.

http://pastebin.com/kJxjwSF6

```
1  require 'spec_helper'
2
3  describe MoviesController do
4    describe 'searching TMDb' do
5      it 'should call the model method that performs TMDb search'
6      it 'should select the Search Results template for rendering'
7      it 'should make the TMDb search results available to that template'
8    end
9  end
```

Figure 5.2: **Skeleton of RSpec examples for MoviesController#search_tmdb. By convention over configuration, the specs for** app/controllers/movies_controller.rb **are expected to be in** spec/controllers/movies_controller_spec.rb, **and so on.**

- It should call a model method to perform the TMDb search, passing it the search terms typed by the user.

- It should select the Search Results HTML view (in Rails parlance, the Search Results *template*) for rendering.

- It should make the TMDb search results available to that template.

Note that none of the methods or templates in this list of desiderata actually exists yet! That is the essence of TDD: write a concrete and concise list of the desired behaviors (the spec), and use it to drive the creation of the methods and templates.

Figure 5.2 shows how we would express these requirements in RSpec. As in Chapter 3, we encourage you to create this file and try the steps as you read this chapter. Line 1 loads some helper methods that will be used by all RSpec tests; in general, for Rails apps this will be the first line of any specfile. Line 3 says that the following specs **describe** the behavior of the **MoviesController** class. Because this class has several methods, line 4 says that this first set of specs describes the behavior of the method that searches TMDb. As you can see, **describe** can be followed by either a class name or a descriptive documentation string.

You can see what they are in `spec/spec_helper.rb`.

The next three lines are placeholders for *examples*, the RSpec term for a short piece of code that tests *one* specific behavior of the **search_tmdb** method. We haven't written any test code yet, but the next screencast shows that we can not only execute these test skeletons with the `rspec` command, but more importantly, automate running them with the `autotest` tool. This automation helps productivity since we don't have to shift our attention between writing code and running tests. For the rest of the chapter, we'll assume that `autotest` is running and that whenever you add tests or application code you will get immediate feedback from RSpec. In the next section we'll create our first tests using TDD.

Screencast 5.2.1: Executing the empty test skeletons and automating execution with `autotest.`

`http://vimeo.com/34754856`

When we run the `spec` command, examples (**it** clauses) containing no code are displayed in yellow as "pending". You can also explicitly mark an example using **pending** and provide a description of why it's pending. Rather than manually running **spec** each time we add or change some code, we can use the `autotest` command, which automatically reruns the appropriate specs whenever you change a specfile or code file.

---

ruby-debug and autotest To use the interactive debugger introduced in Chapter 3 with `autotest`, add **require 'ruby-debug'** to `spec/spec_helper.rb` and insert **debugger** calls wherever you want the action to stop.

1. Before you write any new code, write a test for *one* aspect of the behavior it *should* have. Since the code being tested doesn't exist yet, writing the test forces you to think about how you *wish* the code would behave and interact with its collaborators if it did exist. We call this "exercising the code you wish you had."

2. **Red** step: Run the test, and verify that it fails because you haven't yet implemented the code necessary to make it pass.

3. **Green** step: Write the *simplest possible* code that causes *this* test to pass without breaking any existing tests.

4. **Refactor** step: Look for opportunities to *refactor* either your code or your tests—changing the code's structure to eliminate redundancy, repetition, or other ugliness that may have arisen as a result of adding the new code. The tests ensure that your refactoring doesn't introduce bugs.

5. Repeat until all behaviors necessary to pass a scenario step are complete.

Figure 5.3: The Test-Driven Development (TDD) loop is also known as Red–Green–Refactor because of its skeleton in steps 2, 3 and 4. The last step assumes you are developing code in order to complete a scenario, such as the one you started in Chapter 4.

Summary

- Good tests should be **F**ast, **I**ndependent, **R**epeatable, **S**elf-checking, and **T**imely (FIRST).

- RSpec is a domain-specific language embedded in Ruby for writing tests. Convention over configuration determines where the specfile corresponding to a given class file should reside.

- Within a specfile, a single *example*, introduced by the **it** method, tests a single behavior of a method. **describe** groups examples hierarchically according to the set of behaviors they test.

Self-Check 5.2.1 *A single RSpec test case or* example *is introduced by the keyword _____. A group of related examples is introduced by the keyword _____, which can nested to organize the examples in a file hierarchically.*
◇ **it**; **describe** ∎

Self-Check 5.2.2 *Since RSpec matches tests to classes using convention over configuration, we would put the tests for* `app/models/movie.rb` *in the file _____.*
◇ `spec/models/movie_spec.rb` ∎

5.3 The TDD Cycle: Red–Green–Refactor

Figure 5.3 captures the basic TDD method. You might think we've violated the TDD methodology by writing down three test cases in Figure 5.2 before completing the code for any of those cases, but in practice, there's nothing wrong with creating **it** blocks for tests you know you will want to write. Now, though, it's time to get down to business and start working on the tests.

http://pastebin.com/DwLJrUeG

```
 1  require 'spec_helper'
 2
 3  describe MoviesController do
 4    describe 'searching TMDb' do
 5      it 'should call the model method that performs TMDb search' do
 6        post :search_tmdb, {:search_terms => 'hardware'}
 7      end
 8      it 'should select the Search Results template for rendering'
 9      it 'should make the TMDb search results available to that template'
10    end
11  end
```

Figure 5.4: Filling out the first spec. Whereas a "bare" it (line 8) serves as a placeholder for a yet-to-be-written example, an it accompanied by a do...end block (lines 5–7) is an actual test case.

The first example (test case) in Figure 5.2 states that the **search_tmdb** method should call a model method to perform the TMDb search, passing the keywords typed by the user to that method. In Chapter 4, we modified the **index** view of Rotten Potatoes by adding an HTML form whose submission would be handled by **MoviesController#search_tmdb**; the form contained a single text field called **search_terms** for the user to fill in. Our test case will therefore need to emulate what happens when the user types something into the **search_terms** field and submits the form. As we know, in a Rails app the **params** hash is automatically populated with the data submitted in a form so that the controller method can examine it. Happily, RSpec provides a **post** method that simulates posting a form to a controller action: the first argument is the action name (controller method) that will receive the post, and the second argument is a hash that will become the **params** seen by the controller action. We can now write the first line of our first spec, as Figure 5.4 shows. As the next screencast shows, though, we must overcome a couple of hurdles just to get to the Red phase of Red–Green–Refactor.

Screencast 5.3.1: Developing the first example requires adding an empty controller method and creating an empty view.
http://vimeo.com/34754876
To get past RSpec's errors, we first have to create an empty controller method so that the action (form submission by the user) would have somewhere to go, and then an empty view so that the controller action would have something to render. That one line of test code drove us to ensure that our new controller method and the view it will ultimately render have the correct names.

At this point RSpec reports Green for our first example, but that's not really accurate because the example itself is incomplete: we haven't actually checked whether **search_tmdb** calls a model method to search TMDb, as the spec requires. (We did this deliberately in order to illustrate some of the mechanics necessary to get your first specs running. Usually, since each spec tends to be short, you'd complete a spec before re-running your tests.)

How should we check that **search_tmdb** calls a model method, since no model method exists yet? Again, we will write a test for the behavior of the *code we wish we had*, as directed in step 1 of Figure 5.3. Let's pretend we have a model method that does just what we want. In this case, we'd probably want to pass the method a string and get back a collection of **Movie** objects based on TMDb search results matching that string. *If* that method existed, our controller method might therefore call it like this:

The code we wish we had will be a class method, since finding movies in TMDb is a behavior related to movies in general and not to a particular instance of a **Movie**.

http://pastebin.com/zKnwphQZ

```
1   require 'spec_helper'
2
3   describe MoviesController do
4     describe 'searching TMDb' do
5       it 'should call the model method that performs TMDb search' do
6         fake_results = [mock('Movie'), mock('Movie')]
7         Movie.should_receive(:find_in_tmdb).with('hardware').
8           and_return(fake_results)
9         post :search_tmdb, {:search_terms => 'hardware'}
10      end
11      it 'should select the Search Results template for rendering'
12      it 'should make the TMDb search results available to that template'
13    end
14  end
```

Figure 5.5: Completing the example by asserting that the controller method will call the code we wish we had in the Movie model. Lines 5–10 in this listing replace lines 5–7 in Figure 5.4.

http://pastebin.com/SC8XxMnS

```
1   @movies = Movie.find_in_tmdb(params[:search_terms])
```

Figure 5.5 shows the code for a test case that asserts such a call will occur. In this case, the code we are testing—the *subject code*—is **search_tmdb**. However, part of the behavior we're testing appears to depend on **find_in_tmdb**. Since **find_in_tmdb** is code we don't yet have, the goal of lines 6–8 is to "fake" the behavior it would exhibit if we did have it. Line 6 uses RSpec's **mock** method to create an array of two "test double" **Movie** objects. In particular, whereas a real **Movie** object would respond to methods like **title** and **rating**, the test double would raise an exception if you called any methods on it. Given this fact, why would we use doubles at all? The reason is to isolate these specs from the behavior of the **Movie** class, which might have bugs of its own. Mocks are like puppets whose behavior we completely control, allowing us to isolate unit tests from their collaborator classes and keep tests Independent (the I in FIRST).

> In fact, an alias for **mock** is **double**. For clarity, use **mock** when you're going to ask the fake object to do things, and **double** when you just need a stand-in.

Returning to Figure 5.5, lines 6–7 express the *expectation* that the **Movie** class should receive a call to the method **find_in_tmdb** and that method should receive the single argument **'hardware'**. RSpec will open the **Movie** class and define a class method called **find_in_tmdb** whose only purpose is to track whether it gets called, and if so, whether the right arguments are passed. Critically, *if a method with the same name already existed in the* **Movie** *class, it would be temporarily "overwritten"* by this *method stub*. That's why in our case it doesn't matter that we haven't written the "real" **find_in_tmdb**: it wouldn't get called anyway!

The use of **should_receive** to temporarily replace a "real" method for testing purposes is an example of using a *seam*: "a place where you can alter behavior in your program without editing in that place." (Feathers 2004) In this case, **should_receive** creates a seam by overriding a method in place, without us having to edit the file containing the original method (although in this case, the original method doesn't even exist yet). Seams are also important when it comes to adding new code to your application, but in the rest of this chapter we will see many more examples of seams in testing. Seams are useful in testing because they let us break dependencies between a piece of code we want to test and its collaborators, allowing the collaborators to behave differently under test than they would in real life.

Line 8 (which is just a continuation of line 7) specifies that **find_in_tmdb** should return the collection of doubles we set up in line 6. This completes the illusion of "the code we wish we had": we're calling a method that doesn't yet exist, and supplying the result we wish it would give if it existed! If we omit **with**, RSpec will still check that **find_in_tmdb** gets called, but won't check if the arguments are what we expected. If we omit **and_return**, the fake method call will return **nil** rather than a value chosen by us. In any case, after each example is run, RSpec performs a *teardown* step that restores the classes to their original condition, so if we wanted to perform these same fake-outs in other examples, we'd need to specify them in each one (though we'll soon see a way to DRY out such repetition). This automatic teardown is another important part of keeping tests **I**ndependent.

Technically, in this case it would be OK to omit **and_return**, since this example isn't checking the return value, but we included it for illustrative purposes.

This new version of the test fails because we established an expectation that **search_tmdb** would call **find_in_tmdb**, but the **search_tmdb** isn't even written yet. Therefore the last step is to go from Red to Green by adding just enough code to **search_tmdb** to pass this test. We say the test *drives* the creation of the code, because adding to the test results in a failure that must be addressed by adding new code in the model. Since the only thing this particular example is testing is the method call to **find_in_tmdb**, it suffices to add to **search_tmdb** the single line of code we had in mind as "the code we wished we had":

http://pastebin.com/SHBjb5tk

```
1  @movies = Movie.find_in_tmdb(params[:search_terms])
```

If TDD is new to you, this has been a lot to absorb, especially when testing an app using a powerful framework such as Rails. Don't worry—now that you have been exposed to the main concepts, the next round of specs will go faster. It takes a bit of faith to jump into this system, but we have found that the reward is well worth it. Read the summary below and consider having a sandwich and reviewing the concepts in this section before moving on.

Summary

- The TDD cycle of Red–Green–Refactor begins with writing a test that fails because the *subject code* it's testing doesn't exist yet (Red) and then adding the minimum code necessary to pass just that one example (Green).

- Seams let you change the behavior of your application in a particular place without editing in that place. Typical test setup often establishes seams by using **mock** or its alias **double** to create test double objects, or by using **stub...and_return** to control the return value from a collaborator method. Mocks and stubs are seams that help with testability by isolating the behavior of the code being tested from the behavior of its collaborators.

- Each example sets up preconditions, executes the subject code, and asserts something about the results. Assertions such as **should**, **should_not**, **should_receive**, and **with** make tests **S**elf-checking, eliminating the need for a human programmer to inspect test results.

- After each test, an automatic teardown destroys the mocks and stubs and unsets any expectations, so that tests remain **I**ndependent.

■ *Elaboration: Seams in other languages*

In non-object-oriented languages such as C, seams are hard to create. Since all method calls are resolved at link time, usually the developer creates a library containing the "fake" (test double) version of a desired method, and carefully controls library link order to ensure the test-double version is used. Similarly, since C data structures are accessed by reading directly from memory rather than calling accessor methods, data structure seams (mocks) are usually created by using preprocessor directives such as **#ifdef TESTING** to compile the code differently for testing vs. production use.

In statically-typed OO languages like Java, since method calls are resolved at runtime, one way to create seams is to create a subclass of the class under test and override certain methods when compiling against the test harness. Mocking objects is also possible, though the mock object must satisfy the compiler's expectations for a fully-implemented "real" object, even if the mock is doing only a small part of the work that a real object would. The JMock website[4] shows some examples of inserting testing seams in Java.

In dynamic OO languages like Ruby that let you modify classes at runtime, we can create a seam almost anywhere and anytime. RSpec exploits this ability in allowing us to create just the specific mocks and stubs needed by each test, which makes tests easy to write.

Self-Check 5.3.1 *In Figure 5.5, why must the* **should_receive** *expectation in line 7 come* before *the* **post** *action in line 9?*

◇ The expectation needs to set up a test double for **find_in_tmdb** that can be monitored to make sure it was called. Since the **post** action is eventually going to result in calling **find_in_tmdb**, the double must be set up before the **post** occurs, otherwise the real **find_in_tmdb** would be called. (In this case, **find_in_tmdb** doesn't even exist yet, so the test would fail for that reason.) ■

5.4   More Controller Specs and Refactoring

Returning to our original specfile skeleton from the listing in Figure 5.2, line 6 says that **search_tmdb** should select the "Search Results" view for rendering. Of course, that view doesn't exist yet, but as in the first example we wrote above, that needn't stop us.

Since we know from Chapter 3 that the default behavior of the method **Movies-**
Controller#search_tmdb is to attempt to render the view app/views/movies/ search_tmdb.html.haml (which we created in Chapter 4), our spec just needs to verify that the controller action will indeed try to render that view template. To do this we will use the **response** method of RSpec: once we have done a **get** or **post** action in a controller spec, the object returned by the **response** method will contain the app server's response to that action, and we can assert an expectation that the response *would have rendered* a particular view. This happens in line 16 of Figure 5.6, which illustrates another kind of RSpec assertion: *object*.**should** *match-condition*. In this example, *match-condition* is supplied by **render_template()**, so the assertion is satisfied if the object (in this case the response from the controller action) attempted to render a particular view. We will see the use of **should** with other *match-conditions*. The negative assertion **should_not** can be used to specify that the *match-condition* should not be true.

There are two things to notice about Figure 5.6. First, since each of the two examples (lines 5–10 and 11–16) are self-contained and Independent, we have to create the test doubles and perform the **post** command separately in each. Second, whereas the first example uses **should_receive**, the second example uses **stub**, which creates a test double for a

Is this really necessary? Since the default view is determined by convention over configuration, all we're really doing here is testing Rails' built-in functionality. But if we were rendering one view if the action succeeded but a different view for displaying an error, examples like this would verify that the correct view was selected.

http://pastebin.com/DzhkYLkM

```
1  require 'spec_helper'
2
3  describe MoviesController do
4    describe 'searching TMDb' do
5      it 'should call the model method that performs TMDb search' do
6        fake_results = [mock('Movie'), mock('Movie')]
7        Movie.should_receive(:find_in_tmdb).with('hardware').
8           and_return(fake_results)
9        post :search_tmdb, {:search_terms => 'hardware'}
10     end
11     it 'should select the Search Results template for rendering' do
12       fake_results = [mock('Movie'), mock('Movie')]
13       Movie.stub(:find_in_tmdb).and_return(fake_results)
14       post :search_tmdb, {:search_terms => 'hardware'}
15       response.should render_template('search_tmdb')
16     end
17     it 'should make the TMDb search results available to that template'
18   end
19 end
```

Figure 5.6: **Filling out the second example. Lines 11–16 replace line 11 from Figure 5.5.**

method but *doesn't* establish an expectation that that method will necessarily be called. The double springs into action *if* the method is called, but it's not an error if the method is never called. Make the changes so that your specfile looks like Figure 5.6; autotest should still be running and report that this second example passes.

In this simple example, you could argue that we're splitting hairs by using **should_-receive** in one example and **stub** in another, but the goal is to illustrate that *each example should test a single behavior.* This second example is *only* checking that the correct view is selected for rendering. It's *not* checking that the appropriate model method gets called— that's the job of the first example. In fact, even if the method **Movie.find_in_tmdb** actually *was* implemented already, we'd still stub it out in these examples, because examples should isolate the behaviors under test from the behaviors of other classes with which the subject code collaborates.

Before we write another example, we consider the Refactor step of Red–Green–Refactor. Given that lines 6 and 12 are identical, Figure 5.7 shows one way to DRY them out by *factoring out* common setup code into a **before(:each)** block. As the name implies, this code is executed before *each* of the examples within the **describe** example group, similar to the **Background** section of a Cucumber feature, whose steps are performed before each scenario. There is also **before(:all)**, which runs setup code just once for a whole group of tests; but you risk making your tests dependent on each other by using it, since it's easy for hard-to-debug dependencies to creep in that are only exposed when tests are run in a different order or when only a subset of tests are run.

While the concept of factoring out common setup into a **before** block is straightforward, we had to make one syntactic change to make it work, because of the way RSpec is implemented. Specifically, we had to change **fake_results** into an instance variable **@fake_results**, because local variables occurring inside each test case's **do. . . end** block disappear once that test case finishes running. In contrast, instance variables of an example group are visible to all examples in that group. Since we are setting the value in the **before :each** block, every test case will see the same initial value of **@fake_results**.

There's just one example left to write, to check that the TMDb search results will be made available to the response view. Recall that in Chapter 4, we created views/movies/

Instance variable of what? describe creates and returns a new **Test::-Spec::ExampleGroup** object that represents a group of your test cases. **@fake_results** is an instance variable of this **ExampleGroup** object—not of the class under test (**MoviesController**).

http://pastebin.com/pH6eiERK

```
1  require 'spec_helper'
2
3  describe MoviesController do
4    describe 'searching TMDb' do
5      before :each do
6        @fake_results = [mock('Movie'), mock('Movie')]
7      end
8      it 'should call the model method that performs TMDb search' do
9        Movie.should_receive(:find_in_tmdb).with('hardware').
10          and_return(@fake_results)
11        post :search_tmdb, {:search_terms => 'hardware'}
12      end
13      it 'should select the Search Results template for rendering' do
14        Movie.stub(:find_in_tmdb).and_return(@fake_results)
15        post :search_tmdb, {:search_terms => 'hardware'}
16        response.should render_template('search_tmdb')
17      end
18      it 'should make the TMDb search results available to that template'
19    end
20  end
```

Figure 5.7: DRYing out the controller examples using a before block (lines 5–7).

search_tmdb.html.haml under the assumption that **@movies** would be set up by the controller action to contain the list of matching movies from TMDb. That's why in **MoviesController#search_tmdb** we assigned the result of calling **find_in_tmdb** to the instance variable **@movies**. (Recall that instance variables set in a controller action are available to the view.)

The RSpec **assigns()** method keeps track of what instance variables were assigned in the controller method. Hence **assigns(:movies)** returns whatever value (if any) was assigned to **@movies** in **search_tmdb**, and our spec just has to verify that the controller action correctly sets up this variable. In our case, we've already arranged to return our doubles as the result of the faked-out method call, so the correct behavior for **search_tmdb** would be to set **@movies** to this value, as line 21 of Figure 5.8 asserts.

■ *Elaboration: More than we need?*

Strictly speaking, for the purposes of this example the stubbed **find_in_tmdb** could have returned any value at all, such as the string "I am a movie", because the *only* behavior tested by this example is whether the correct instance variable is being set up and made available to the view. In particular, this example doesn't care what the *value* of that variable is, or whether **find_in_tmdb** is returning something sensible. But since we already had doubles set up, it was easy enough to use them in this example.

Our last task in Red–Green–Refactor is the Refactor step. The second and third examples are identical except for the last line in each one (lines 16 and 21). To DRY them out, Figure 5.9 starts a separate nested example group with **describe**, grouping the common behaviors of the last two examples into their own **before** block. We chose the description string after valid search to name this **describe** block because the examples in this subgroup all assume that a valid call to **find_in_tmdb** has occurred. (That assumption itself is tested by the first example.)

When example groups are nested, any **before** blocks associated with the outer nesting are executed prior to those associated with the inner nesting. So, for example, considering the test case in lines 18–20 of Figure 5.9, the setup code in lines 5–7 is run first, followed by the setup code in lines 14–17, and finally the example itself (lines 18–20).

http://pastebin.com/JPW8B3bQ

```
 1  require 'spec_helper'
 2
 3  describe MoviesController do
 4    describe 'searching TMDb' do
 5      before :each do
 6        @fake_results = [mock('Movie'), mock('Movie')]
 7      end
 8      it 'should call the model method that performs TMDb search' do
 9        Movie.should_receive(:find_in_tmdb).with('hardware').
10          and_return(@fake_results)
11        post :search_tmdb, {:search_terms => 'hardware'}
12      end
13      it 'should select the Search Results template for rendering' do
14        Movie.stub(:find_in_tmdb).and_return(@fake_results)
15        post :search_tmdb, {:search_terms => 'hardware'}
16        response.should render_template('search_tmdb')
17      end
18      it 'should make the TMDb search results available to that template' do
19        Movie.stub(:find_in_tmdb).and_return(@fake_results)
20        post :search_tmdb, {:search_terms => 'hardware'}
21        assigns(:movies).should == @fake_results
22      end
23    end
24  end
```

Figure 5.8: Asserting that @movie is set up correctly by search_tmdb. Lines 18–22 in this listing replace line 18 in Figure 5.7.

http://pastebin.com/Q7wMTZUZ

```
 1  require 'spec_helper'
 2
 3  describe MoviesController do
 4    describe 'searching TMDb' do
 5      before :each do
 6        @fake_results = [mock('Movie'), mock('Movie')]
 7      end
 8      it 'should call the model method that performs TMDb search' do
 9        Movie.should_receive(:find_in_tmdb).with('hardware').
10          and_return(@fake_results)
11        post :search_tmdb, {:search_terms => 'hardware'}
12      end
13      describe 'after valid search' do
14        before :each do
15          Movie.stub(:find_in_tmdb).and_return(@fake_results)
16          post :search_tmdb, {:search_terms => 'hardware'}
17        end
18        it 'should select the Search Results template for rendering' do
19          response.should render_template('search_tmdb')
20        end
21        it 'should make the TMDb search results available to that template' do
22          assigns(:movies).should == @fake_results
23        end
24      end
25    end
26  end
```

Figure 5.9: Completed and refactored spec for search_tmdb. The nested group starting at line 13 allows DRYing out the duplication between lines 14–15 and 19–20 in Figure 5.8.

Our next task will be to use TDD to create the model method **find_in_tmdb** that we've so far been stubbing out. Since this method is supposed to call the actual TMDb service, we will again need to use stubbing, this time to avoid having our examples depend on the behavior of a remote Internet service.

Summary

- An example of the Refactor step of Red–Green–Refactor is to move common setup code into a **before** block, thus DRYing out your specs.

- Like **should_receive**, stubbing with **stub** creates a "test double" method for use in tests, but unlike **should_receive**, **stub** doesn't require that the method actually be called.

- **assigns()** allows a controller test to inspect the values of instance variables set by a controller action.

Self-Check 5.4.1 *Specify whether each of the following RSpec constructs is used to (a) create a seam, (b) determine the behavior of a seam, (c) neither: (1)* **assigns()**; *(2)* **should_receive**; *(3)* **stub**; *(4)* **and_return**.
◇ (1) c, (2) a, (3) a, (4) b ∎

Self-Check 5.4.2 *Why is it usually preferable to use* **before(:each)** *rather than* **before(:all)**?
◇ Code in a **before(:each)** block is run before each spec in that block, setting up identical preconditions for all those specs and thereby keeping them Independent. ∎

5.5   Fixtures and Factories

Mocks and stubs are appropriate when you need a stand-in with a small amount of functionality to express a test case. But suppose you were testing a new method **Movie#name_with_rating** that you know will examine the **title** and **rating** attributes of a **Movie** object. You could create a mock that knows all that information, and pass that mock:

http://pastebin.com/N3s1A193

```
1  fake_movie = mock('Movie')
2  fake_movie.stub(:title).and_return('Casablanca')
3  fake_movie.stub(:rating).and_return('PG')
4  fake_movie.name_with_rating.should == 'Casablanca (PG)'
```

But there are two reasons not to use a mock here. First, this mock object needs almost as much functionality as a real **Movie** object, so you're probably better off using a real object. Second, since the instance method being tested is part of the **Movie** class itself, it makes sense to use a real object since this isn't a case of isolating the test code from collaborator classes.

You have two choices for where to get a real **Movie** object to use in such tests. One choice is to set up one or more *fixtures*—a fixed state used as a baseline for one or more tests. The term *fixture* comes from the manufacturing world: a test fixture is a device that holds or supports the item under test. Since all state in Rails SaaS apps is kept in the database, a fixture file defines a set of objects that is automatically loaded into the test database before tests are run, so you can use those objects in your tests without first

http://pastebin.com/16xhen5y

```
 1  # spec/fixtures/movies.yml
 2  milk_movie:
 3    id: 1
 4    title: Milk
 5    rating: R
 6    release_date: 2008-11-26
 7
 8  documentary_movie:
 9    id: 2
10    title: Food, Inc.
11    release_date: 2008-09-07
```

http://pastebin.com/NA71rdQf

```
 1  # spec/models/movie_spec.rb:
 2
 3  describe Movie do
 4    fixtures :movies
 5    it 'should include rating and year in full name' do
 6      movie = movies(:milk_movie)
 7      movie.name_with_rating.should == 'Milk (R)'
 8    end
 9  end
```

Figure 5.10: **Fixtures declared in YAML files (top) are automatically loaded into the test database before each spec is executed (bottom).**

setting them up. Like setup and teardown of mocks and stubs, the test database is erased and reloaded with the fixtures before *each spec*, keeping tests Independent. Rails looks for fixtures in a file containing **YAML** (Yet Another Markup Language) objects. As Figure 5.10 shows, YAML is a very simple-minded way of representing hierarchies of objects with attributes, similar to XML, which we saw at the beginning of the chapter. The fixtures for the **Movie** model are loaded from spec/fixtures/movies.yml, and are available to your specs via their symbolic names, as Figure 5.10 shows.

Strictly speaking, it's not erased, but each spec is run inside a ***database transaction*** that is rolled back when the spec finishes.

But unless used carefully, fixtures can interfere with tests being Independent, as every test now depends implicitly on the fixture state, so changing the fixtures might change the behavior of tests. In addition, although each individual test probably relies on only one or two fixtures, the union of fixtures required by all tests can become unwieldy. For this reason, many programmers prefer to use a ***factory***—a framework designed to allow quick creation of full-featured objects (rather than mocks) at testing time. For example, the popular FactoryGirl[5] tool for Rails lets you define a factory for Movie objects and create just the objects you need quickly for each test, selectively overriding only certain attributes, as Figure 5.11 shows. (FactoryGirl is part of the bookware.) In our simple app, using a factory doesn't confer much benefit over just calling **Movie.new** to create a new Movie directly. But in more complicated apps in which object creation and initialization involve many steps—for example, objects that have many attributes that must be initialized at creation time—a factory helps DRY out your test preconditions (**before** blocks) and streamline your test code.

Before adding more functionality, let's dig a bit more deeply into how RSpec works. RSpec's **should** is a great example of the use of Ruby language features to improve readability and blur the line between tests and documentation. The following screencast explains in a bit more detail how an expression such as **value.should == 5** is actually handled.

http://pastebin.com/N3fS70BC

```
1   # spec/factories/movie.rb
2
3   FactoryGirl.define do
4     factory :movie do
5       title 'A Fake Title' # default values
6       rating 'PG'
7       release_date { 10.years.ago }
8     end
9   end
```

http://pastebin.com/s3u2hKyx

```
1   # spec/models/movie_spec.rb
2
3   describe Movie do
4     it 'should include rating and year in full name' do
5       movie = FactoryGirl.build(:movie, :title => 'Milk', :rating => 'R')
6       movie.name_with_rating.should == 'Milk (R)'
7     end
8   end
9
10  # or if you mix in FactoryGirl's syntax methods (see FactoryGirl README):
11
12  describe Movie do
13    subject { create :movie, :title => 'Milk', :rating => 'R' }
14    its :name_with_rating { should == 'Milk (R)' }
15  end
```

Figure 5.11: An example of using FactoryGirl instead of fixtures to create real (not mock) objects for use in tests. Factory frameworks streamline the creation of such objects while preserving Independence among tests.

Screencast 5.5.1: How Ruby's dynamic language features make specs more readable.
`http://vimeo.com/34754890`
RSpec mixes a module containing the **should** method into the **Object** (root) class. **should** expects to be passed a *matcher* that can be evaluated to the condition being asserted. RSpec methods such as **be** can be used to construct such a matcher; because of Ruby's flexible syntax and optional parentheses, an assertion such as **value.should be < 5** can be understood by fully parenthesizing and de-sugaring it to **value.should(be.>(5))**. In addition, RSpec uses Ruby's **method_missing** feature (described in Chapter 3) to detect matchers beginning with **be_** or **be_a_**, allowing you to create assertions such as **cheater.should be_disqualified**.

Summary

- When a test needs to operate on a real object rather than a mock, the real object can be created on the fly by a factory or preloaded as a fixture. But beware that fixtures can create subtle interdependencies between tests, breaking Independence.

- Tests are a form of internal documentation. RSpec exploits Ruby language features to let you write exceptionally readable test code. Like application code, test code is there for humans, not for the computer, so taking the time to make your tests readable not only deepens your understanding of them but also documents your thoughts more effectively for those who will work with the code after you've moved on.

Self-Check 5.5.1 *Suppose a test suite contains a test that adds a model object to a table and then expects to find a certain number of model objects in the table as a result. Explain how the use of fixtures may affect the Independence of the tests in this suite, and how the use of Factories can remedy this problem.*

◇ If the fixtures file is ever changed so that the number of items initially populating that table changes, this test may suddenly start failing because its assumptions about the initial state of the table no longer hold. In contrast, a factory can be used to quickly create only those objects needed for each test or example group on demand, so no test needs to depend on any global "initial state" of the database. ∎

5.6 TDD for the Model

We've now created two of the three parts of the new "Search TMDb" feature: we created the view in Chapter 4 and we used TDD to drive the creation of the controller action in the previous sections. All that remains to finish the user story we started in Chapter 4 is the model method **find_in_tmdb**, which actually uses Service-Oriented Architecture technology to communicate with TMDb. Using TDD to drive its implementation will go quickly now that we know the basics.

By convention over configuration, specs for the **Movie** model go in spec/models/ movie_spec.rb. Figure 5.12 shows the happy path for calling **find_in_tmdb**, which describes what happens when everything works correctly. (Complete specs must also cover the sad paths, as we'll soon see.) Inside the overall **describe Movie**, we've added a nested **describe** block for the keyword-search function. Our first spec says that when **find_in_tmdb** is called with a string parameter, it should pass that string parameter as the value of the :title option to the TMDb gem's **TmdbMovie.find** method. We express this using **hash_including**, a matcher that specifies that a particular argument (in this case, the only argument) must be a hash including the key/value paper :title =>'Inception'. This spec should immediately fail because we haven't defined **find_in_tmdb** yet, so we are at the Red stage already. Of course at this stage **find_in_tmdb** is trivial, so the bottom of Figure 5.12 shows its initial implementation that gets us from Red to Green. (As with the controller spec, for brevity we will omit the line that loads spec_helper from the rest of the listings of this specfile.)

However, this spec is subtly incomplete! So far, all of our test cases have been based

http://pastebin.com/5a5SwtuV

```
 1   require 'spec_helper'
 2
 3   describe Movie do
 4     describe 'searching Tmdb by keyword' do
 5       it 'should call Tmdb with title keywords' do
 6         TmdbMovie.should_receive(:find).with(hash_including :title => '
                 Inception')
 7         Movie.find_in_tmdb('Inception')
 8       end
 9     end
10   end
```

http://pastebin.com/30ACnD2m

```
 1   class Movie < ActiveRecord::Base
 2
 3     def self.find_in_tmdb(string)
 4       TmdbMovie.find(:title => string)
 5     end
 6
 7     # rest of file elided for brevity
 8   end
```

Figure 5.12: (Top) the happy path spec for calling the Tmdb gem; (bottom) Initial happy path implementation driven by happy path spec.

on the **explicit requirement** described in the user story of Chapter 4: when the user types in the name of a movie and clicks *Search TMDb*, she should see a page showing matching results. However, Screencast 5.1.1 revealed the additional **implicit requirement** that every TMDb request must include a valid API key. Further, Screencast 5.1.2 showed that the ruby-tmdb gem gives a *different* error for a blank API key than for an invalid one, so we must be prepared to handle both kinds of errors. Our specs so far do not cover these implicit requirements, and since we have been stubbing the call to **TmdbMovie.find**, we have been masking the errors that would otherwise occur.

So we must augment our description of the model method to capture these implicit requirements:

- It should raise an exception if an invalid key is provided.

- It should raise an exception if a blank key is provided.

Unfortunately, the way ruby-tmdb is implemented, it raises a **RuntimeError**, the most generic kind of Ruby exception. For Rotten Potatoes, we would prefer that **find_in_tmdb** raise an exception specific to this type of error, as the revised spec in Figure 5.13 demands. Note that we have renamed our first spec to indicate that it applies to the revised case when the API key is valid, and added a new spec to cover the case when the API key hasn't been initialized.

Let's take a moment to understand both the code itself and why it fails with Red. Notice first that we had to "wrap" the call to **find_in_tmdb** in a **lambda**. We *expect* the call to raise an exception, but if a spec raises an exception it stops the testing run! So in order to make the spec **Self-checking**, we invoke **should** on the callable **lambda** object, which will cause the lambda to be executed in a "controlled environment" where RSpec can catch any exceptions and match them to our expectation.

Nevertheless, the test fails with the message uninitialized constant Movie::- InvalidKeyError. Recall that a Ruby class is simply a constant that names a class

http://pastebin.com/rmS67MZp

```
 1   require 'spec_helper'
 2
 3   describe Movie do
 4     describe 'searching Tmdb by keyword' do
 5       it 'should call Tmdb with title keywords given valid API key' do
 6         TmdbMovie.should_receive(:find).
 7           with(hash_including :title => 'Inception')
 8         Movie.find_in_tmdb('Inception')
 9       end
10       it 'should raise an InvalidKeyError with no API key' do
11         lambda { Movie.find_in_tmdb('Inception') }.
12           should raise_error(Movie::InvalidKeyError)
13       end
14     end
15   end
```

Figure 5.13: The code we wish we had would raise a very specific exception to signal a missing API key (lines 11–12), but this spec fails because find_in_tmdb raises its own generic exception instead.

http://pastebin.com/NPDWxUk3

```
 1   class Movie < ActiveRecord::Base
 2
 3     class Movie::InvalidKeyError < StandardError ; end
 4
 5     def self.find_in_tmdb(string)
 6       begin
 7         TmdbMovie.find(:title => string)
 8       rescue ArgumentError => tmdb_error
 9         raise Movie::InvalidKeyError, tmdb_error.message
10       end
11     end
12
13     # rest of file elided for brevity
14   end
```

Figure 5.14: Defining our new exception type within class Movie (line 3) and getting the behavior we want by rescuing the exception thrown by TmdbMovie.find and re-raising our new exception type (lines 6–10).

object; this message is telling us that we've referenced an exception class called **Movie::InvalidKeyError** but haven't defined it anywhere. Line 3 of Figure 5.14 fixes this by defining this new class within **Movie**'s namespace (hence the notation **Movie::InvalidKeyError** in line 12 of the spec). When you make this change, the test will still fail, but now it will fail for the right reason: we've asserted that a **Movie::InvalidKeyError** should be raised, but instead got an **ArgumentError** from **TmdbMovie.find**. Figure 5.14 shows the easy fix that makes the test pass Green. Notice in line 9 that we pass the error message from the original **ArgumentError** exception as the descriptive message of our new exception.

Summary

- If we need to check that the subject code raises an exception, we can do so by making a lambda-expression the receiver of an expectation like **should** or **should_not** and using the matcher **raise_error**.

- As an example of how to perform only a partial check on arguments using **with**, we matched the argument using **hash_including**, which checks that the argument quacks like a hash and contains a particular key/value pair but makes no assertions about its other contents.

■*Elaboration: Declared vs. undeclared exceptions*

In statically-typed languages such as Java, the compiler enforces that a method must declare any exceptions it might throw. If the callee wants to add a new type of exception, the callee's method signature changes, requiring the callee and all callers to be recompiled.

This approach doesn't extend well to SaaS apps, which may communicate with other services like Tmdb whose evolution and behavior are not under our control. We must rely on the remote service's API documentation to tell us what could go wrong, but we must also assume that other undocumented failures can also happen. In those cases the best we can do is catch the exception, log detailed information, and (depending on our judgment) notify the maintainers of Rotten Potatoes that an unexpected error occurred.

Self-Check 5.6.1 *Considering line 11 of Figure 5.13, suppose we didn't wrap the call to* **find_in_tmdb** *in a lambda-expression. What would happen and why?*

◇ If **find_in_tmdb** correctly raises the exception, the spec will fail because the exception will stop the run. If **find_in_tmdb** incorrectly fails to raise an exception, the spec will fail because the assertion **should raise_error** expects one. Therefore the test would always fail whether **find_in_tmdb** was correct or not. ■

Self-Check 5.6.2 *Given that failing to initialize a valid API key raises an exception, why doesn't line 8 of Figure 5.13 raise an exception?*

◇ Because lines 6–7 replace the **TmdbMovie.find** call with a stub, preventing the "real" method from executing and raising an exception. ■

5.7   Stubbing the Internet

The above sad path captures the case of not initializing the API key at all, but what if we specify a TMDb API key but it's an invalid one? This requires us to finally add some code to actually initialize the API key. Figure 5.15 adds an accessor method for the key and sets the key's value in every call to **find_in_tmdb**.

But if your key is valid, this change should result in a failing spec, since the spec in line 12 will no longer raise an exception. We must modify the spec to deliberately set the API key to the empty string (as it would be if we didn't initialize it). Happily, we already know how to do this: we stub out the **Movie.api_key** accessor and return an empty string, as shown in Figure 5.16. This change makes the spec in line 12 revert to Green. Note that setting the key by calling an accessor method creates a seam that we can stub to force a failing value in this test. If the key had been set from a variable, this would have been harder to do. With this seam in place, we can finally test the behavior of having a non-blank

Be sure to acquire and use your own TMDb API key[6] rather than the one hardcoded in the example listing!

Why set the key before every find rather than just once? Setting the key is an inexpensive operation, so the extra code required to check if the key has been initialized would hurt conciseness without improving performance. If setting the key were expensive, one-time initialization might make sense.

http://pastebin.com/wJHTfTC9

```
 1  class Movie < ActiveRecord::Base
 2
 3    class Movie::InvalidKeyError < StandardError ; end
 4
 5    def self.api_key
 6      'cc4b67c52acb514bdf4931f7cedfd12b' # replace with YOUR Tmdb key
 7    end
 8
 9    def self.find_in_tmdb(string)
10      Tmdb.api_key = self.api_key
11      begin
12        TmdbMovie.find(:title => string)
13      rescue ArgumentError => tmdb_error
14        raise Movie::InvalidKeyError, tmdb_error.message
15      rescue RuntimeError => tmdb_error
16        if tmdb_error.message =~ /status code '404'/
17          raise Movie::InvalidKeyError, tmdb_error.message
18        else
19          raise RuntimeError, tmdb_error.message
20        end
21      end
22    end
23    # rest of file elided for brevity
24  end
```

Figure 5.15: A simple method to initialize the API key, defined in lines 5–7 and used in line 10. In a real application, the key string would probably be read from a configuration file, but creating this accessor method lets us change the implementation of how the key is retrieved without affecting other code.

but invalid API key. The spec in Figure 5.17 is easy to write since all the pieces are in place. Perhaps surprisingly, the spec doesn't pass:

http://pastebin.com/GAj3PkDP

```
 1  expected Movie::InvalidKeyError, got #<RuntimeError: Tmdb API returned
 2  status code '404' for URL:
 3  'http://api.themoviedb.org/2.1/Movie.search/en/json/INVALID/Inception'>
```

There are two problems here. First, as Screencast 5.1.2 showed, **TmdbMovie.find** raises **ArgumentError** if the key is blank but **RuntimeError** if the key is invalid. (Presumably the reason is that a blank key is obviously invalid, but a nonblank key can only be tested by calling the TMDb service with it.) The problem of raising a different exception can be fixed by adding another **rescue** clause to catch the **RuntimeError** exception, as Figure 5.18 shows.

http://pastebin.com/N5PCsarU

```
 1  require 'spec_helper'
 2
 3  describe Movie do
 4    describe 'searching Tmdb by keyword' do
 5      # first spec elided for brevity
 6      it 'should raise an InvalidKeyError with no API key' do
 7        Movie.stub(:api_key).and_return('')
 8        lambda { Movie.find_in_tmdb('Inception') }.
 9          should raise_error(Movie::InvalidKeyError)
10      end
11    end
12  end
```

Figure 5.16: Because Figure 5.15 uses an accessor method Movie.api_ key for getting the key's value rather than assigning it from a variable, it provides a seam that enables us to control test behavior.

http://pastebin.com/60vFPeuw

```
 1  require 'spec_helper'
 2
 3  describe Movie do
 4    describe 'searching Tmdb by keyword' do
 5      # first 2 specs elided for brevity
 6      it 'should raise an InvalidKeyError with invalid API key' do
 7        Movie.stub(:api_key).and_return('INVALID')
 8        lambda { Movie.find_in_tmdb('Inception') }.
 9          should raise_error(Movie::InvalidKeyError)
10      end
11    end
12  end
```

Figure 5.17: **Testing for a nonblank but invalid key causes a failure because TmdbMovie.find raises a different exception for an invalid key than it does for a blank or uninitialized key.**

http://pastebin.com/wJHTfTC9

```
 1  class Movie < ActiveRecord::Base
 2
 3    class Movie::InvalidKeyError < StandardError ; end
 4
 5    def self.api_key
 6      'cc4b67c52acb514bdf4931f7cedfd12b' # replace with YOUR Tmdb key
 7    end
 8
 9    def self.find_in_tmdb(string)
10      Tmdb.api_key = self.api_key
11      begin
12        TmdbMovie.find(:title => string)
13      rescue ArgumentError => tmdb_error
14        raise Movie::InvalidKeyError, tmdb_error.message
15      rescue RuntimeError => tmdb_error
16        if tmdb_error.message =~ /status code '404'/
17          raise Movie::InvalidKeyError, tmdb_error.message
18        else
19          raise RuntimeError, tmdb_error.message
20        end
21      end
22    end
23    # rest of file elided for brevity
24  end
```

Figure 5.18: **Rescuing RuntimeError as well as ArgumentError makes the test pass. Rescuing from RuntimeError can be dangerous since it's a generic catch-all for runtime exceptions that aren't otherwise handled, so we specifically check that the exception message matches the TMDb error message we saw in Screencast 5.1.1; if it doesn't, we just re-raise the RuntimeError.**

http://pastebin.com/cbmkMBK1

```
 1   require 'spec_helper'
 2
 3   describe Movie do
 4     describe 'searching Tmdb by keyword' do
 5       it 'should call Tmdb with title keywords given valid API key' do
 6         TmdbMovie.should_receive(:find).
 7           with(hash_including :title => 'Inception')
 8         Movie.find_in_tmdb('Inception')
 9       end
10       it 'should raise an InvalidKeyError with no API key' do
11         Movie.stub(:api_key).and_return('')
12         lambda { Movie.find_in_tmdb('Inception') }.
13           should raise_error(Movie::InvalidKeyError)
14       end
15       it 'should raise an InvalidKeyError with invalid API key' do
16         TmdbMovie.stub(:find).
17           and_raise(RuntimeError.new('API returned code 404'))
18         lambda { Movie.find_in_tmdb('Inception') }.
19           should raise_error(Movie::InvalidKeyError)
20       end
21     end
22   end
```

Figure 5.19: **Mimicking the behavior of the TMDb API when an invalid key is passed (lines 16–17) breaks the dependency between the invalid-API-key spec and TMDb itself.**

That leads us to the second problem, which is more serious: this spec actually calls the TMDb service every time it's executed, making it neither **F**ast (it can take a few seconds for each call to complete) nor **R**epeatable (the test will behave differently if TMDb is down or your computer is not connected to the Internet).

We already know how to fix this: introduce a seam that isolates the caller from the callee, as we did earlier with **TmdbMovie.find**. Since we now know that **TmdbMovie.find** raises a **RuntimeError** when given an invalid key, we can mimic that behavior with a stub that does just that. Note that this stub obsoletes the need for stubbing an invalid key value, since we are faking the behavior of the TMDb remote service itself. Figure 5.19 shows the complete `movie_spec.rb` including this change, which keeps the spec Green but "disconnects" it from the real TMDb service.

Summary

- To test code that communicates with an external service, we create stubs to mimic the service's behavior in order to keep our tests **F**ast and **R**epeatable.

- We can learn about the behavior we need to mimic both by reading the service's API documentation and by directly observing the service's real behavior under a variety of conditions.

■ *Elaboration: Red–Refactor–Green–Refactor?*

Sometimes getting from Red to Green is not just a matter of adding new code, but may first require refactoring existing code. For example, if line 10 of Figure 5.15 had set the API key from a variable (**Tmdb.api_key=@api_key**) rather than by calling the accessor method in lines 5–7, we would have refactored to create the accessor method in order to have the testing seam needed in line 7 of Figure 5.16. This refactoring would have been simple, but more complex refactorings may require code changes that temporarily make some Green tests go Red. It's important to change those tests as necessary to make them pass again before continuing with your new test. Remember that the goal is to always have working code.

■ *Elaboration: Where should we stub external services?*

We chose to test TMDb integration by stubbing **find_in_tmdb** but there are multiple places we could have stubbed. Stubbing the methods of the ruby-tmdb gem would allow our tests to catch errors in the interaction between **Movie.find_in_tmdb** and ruby-tmdb itself. More radically, we could use a gem like FakeWeb[7] to stub out the entire Web except for particular URIs that return a canned response when accessed from a Ruby program. (You can think of FakeWeb as **stub...with...and_return** for the whole Web.) For example, we could create a canned XML document by cutting and pasting the result of a live call, and use FakeWeb to arrange to return that document when the app uses the appropriate RESTful URI to attempt to contact TMDb. From an integration testing standpoint, this is the most realistic way to test, because the stubbed behavior is "farthest away"—we are stubbing as late as possible in the flow of the request. Therefore, when creating Cucumber scenarios to test external service integration, FakeWeb is an appropriate choice. From a unit testing point of view (as we've adopted in this chapter) it's less compelling, since we are concerned with the correct behavior of specific class methods, and we don't mind stubbing "close by" in order to observe those behaviors in a controlled environment.

Self-Check 5.7.1 *Name two likely violations of FIRST that arise when unit tests actually call an external service as part of testing.*

◇ The test may no longer be Fast, since it takes much longer to call an external service than to compute locally. The test may no longer be Repeatable, since circumstances beyond our control could affect its outcome, such as the temporary unavailability of the external service. ■

Self-Check 5.7.2 *How would the spec in Figure 5.19 be simplified if* **TmdbMovie** *raised the* same *exception for either a blank or an invalid key?*

◇ With only one condition to check, either lines 10–14 or 15–19 could be eliminated from the spec. ■

5.8 Coverage Concepts and Unit vs. Integration Tests

How much testing is enough? A poor but unfortunately widely-given answer is "As much as you can do before the shipping deadline." A very coarse-grained alternative is the *code-to-test ratio*, the number of non-comment lines of code divided by number of lines of tests of all types. In production systems, this ratio is usually less than 1, that is, there are more lines of test than lines of app code. The command `rake stats` issued in the root directory

Structure of test cases	
before(:each) do. . . end	Set up preconditions executed before each spec (use **before(:all)** to do just once, at your own risk)
it 'should do something' do. . . end	A single example (test case) for one behavior
describe 'collection of behaviors' do. . . end	Groups a set of related examples
Mocks and stubs	
m=mock('movie')	Creates a mock object with no predefined methods
m.stub(:rating).and_return('R')	Replaces the existing **rating** method on **m**, or defines a new **rating** method if none exists, that returns the canned response **'R'**
m=mock('movie', :rating=>'R')	Shortcut that combines the 2 previous examples
Movie.stub(:find).and_return(@fake_movie)	Forces **@fake_movie** to be returned *if* **Movie.find** is called, but doesn't require that it be called
Useful methods and objects for controller specs	
post '/movies/create', {:title=>'Milk', :rating=>'R'}	Causes a POST request to /movies/create and passes the given hash as the value of **params**. **get**, **put**, **delete** also available.
response.should render_template('show')	Checks that the controller action renders the **show** template for this controller's model
response.should redirect_to(:controller => 'movies', :action => 'new')	Checks that the controller action redirects to **MoviesController#new** rather than rendering a view
Assertions on method calls: can also negate, e.g. **should_not_receive**	
Movie.should_receive(:find).exactly(2).times	Stubs **Movie.find** and ensures it's called exactly twice (omit **exactly** if you don't care how many calls; **at_least()** and **at_most()** also available
Movie.should_receive(:find).with('Milk','R')	Checks that **Movie.find** is called with exactly 2 arguments having these values
Movie.should_receive(:find).with(anything())	Checks that **Movie.find** is called with 1 argument whose value isn't checked
Movie.should_receive(:find). with(hash_including :title=>'Milk')	Checks that **Movie.find** is called with 1 argument that must be a hash (or something that quacks like one) that includes the key **:title** with the value **'Milk'**
Movie.should_receive(:find).with(no_args())	Checks that **Movie.find** is called with zero arguments
Matchers	
greeting.should == 'bonjour'	Compares its argument for equality with receiver of assertion
result.should be_odd	Calls **odd?** (note question mark) on **result**

Figure 5.20: A few useful RSpec methods, some of which were introduced in this chapter. See the full RSpec documentation[9] for details and additional methods not listed here.

http://pastebin.com/yGBF2QPM

```
1  class MyClass
2    def foo(x,y,z)
3      if x
4        if (y && z) then bar(0) end
5      else
6        bar(1)
7      end
8    end
9    def bar(x) ; @w = x ; end
10 end
```

Figure 5.21: A simple code example to illustrate basic coverage concepts.

of a Rails app computes this ratio based on the number of lines of RSpec tests (it doesn't count Cucumber scenarios).

A more precise way to approach the question is in terms of ***code coverage***. Since the goal of testing is to exercise the subject code in at least the same ways it would be exercised in production, what fraction of those possibilities is actually exercised by the test suite? Surprisingly, measuring coverage is not as straightforward as you might suspect. Here is a simple fragment of code and the definitions of several commonly-used coverage terms as they apply to the example.

- S0 or Method coverage: Is every method executed at least once by the test suite? Satisfying S0 requires calling **foo** and **bar** at least once each.

  Sometimes written with a subscript, S_0.

- S1 or Call coverage or Entry/Exit coverage: Has each method been called from every place it could be called? Satisfying S1 requires calling **bar** from both line 4 and line 6.

- C0 or Statement coverage: Is every statement of the source code executed at least once by the test suite, counting both branches of a conditional as a single statement? In addition to calling **bar**, satisfying C0 would require calling **foo** at least once with **x** true (otherwise the statement in line 4 will never be executed), and at least once with **y** false.

- C1 or Branch coverage: Has each branch been taken in each direction at least once? Satisfying C1 would require calling **foo** with both false and true values of **x** and with values of **y** and **z** such that **y && z** in line 4 evaluates once to true and once to false. A more stringent condition, ***decision coverage***, requires that each *subexpression* that independently affects a conditional expression be evaluated to true and false. In this example, a test would additionally have to separately set **y** and **z** so that the condition **y && z** fails once for **y** being false and once for **z** being false.

- C2 or Path coverage: Has every possible route through the code been executed? In this simple example, where **x,y,z** are treated as booleans, there are 8 possible paths.

- Modified Condition/Decision Coverage (MCDC) combines a subset of the above levels: Every point of entry and exit in the program has been invoked at least once, every decision in the program has taken all possible outcomes at least once, and each condition in a decision has been shown to independently affect that decision's outcome.

Achieving C0 coverage is relatively straightforward, and a goal of 100% C0 coverage is not unreasonable. Achieving C1 coverage is more difficult since test cases must be constructed more carefully to ensure each branch is taken at least once in each direction. C2 coverage is most difficult of all, and not all testing experts agree on the additional value of achieving 100% path coverage. Therefore, code coverage statistics are most valuable to the extent that they highlight undertested or untested parts of the code and show the overall comprehensiveness of your test suite. The next screencast shows how to use the SimpleCov[10] Ruby gem (included in the bookware) to quickly check the C0 coverage of your RSpec tests.

Screencast 5.8.1: Using SimpleCov to check C0 coverage.
`http://vimeo.com/34754907`
The SimpleCov tool, provided as a Ruby gem, measures and displays the C0 coverage of your specs. You can zoom in on each file and see which specific lines were covered by your tests. You cannot run coverage if you have any failing tests, but unimplemented or pending tests are okay.

This chapter, and the above discussion of coverage, have focused on unit tests. Chapter 4 explained how user stories could become automated acceptance tests; those are *integration tests* or *system tests* because each test (that is, each scenario) exercises a lot of code in many different parts of the application, rather than relying on fake objects such as mocks and stubs to isolate classes from their collaborators. Integration tests are important, but insufficient. Their resolution is poor: if an integration test fails, it is harder to pinpoint the cause since the test touches many parts of the code. Their coverage tends to be poor because even though a single scenario touches many classes, it executes only a few code paths in each class. For the same reason, integration tests also tend to take longer to run. On the other hand, while unit tests run quickly and can isolate the subject code with great precision (improving both coverage resolution and error localization), because they rely on fake objects to isolate the subject code, they may mask problems that would only arise in integration tests.

Somewhere in between these levels are *functional tests*, which exercise a well-defined subset of the code. They rely on mocks and stubs to isolate a set of cooperating classes rather than a single class or method. For example, controller specs such as Figure 5.9 use **get** and **post** methods to submit URIs to the app, which means they rely on the routing subsystem to work correctly in routing those calls to the appropriate controller methods. (To see this for yourself, temporarily remove the line **map.resources :movies** from `config/routes.rb` and try re-running the controller specs.) However, the controller specs are still isolated from the database by stubbing out the model method **find_in_tmdb** that would normally communicate with the database.

In other words, high assurance requires both good coverage and a mix of all three kinds of tests. Figure 5.22 summarizes the relative strengths and weaknesses of different types of tests.

	Unit	Functional	Integration/System
What is tested	One method/class	Several methods/classes	Large chunks of system
Rails example	Model specs	Controller specs	Cucumber scenarios
Preferred tool	RSpec	Rspec	Cucumber
Running time	Very fast	Fast	Slow
Error localization	Excellent	Moderate	Poor
Coverage	Excellent	Moderate	Poor
Use of mocks & stubs	Heavy	Moderate	Little/none

Figure 5.22: **Summary of the differences among unit tests, functional tests, and integration or whole-system tests.**

Summary

- Static and dynamic measures of coverage, including code-to-test ratio (reported by `rake stats`), C0 coverage (reported by SimpleCov), and C1–C2 coverage, measure the extent to which your test suite exercises different paths in your code.

- Unit, functional, and integration tests differ in terms of their running time, resolution (ability to localize errors), ability to exercise a variety of code paths, and ability to "sanity-check" the whole application. All three are vital to software assurance.

Self-Check 5.8.1 *Why does high test coverage not necessarily imply a well-tested application?*

◇ Coverage says nothing about the quality of the tests. However, low coverage certainly implies a poorly-tested application. ∎

Self-Check 5.8.2 *What is the difference between C0 code coverage and code-to-test ratio?*

◇ C0 coverage is a *dynamic* measurement of what fraction of all statements are executed by a test suite. Code-to-test ratio is a *static* measurement comparing the total number of lines of code to the total number of lines of tests. ∎

Self-Check 5.8.3 *Why is it usually a bad idea to make extensive use of* **mock** *or* **stub** *in Cucumber scenarios such as those described in Chapter 4?*

◇ Cucumber is a tool for full-system testing and acceptance testing. Such testing is specifically intended to exercise the entire system, rather than "faking" certain parts of it as we have done using seams in this chapter. (However, if the "full system" includes interacting with outside services we don't control, such as the interaction with TMDb in this example, we do need a way to "fake" their behavior for testing. That topic is the subject of Exercise 5.1.) ∎

5.9 Other Testing Approaches and Terminology

The field of software testing is as broad and long-lived as software engineering and has its own literature. Its range of techniques includes formalisms for proving things about coverage, empirical techniques for selecting which tests to create, and directed-random testing.

Depending on an organization's "testing culture," you may hear different terminology than we've used in this chapter. Ammann and Offutt's *Introduction to Software Testing* (Ammann and Offutt 2008) is one of the best comprehensive references on the subject. Their approach is to divide a piece of code into **basic blocks**, each of which executes from the beginning to the end with no possibility of branching, and then join these basic blocks into a graph in which conditionals in the code result in graph nodes with multiple out-edges. We can then think of testing as "covering the graph": each test case tracks which nodes in the graph it visits, and the fraction of all nodes visited at the end of the test suite is the test coverage. Ammann and Offutt go on to analyze various structural aspects of software from which such graphs can be extracted, and present systematic automated techniques for achieving and measuring coverage of those graphs.

One insight that emerges from this approach is that the levels of testing described in the previous section refer to **control flow coverage**, since they are only concerned with whether specific parts of the code are executed or not. Another important coverage criterion is **define–use coverage** or **DU-coverage**: given a variable **x** in some program, if we consider every place that **x** is assigned a value and every place that the value of **x** is used, DU-coverage asks what fraction of all *pairs* of define and use sites are exercised by a test suite. This condition is weaker than all-paths coverage but can find errors that control-flow coverage alone would miss.

Another approach, less common today, distinguishes **black-box tests**, whose design is based solely on the software's external specifications, form **white-box tests** (also called **glass-box tests**), whose design reflects knowledge about the software's implementation that is not implied by external specifications. For example, the external specification of a hash table might just state that when we store a key/value pair and later read that key, we should get back the stored value. A black-box test would specify a random set of key/value pairs to test this behavior, whereas a white-box test might exploit knowledge about the hash function to construct worst-case test data that results in many hash collisions.

Mutation testing, invented by Ammann and Offutt, is a test-automation technique in which small but syntactically legal changes are automatically made to the program's source code, such as replacing **a+b** with **a-b** or replacing **if (c)** with **if (!c)**. Most such changes should cause at least one test to fail, so a mutation that causes *no* test to fail indicates either a lack of test coverage or a very strange program. The Ruby gem Heckle performs mutation testing in conjunction with RSpec, but is unfortunately incompatible with Ruby 1.9, the version of the language we use in this book. As of this writing, no solid tool for Ruby 1.9 mutation testing has yet emerged, though given the importance of testing in the Ruby community, this will likely change soon.

Fuzz testing consists of throwing random data at your application and seeing what breaks. About 1/4 of common Unix utilities can be made to crash by fuzz testing, and Microsoft estimates that 20–25% of their bugs are found this way. *Dumb fuzzing* generates completely random data, while *smart fuzzing* includes knowledge about the app's structure. For example, smart fuzzing for a Rails app might include randomizing the variables and values occurring in form postings or in URIs embedded in page views, creating URIs that are syntactically valid but might expose a bug. Smart fuzzing for SaaS can also include attacks such as cross-site scripting or SQL injection, which we'll discuss in Chapter 10. Tarantula[11] (a fuzzy spider that crawls your site) is a Ruby gem for fuzz-testing Rails applications.

Self-Check 5.9.1 *The Microsoft Zune music player had an infamous bug that caused all*

*Zunes to "lock up" on December 31, 2008. Later analysis showed that the bug would
be triggered on the last day of any leap year. What kinds of tests—black-box, glass-box,
mutation or fuzz—would have been likely to catch this bug?*
⋄ A glass-box test for the special code paths used for leap years would have been effective.
Fuzz testing might have been effective: since the bug occurs roughly once in every 1460
days, a few thousand fuzz tests would likely have found it. ∎

5.10 Fallacies and Pitfalls

 Fallacy: **100% test coverage with all tests passing means no bugs.**

There are many reasons this statement can be false. Complete test coverage says nothing about the quality of the individual tests. As well, some bugs may require passing a
certain value as a method argument (for example, to trigger a divide-by-zero error), and
control flow testing often cannot reveal such a bug. There may be bugs in the interaction
between your app and an external service such as TMDb; stubbing out the service so you
can perform local testing might mask such bugs.

 Pitfall: **Dogmatically insisting on 100% test coverage all passing (green) before you ship.**

As we saw above, 100% test coverage is not only difficult to achieve at levels higher
than C1, but gives no guarantees of bug-freedom even if you do achieve it. Test coverage
is a useful tool for estimating the overall comprehensiveness of your test suite, but high
confidence requires a variety of testing methods—integration as well as unit, fuzzing as
well as hand-constructing test cases, define-use coverage as well as control-flow coverage,
mutation testing to expose additional holes in the test strategy, and so on. Indeed, in Chapter 10 we will discuss operational issues such as security and performance, which call for
additional testing strategies beyond the correctness-oriented ones described in this chapter.

 Fallacy: **You don't need much test code to be confident in the application.**

While insisting on 100% coverage may be counterproductive, so is going to the other
extreme. The *code-to-test ratio* in production systems (lines of noncomment code divided
by lines of tests of all types) is usually less than 1, that is, there are more lines of test
than lines of app code. As an extreme example, the SQLite database included with Rails
contains over 1200 times as much test code as application code[12] because of the wide
variety of ways in which it can be used and the wide variety of different kinds of systems
on which it must work properly! While there is controversy over how useful a measure
the test-to-code ratio is, given the high productivity of Ruby and its superior facilities for
DRYing out your test code, a `rake stats` ratio between 0.2 and 0.5 is a reasonable target.

 Pitfall: **Relying too heavily on just one kind of test (unit, functional, integration).**

Even 100% unit test coverage tells you nothing about interactions among classes. You
still need to create tests to exercise the interactions between classes (functional or module
testing) and to exercise complete paths through the application that touch many classes and
change state in many places (integration testing). Conversely, integration tests touch only

a tiny fraction of all possible application paths, and therefore exercise only a few behaviors in each method, so they are not a substitute for good unit test coverage to get assurance that your lower-level code is working correctly.

 Pitfall: **Writing tests after the code rather than before.**

Thinking about "the code we wish we had" from the perspective of a test for that code tends to result in code that is testable. This seems like an obvious tautology until you try writing the code first without testability in mind, only to discover that surprisingly often you end up with mock trainwrecks (see next pitfall) when you do try to write the test.

In addition, in the traditional Waterfall lifecycle described in Chapter 1, testing comes after code development, but with SaaS that can be in "public beta" for months, no one would suggest that testing should only begin after the beta period. Writing the tests first, whether for fixing bugs or creating new features, eliminates this pitfall.

 Pitfall: **Mock Trainwrecks.**

Mocks exist to help isolate your tests from their collaborators, but what about the collaborators' collaborators? Suppose our **Movie** object has a **pics** attribute that returns a list of images associated with the movie, each of which is a **Picture** object that has a **format** attribute. You're trying to mock a **Movie** object for use in a test, but you realize that the method to which you're passing the **Movie** object is going to expect to call methods on its **pics**, so you find yourself doing something like this:

http://pastebin.com/EmQusZd4

```
1  movie = mock('Movie', :pics => [mock('Picture', :format => 'gif')])
2  Movie.count_pics(movie).should == 1
```

This is called a *mock trainwreck*, and it's a sign that the method under test (**count_pics**) has excessive knowledge of the innards of a **Picture**. In the Chapters 7 and 9 we'll encounter a set of additional guidelines to help you detect and resolve such *code smells*.

 Pitfall: **Inadvertently creating dependencies regarding the order in which specs are run, for example by using before(:all).**

If you specify actions to be performed only once for a whole group of test cases, you may introduce dependencies among those test cases without noticing. For example, if a **before :all** block sets a variable and test example A changes the variable's value, test example B could come to rely on that change if A is usually run before B. Then B's behavior in the future might suddenly be different if B is run first, which might happen because autospec prioritizes running tests related to recently-changed code. Therefore it's best to use **before :each** and **after :each** whenever possible.

5.11 Concluding Remarks: TDD vs. Conventional Debugging

In this chapter we've used RSpec to develop a method using TDD with unit tests. Although TDD may feel strange at first, most people who try it quickly realize that they already use the unit-testing techniques it calls for, but in a different workflow. Often, a typical developer will write some code, assume it probably works, test it by running the whole application, and hit a bug. As an MIT programmer lamented at the first software engineering conference in 1968: "We build systems like the Wright brothers built airplanes—build the whole thing, push it off a cliff, let it crash, and start over again."

Once a bug has been hit, if inspecting the code doesn't reveal the problem, the typical developer would next try inserting print statements around the suspect area to print out the values of relevant variables or indicate which path of a conditional was followed. The TDD developer would instead write assertions using **should** constructs.

If the bug still can't be found, the typical developer might isolate part of the code by carefully setting up conditions to skip over method calls he doesn't care about or change variable values to force the code to go down the suspected buggy path. For example, he might do this by setting a breakpoint using a debugger and manually inspecting or manipulating variable values before continuing past the breakpoint. In contrast, the TDD developer would isolate the suspect code path using stubs and mocks to control what happens when certain methods are called and which direction conditionals will go.

By now, the typical developer is absolutely convinced that he'll certainly find the bug and won't have to repeat this tedious manual process, though this usually turns out to be wrong. The TDD developer has isolated each behavior in its own spec, so repeating the process just means re-running the spec, which can even happen automatically using `autotest`.

In other words: If we write the code first and have to fix bugs, we end up using the same techniques required in TDD, but less efficiently and more manually, hence less productively.

But if we use TDD, bugs can be spotted immediately as the code is written. If our code works the first time, using TDD still gives us a regression test to catch bugs that might creep into this part of the code in the future.

5.12 To Learn More

* The online RSpec documentation[13] gives complete details and additional features used in advanced testing scenarios.

P. Ammann and J. Offutt. *Introduction to Software Testing.* Cambridge University Press, 2008. ISBN 0521880386. URL http://www.amazon.com/Introduction-Software-Testing-Paul-Ammann/dp/0521880386.

M. Feathers. *Working Effectively with Legacy Code.* Prentice Hall, 2004. ISBN 9780131177055. URL http://www.amazon.com/Working-Effectively-Legacy-Michael-Feathers/dp/0131177052.

Notes

[1] http://themoviedb.org
[2] http://nokogiri.org
[3] http://en.wikipedia.org/wiki/Y2k
[4] http://www.jmock.org/getting-started.html
[5] https://github.com/thoughtbot/factory_girl_rails/blob/master/GETTING_STARTED.md
[6] http://api.themoviedb.org
[7] http://fakeweb.rubyforge.org
[8] http://rspec.info
[9] http://rspec.info

5.13 Exercises

Exercise 5.1 *Complete the happy path of the Cucumber scenario started in Chapter 4 for retrieving movie info from TMDb. To keep the scenario **Independent** of the real TMDb service, you'll need to download and use the* FakeWeb *gem to "stub out" calls to the TMDb service.*

Exercise 5.2 *Our current controller specs only cover the happy path of testing* **search_tmdb**: *since* **find_in_tmdb** *can now raise an* **InvalidKeyError**, *the controller specs are incomplete because we don't test what the controller method does in that case. Use TDD to create specs and controller code to handle this case.*

Exercise 5.3 *In Section 5.3, we stubbed the method* **find_in_tmdb** *both to isolate the testing of the controller from other classes and because the method did not yet exist. How would such stubbing be handled in Java?*

◇ You would need to create a separate copy of the **Movie** class for use with the controller specs and stub the appropriate methods there. ∎

Exercise 5.4 *Based on the specfile below, to what method(s) must instances of* **Foo** *respond in order for the tests to pass?*

http://pastebin.com/dFp71CBp

```
 1  require 'foo'
 2  describe Foo do
 3    describe "a new foo" do
 4      before :each do ; @foo = Foo.new ; end
 5      it "should be a pain in the butt" do
 6        @foo.should be_a_pain_in_the_butt
 7      end
 8      it "should be awesome" do
 9        @foo.should be_awesome
10      end
11      it "should not be nil" do
12        @foo.should_not  be_nil
13      end
14      it "should not be the empty string" do
15        @foo.should_not == ""
16      end
17    end
18  end
```

◇ Instances of **foo** must respond to **pain_in_the_butt?**, **awesome?**, **nil?** (which is defined on **Object** and usually inherited), and **==**, which must be prepared to accept a string argument. ∎

Exercise 5.5 *(Hard) In the previous exercise, explain why incorrect test behavior would result from rewriting line 15 as:*

http://pastebin.com/hQsQZqYJ

```
 1  @foo.should != ""
```

Exercise 5.6 *In Chapter 4, we created a "Find in TMDb" button on the index page of Rotten Potatoes that would post to* **search_tmdb**, *but we never wrote a spec that verifies that the button routes to the correct action. Write this spec using RSpec's* **route_to** *assertion matcher and add it to the controller spec. (Hint: since this route doesn't correspond to a basic CRUD action, you won't be able to use the built-in RESTful URI helpers to specify the route, but you can use the* **:controller** *and* **:action** *arguments to* **route_to** *to specify the action explicitly.)*

http://pastebin.com/WJQ2AA05

```
1  # in movies_controller_spec.rb
2  it 'recognizes and generates routing for Find In TMDb' do
3    { :post => '/movies/find_in_tmdb' }.should route_to(
4      :controller => 'movies', :action => 'find_in_tmdb')
5  end
```

■

Exercise 5.7 *Increase the C0 coverage of* `movies_controller.rb` *to 100% by creating additional specs in* `movies_controller_spec.rb`.

Exercise 5.8 *In 1999, the $165 million Mars Climate Orbiter spacecraft burned up while entering the Martian atmosphere because one team working on thruster software had expressed thrust in metric (SI) units while another team working on a different part of the thruster software had expressed them in Imperial units. What kind(s) of correctness tests—unit, functional, or integration—would have been necessary to catch this bug?*

Improving Productivity: DRY and Concise Rails

This chapter will be added to the Alpha Edition before May 1, 2012. Purchasers of the ebook will be notified by email from Amazon when a free update for their ebook is available.

7 Software Maintenance: Using Agile Methods on Legacy Software

This chapter is not present in the Alpha Edition.

8 Working In Teams vs. Individually

This chapter will be added to the Alpha Edition before May 1, 2012. Purchasers of the ebook will be notified by email from Amazon when a free update for their ebook is available.

9 Software Design Patterns for SaaS

This chapter is not present in the Alpha Edition.

10 Operations: Performance, Scaling, and Practical Security

This chapter is not present in the Alpha Edition.

Looking Backwards and Looking Forwards

Well, the <omitted> paper is in good company (and for the same reason).
The B-tree paper was rejected at first.
The Transaction paper was rejected at first.
The data cube paper was rejected at first.
The five-minute rule paper was rejected at first.
But linear extensions of previous work get accepted.
So, resubmit! PLEASE!!! —Jim Gray, Email to Jim Larus about a rejected paper, 2000

In this chapter we give perspectives on the big ideas in this book—Agile, Cloud Computing, Rails, SaaS, and SOA—and show how Berkeley students who have graduated and taken jobs in industry rank their importance.

Jim Gray (1944–Lost at sea 2007) was a friendly giant in computer science. He was the first PhD in Computer Science from UC Berkeley, and he mentored hundreds of PhD students and faculty around the world. He received the 1998 Turing Award for contributions to database and transaction processing research and technical leadership in system implementation.

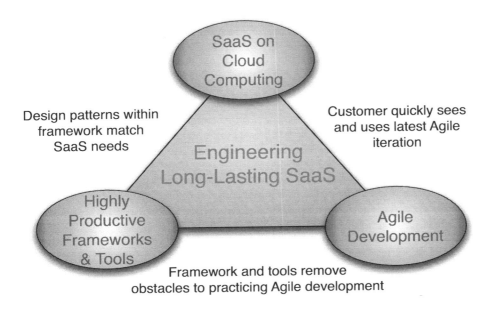

Figure 11.1: The Virtuous Triangle of Engineering Long-Lived SaaS is formed from the three software engineering crown jewels of (1) SaaS on Cloud Computing, (2) Highly Productive Framework and Tools, and (3) Agile Development.

11.1 Looking Backwards

Figure 11.1, first seen in Chapter 1, shows the three "crown jewels" on which the material in this book is based. To understand this virtuous triangle you needed to learn many new terms; Figure 11.2 lists nearly 120 terms from just the first three chapters!

Each pair of jewels form synergistic bounds that support each other, as Figure 11.1 shows. In particular, the tools and related services of Rails makes it much easier to follow the Agile lifecycle. Figure 11.3 shows our oft repeated Agile iteration, but this time it is decorated with the tools and services that we use in this book. Without these ten tools and services, it would be a lot harder to follow the Agile lifecycle *and* to develop SaaS apps.

11.2 Perspectives on SaaS and Service-Oriented Architecture

In this book you've been mainly a user of a successful distributed architecture (the Web, SOA) and framework (Rails). As a successful software engineer you'll likely need to create such frameworks, or extend existing ones. Paying careful attention to principles that made these frameworks successful will help.

In Chapter 2 we pointed out that by choosing to build SaaS, some architectural choices are made for you. In building different kinds of systems, other choices might be appropriate, but for reasons of scope, we have focused on this one set of choices. But it's worth pointing out that some of the important architectural principles underlying SaaS and SOA apply in other architectures as well, and as Jim Gray's quote at the front of this chapter suggests, good ideas took time to mature.

For example, Rails is very powerful but has evolved tremendously since version 1.0, which was originally *extracted* from a specific application. Indeed, the Web itself evolved

Chapter 1	Chapter 2 (cont'd)	Chapter 3
acceptance test	HTTP cookie	accessor method
agile development process	HTTP method	anonymous lambda expression
automatic theorem proving	HTTP server	app root
cloud computing	interpolated	backtrace
cluster	IP address	block
DRY(Don't Repeat Yourself)	load balancer	class variable
formal methods	logic tier	closure
functional test	markup language	duck typing
integration test	master-slave	dynamically typed
legacy code	middleware	encapsulation
lifecycle	model	functional programming
model checking	multi-homed	gem
module test	MVC (Model-View-Controller)	generator
object oriented programming	network interface	getter method
public cloud service	network protocol	idempotent
regression test	peer-to-peer architecture	instance variable
SaaS (Software as a Service)	persistence tier	instrumentation
SOA (Service Oriented Arch.)	primary key	iterator
system test	public-key cryptography	lexical scoping
test coverage	push-based	looking up a method
unit test	RDBMS (relational database management system)	metaprogramming
utility computing	relational algebra	method chaining
validation	relational database	migration
verification	request-reply protocol	mix-ins
virtual machine	route	mutator method
warehouse scale computer	selector notation	poetry mode
waterfall development process	session	receiver
Chapter 2	SGML (Standard Generalized Markup Language)	reflection
action	sharding	regex
application server	shared-nothing architecture	regular expressions
client-server architecture	stateless protocol	root class
controller	structured storage	setter method
CSS (Cascading Style Sheet)	TCP port number	static variable
CRUD (Create, Read, Update, Delete)	TCP/IP (Transmission Control Protocol/Internet Protocol)	symbol
data consistency	URI (Uniform Resource Identifier)	syntactic sugar
design pattern	view	type casting
DNS (Domain Name System)	web application framework	yield
HAML (HTML Abstraction Markup Language)	Web server	
hostnames	XHTML (eXtended HyperText Markup Language)	
HTML (HyperText Markup Language)	XML (eXtensible Markup Language)	
HTTP (HyperText Transfer Protocol)		

Figure 11.2: Terms introduced in the first three chapters of this book.

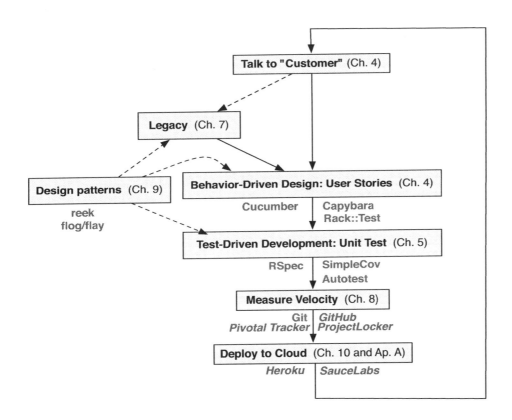

Figure 11.3: An iteration of the Agile software lifecycle and its relationship to the chapters in this book, with the supporting tools (red bold letters) and supporting services (blue italic letters) identified with each step.

from specific details to more general architectural patterns:

- From static documents in 1990 to dynamic content by 1995;

- From opaque URIs in the early 1990s to REST by the early 2000s;

- From session "hacks" (fat URIs, hidden fields, and so on) in the early 1990s to cookies and real sessions by the mid 1990s; and

- From setting up and administering your own ad-hoc servers in 1990 to deployment on "curated" cloud platforms in the 2000s.

11.3 It Takes Time

As Jim Gray suggests in the opening quote, good incremental ideas can be embraced quickly but great radical ideas take time before they are accepted.

Ruby and Java are the same age, both appearing in 1995. Within a few years Java became one of the most popular programming languages, while Ruby remained primarily of interest to the programming languages literati. Ruby's popularity came a decade later with the release of Rails. Ruby and Rails demonstrate that big ideas in programming languages really can deliver productivity through extensive software reuse. Comparing to Java and its frameworks to Ruby and Rails, Stella et al. 2008 and Ji and Sedano 2011 found factors of 3 to 5 reductions in number of lines of code, which is one indication of productivity.

Rails itself took off with the shift in the software industry towards Software as a Service (SaaS) using Agile development and deployed via cloud computing. Today virtually every traditional buy-and-install program is offered as a service, including PC standard-bearers like Office (see Office 365) and TurboTax (see TurboTax Online). Tools like Rails made Agile much easier to use and practice than earlier software development methods. Remarkably, not only has the future of software been revolutionized, software development is now easier to learn!

11.4 Evaluating the Book in the Classroom

The tools and services in Figure 11.3 and their resulting productivity allow college students to experience the whole software life cycle repeatedly in a single course. A typical undergraduate workload of four courses per term and a 50-hour work week gives students about 12 hours per week per course, including lectures, labs, exams, and so forth. This works out to roughly 120 hours per quarter to 180 hours per semester, or just three to four weeks for a full-time developer! The productivity of Rails and its ecosystem of tools and the automation of tasks via services allow students to learn and practice software engineering fundamentals within the time budget of the classroom.

The ideas in this book are useful as well as enlightening. Figure 11.4 shows the survey results of Berkeley students from two course offerings of a class based on the material in this book. Just 22 of the 47 respondents had graduated, and just 19 had done significant software projects. The figures below show the results of their 26 software projects. We were surprised that Agile software development was so popular (68%) and that the cloud was such a popular platform (50%). Given that no language was used in more than 22% of the projects, our alumni must be using Agile in projects that use languages other than Ruby

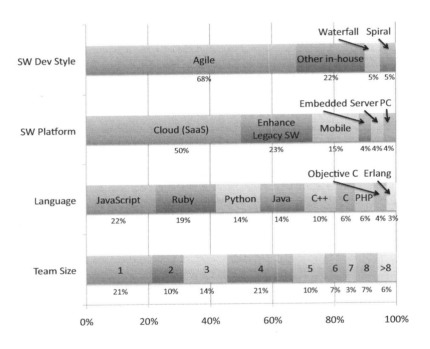

Figure 11.4: A survey of former Berkeley students now in industry concerning software development styles, software platforms, programming languages used, and size of programming teams. The Waterfall software development process is characterized by much of the design being done in advance in coding, completing each phase before going on to the next one. The Spiral model combines features of a prototyping model and the Waterfall model and is intended for large projects.

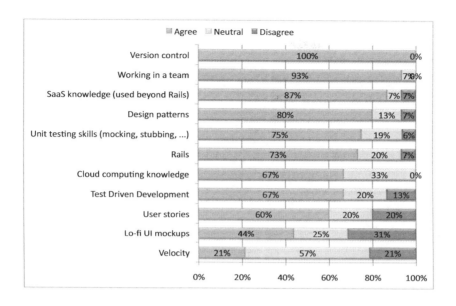

Figure 11.5: A survey of former Berkeley students asking if the topics in this book were useful in their industrial projects.

or Python. All the class teams had four or five students, which happily matches the average team size from the survey.

Agile development and Rails were not selected because we expected them to dominate students' professional careers upon graduation, but because their productivity allows us to fit several critical ideas into a single college course in the hope that students will later apply them to other methodologies, languages, and frameworks.

Figure 11.5 shows the students' ranking of the topics in the book in terms of usefulness in their industrial projects. Most students agreed that the concepts in the course were useful in their jobs. Once again, we were pleased to see that these ideas were still being used, even in industrial projects that did not rely on Agile or on Rails. The two lower ranked topics were Lo-Fi User Interface Mockups, which makes sense since few developers work on the UI of a user-facing project, and Velocity, as progress can be measured in other ways in industry.

Although a small sample and not a conclusive user study, we think our survey offers at least anecdotal evidence that people who study this material continue to use successful software development techniques in later software projects of all kinds.

We believe the approach of this book pleases three groups of stakeholders:

1. Students like it because they get the pride of accomplishment in shipping code that works and is used by people other than their instructors, plus they get experience that can help land internships or jobs.

2. Faculty like it because students actually use what they hear in lecture, they can see how big computer science ideas genuinely improve productivity, and they use what they learn beyond the classroom.

3. Colleagues in industry like it because it addresses several of their concerns. An example is this quote from a Google engineer:

   "I'd be far more likely to prefer graduates of this program than any other I've seen. As you know, we're not a Ruby shop, but I feel this is a good choice for the class to be able to get real features done. Java or C++ would take forever."

11.5   Last Words

> *To me programming is more than an important practical art. It is also a gigantic undertaking in the foundations of knowledge.*
> —Grace Murray Hopper, *Management and the Computer of the Future*, 1962.

Grace Murray Hopper (1906–1992) was one of the first programmers, developed the first compiler, and was refered to as "Amazing Grace." She became a rear admiral in the US Navy, and in 1997 a warship was named for her: the USS Hopper.

Software helped put humans on the moon, led to the invention of lifesaving CAT scans, and enables eyewitness citizen journalism. By working as a software developer, you become part of a community that has the power to change the world.

But with great power comes great responsibility. Faulty software caused the loss of the Ariane V rocket[1] and Mars Observer[2] as well as the deaths of several patients due to radiation overdoses from the Therac-25 machine[3].

While the early stories of computers and software are dominated by "frontier narratives" of lone geniuses working in garages or at startups, software today is too important to be left to any one individual, however talented. As we said in Chapter 8, it is now a team sport.

We believe the concepts in this book increase the chances of you being both a responsible software developer *and* a part of a winning team. There's no textbook for getting there; just keep writing, learning, and refactoring to apply your lessons as you go.

And as we said in the first chapter, we look forward to becoming passionate fans of the beautiful and long-lasting code that you and your team create!

11.6   To Learn More

F. Ji and T. Sedano. Comparing extreme programming and waterfall project results. *Conference on Software Engineering Education and Training*, pages 482–486, 2011.

L. Stella, S. Jarzabek, and B. Wadhwa. A comparative study of maintainability of web applications on J2EE, .NET and Ruby on Rails. *10th International Symposium on Web Site Evolution*, pages 93–99, October 2008.

Notes

[1]http://en.wikipedia.org/wiki/Ariane_5_Flight_501
[2]http://en.wikipedia.org/wiki/Mars_Observer
[3]http://en.wikipedia.org/wiki/Therac-25

A Using the Bookware

All the things I do are of a piece. I'm exploring the edges, finding new ways of doing things. It keeps me very, very engaged.
—Fran Allen, from Computer History Museum Fellow Award Plaque, 2000

Frances Allen (1932–) received the 2006 Turing Award for pioneering contributions to the theory and practice of optimizing compiler techniques that laid the foundation for modern optimizing compilers and automatic parallel execution.

A.1 Alpha Edition Guidance

Although we take steps in this book to minimize the pain, such as using Test-Driven Development (Chapter 5) to catch problems quickly and providing a VM image with a consistent environment, errors *will* occur. In addition, the Alpha test of the book is going to be 300 times larger than we originally planned and used in 140 countries rather than just in one classroom, so we expect there will be problems with the bookware that we had not anticipated. You can react most productively by remembering the acronym **RASP**: Read, Ask, Search, Post.

Read the error message. Error messages can look disconcertingly long, but a long error message is often your friend because it gives a strong hint of the problem. There will be places to look in the online information associated with the class given the error message.

Ask a coworker. If you have friends in the class, or have instant messaging enabled, put the message out there.

Search for the error message. You'd be amazed at how often experienced developers deal with an error by using a search engine such as Google to look up key words or key phrases in the error message.

Post a question on a site like StackOverflow[1] or ServerFault[2] (*after* searching to see if a similar question has been asked!), sites that specialize in helping out developers and allow you to vote for the most helpful answers to particular questions so that they eventually percolate to the top of the answer list.

Thanks again for your help with the Alpha test, and we appreciate your patience.

A.2 Overview of the Bookware

The bookware consists of three parts.

The first is a uniform development environment preloaded with all the tools referenced in the book. For convenience and uniformity, this environment is provided as a ***virtual machine image***.

The second comprises a set of excellent SaaS sites aimed at developers: GitHub[3], ProjectLocker[4], Heroku[5], and Pivotal Tracker[6]. **Disclaimer:** At the time of this writing, the *free* offerings from the above sites were sufficient to do the work in this book. However, the providers of those services or tools may decide at any time to start charging, which would be beyond our control.

The third is supplementary material connected to the book, which is free whether you've purchased the book or not:

- The book's web site (http://saasbook.info[7]) contains the latest errata for each book version, links to supplementary material online, a bug reporting mechanism if you find errors, and high-resolution renderings of the figures and tables in case you have trouble reading them on your ebook reader

- GitHub (http://github.com/saasbook[8]) contains complete code for the various Rotten Potatoes examples used throughout the book

- Pastebin (http://pastebin.com/u/saasbook[9]) contains syntax-highlighted, copy-and-pastable code excerpts for every example in the book

- Vimeo (http://vimeo.com/saasbook[10]) hosts all the screencasts referenced in the book

A.3 Using the Bookware VM With VirtualBox

Virtual machine (VM) technology allows a single physical machine (your laptop or PC) to run one or more *guest operating systems (OS)* "on top of" your machine's built-in OS, in such a way that each guest believes it is running on the real hardware. These virtual machines can be "powered on" and "powered off" at will, without interfering with your computer's built-in OS (the *host OS*). A *hypervisor* is an application that facilitates running VMs. The bookware VM runs on VirtualBox[11], a free and open-source hypervisor originally developed by Sun Microsystems (now part of Oracle). VirtualBox runs on Linux, Windows, or Mac OS X, as long as the host computer has an Intel-compatible processor.

The development environment in the VM is based on GNU/Linux. Linux is an open-source implementation of the *kernel* (core functionality) of Unix, one of the most influential operating systems ever created and the most widely-used environment for SaaS development and deployment. GNU (a recursive acronym for GNU's Not Unix) is a collection of open-source implementations of nearly all of the important Unix applications, especially those used by developers.

■ *Elaboration: Thinking about installing your own software locally?*

The explanations and examples in each version of the book have been cross-checked against the *specific* versions of Ruby, Rails, and other software included in the VM. Changes across versions are significant, and running the book examples with the wrong software versions may result in syntax errors, incorrect behavior, differing messages, silent failure, or other problems. To avoid confusion, we strongly recommend you use the VM until you are familiar enough with the environment to distinguish errors in your own code from problems arising from incompatible versions of software components. The book's web site[12] includes a manifest of everything we installed for each version of the VM and an Amazon EC2-compatible version of the VM in case you have trouble using Virtualbox.

Follow the instructions at http://saasbook.info/bookware-vm-instructions[13] to download and setup the VM on your computer. Once it's set up, a typical work session will go like this:

1. Start VirtualBox, select the `saasbook` VM, and click the Start button.

2. Do your work.

3. When you're ready to quit, select Quit from the VirtualBox File menu. You have three choices of what to do with your VM state.

    - *Save virtual machine state* means the next time you resume, the VM will be exactly as you left it, like standby/resume on your host OS.

    - *Send shutdown signal* will shut down the guest OS in an orderly way; your changes will be saved, but the next time you restart the VM, any programs that were running *in the VM* will have been shut down. This is like using the `shutdown` command in Figure A.1.

    - *Power off* is like pulling the plug on the VM, and there is a risk that some data may be lost; not recommended except as a last resort if the other options don't work. This is like using the `reboot -q` command in Figure A.1.

Restart VM networking (when host computer is suspended and then resumed on a different network)	`sudo /etc/init.d/networking restart`
Reboot VM gracefully	`sudo /sbin/reboot`
Reboot VM forcibly (if gracefully doesn't work)	`sudo /sbin/reboot -q`
Shutdown VM gracefully or forcibly	Substitute `shutdown` for `reboot` in above 2 lines

Figure A.1: Some useful "housekeeping" commands that you can type at the Terminal prompt of your VM. Some of these are available via the GUI in the VM, but in the Unix world, it's best to understand the command-line equivalents in case the GUI itself is having problems.

If your host computer is connected to the Internet, your VM will be too. However, if you suspend (sleep) your *host* computer and then wake it up on a different physical network (for example, sleep your computer at work, then travel home and wake it up there), you will need to restart your VM's networking subsystem. To do this, type `sudo /etc/init.d/networking restart` in a Terminal window in the VM. If this doesn't work, reboot your VM. Figure A.1 gives some useful commands when working in the VM.

VM networking uses NAT by default, giving your VM a 10.0.0.* address that is routable from your host computer but not from the outside world. VirtualBox offers other networking options if this doesn't work in your setup.

■ *Elaboration: Free and Open Source Software*

Linux was originally created by Finnish programmer Linus Torvalds for his own use. The GNU project was started by Richard Stallman, creator of the Emacs editor and founder of the Free Software Foundation (which stewards GNU), an illustrious developer with very strong opinions about the role of open source software. Both Linux and GNU are constantly being improved by contributions from thousands of collaborators worldwide; in fact, Linus later created Git to manage this large-scale collaboration. Despite the apparent lack of centralized authority in their development, the robustness of GNU and Linux compare favorably to proprietary software developed under a traditional centralized model. This phenomenon is explored in Eric Raymond's *The Cathedral and the Bazaar*[14], which some consider the seminal manifesto of the Free and Open Source Software (FOSS) movement.

A.4 Working With Code: Editors and Unix Survival Skills

You will save yourself a great deal of grief by working with an editor that supports syntax highlighting and automatic indentation for the language you use. You can either edit files directly on the VM, or use the VirtualBox "shared folders" feature to make some directories on your VM available as folders on your Mac or Windows PC so that you can run a native editor on your Mac or PC.

Many *Integrated Development Environments* (IDEs) that support Ruby, including Aptana, NetBeans and RubyMine, perform syntax highlighting, indentation and other useful tasks. Note that while these IDEs also provide a GUI for other development-related tasks such as running tests, in this book we use command-line tools for these tasks for three reasons. First, unlike some IDEs, the command line tools are standard across all platforms. Second, we place heavy emphasis in the book on automation to avoid mistakes and improve productivity; GUI tasks cannot generally be automated, whereas command line tools can be composed into scripts that automate various tasks, an approach central to the Unix philosophy. Third, understanding what specific tools are involved in each aspect of development helps roll back the "magic curtain" of IDE GUIs. We believe this is helpful when learning a new system because if something goes wrong while using the GUI, in order to find the problem you need some understanding of how the GUI actually does the tasks.

There are two ways to edit files on the VM. The first is to run an editor on the VM itself. Aptana and Emacs are both installed in the VM. Aptana is an open-source IDE specifically for Ruby. It has lots of features and therefore a bit of a steep learning curve. Various tutorials[15] are available in screencast form. Emacs is the granddaddy of customizable editors and one of the creations of the illustrious Richard Stallman.

(TBD more details on using, tutorials, etc.)

If you choose to edit natively on your Mac or Windows computer, free editors that support Ruby include TextWrangler[16] for Mac OS X or Notepad++[17] for Windows. You'll have to setup the Shared Folders feature of VirtualBox (as explained at `http://saasbook.info/bookware-vm-instructions`[18]) to use this approach.

A.5 Getting Started With Git for Version Control

Version control, also called source code control or software configuration management (SCM), is the process of keeping track of the history of changes to a set of files such that we can tell who made each change and when, reconstruct one or more files as they existed at some point in the past, or selectively combine changes made by different people. A version control system (VCS) is a tool that helps manage this process. For individual developers, SCM provides a timestamped and annotated history of changes to the project and an easy way to undo changes that introduce bugs. Chapter 8 discusses the many additional benefits of SCM for small teams.

SCM or VCS?
Confusingly, the abbreviations SCM and VCS are often used interchangeably.

We will be using Git for version control. Cloud-based Git hosting services like GitHub and ProjectLocker, while not required for Git, are highly desirable because they enable small teams to collaborate conveniently (as Chapter 8 describes) and give individual developers a place to back up their code. We include setup examples for both GitHub and ProjectLocker; once the initial setup is complete, the project management commands work the same way for both. This section covers the basics of Git, and the next two sections cover one-time setup instructions for GitHub and ProjectLocker.

Linus Torvalds invented Git to assist with version control on the Linux project. You should read this section even if you've used other VCSs like Subversion, as Git's conceptual model is quite different.

Like all version control systems, a key concept in Git is the project ***repository***, usually shortened to ***repo***, which holds the complete change history of some set of files that make up a project. To start using Git to track a project, you first cd to the project's top-level directory and use the command `git init`, which initializes an empty repo based in that directory. ***Tracked files*** are those that are a permanent part of the repo, so their revision information is maintained and they are backed up; `git add` is used to add a file to the set of tracked files. Not every project file needs to be tracked—for example, intermediate files created automatically as part of the development process, such as log files, are usually untracked.

Screencast A.5.1 illustrates the basic Git workflow. When you start a new project, `git init` sets up the project's root directory as a Git repo. As you create files in your project, for each new file you use `git add` *filename* to cause the new file to be tracked by Git. When you reach a point where you're happy with the current state of the project, you ***commit*** the changes: Git prepares a list of all of the changes that will be part of this commit, and opens that list in an editor so you can add a descriptive comment. Which editor to use is determined by a ***configuration setting***, as described below. Committing causes a snapshot of the tracked files to be recorded permanently along with the comments. This snapshot is assigned a ***commit ID***, a 40-digit hexadecimal number that, surprisingly, is unique in the universe (not just within this Git repo, but across all repos); an example might be

1623f899bda026eb9273cd93c359326b47201f62. This commit ID is the canonical way to refer to the state of the project at that point in time, but as we'll see, Git provides more convenient ways to refer to a commit besides the cumbersome commit ID. One common way is to specify a prefix of the commit that is unique within this repo, such as 1623f8 for the example above.

The *SHA-1* algorithm is used to compute the 40-digit one-way hash of a representation of the entire tree representing the project at that point in time.

To specify that Git should use the vim editor to let you make your changes, you would say git config --global core.editor 'vim'. It doesn't matter what directory you're in when you do this, since --global specifies that this option should apply to *all* your Git operations in *all* repos. (Most Git configuration variables can also be set on a per-repo basis.) Other useful values for this particular setting are 'mate -w' for the TextMate editor on MacOS, 'edit -w' for TextWrangler on MacOS, and the rather unwieldy "'C:/Program Files/Notepad++/notepad++.exe' -multiInst -notabbar -nosession -noPlugin" for Windows. In all cases, the various quote marks are necessary to prevent spaces from dividing up the name of the editor into multiple command-line arguments.

Unlike MacOS, the Windows shell (command prompt) diverges from Unix conventions, so it's often awkward to get Unix tools to work properly in Windows.

> **Screencast A.5.1: Basic Git flow for a single developer.**
> http://vimeo.com/34754947
> In this simple workflow, git init is used to start tracking a project with Git, git add and git commit are used to add and commit two files. One file is then modified, and when git status shows that a tracked file has some changes, git diff is used to preview the changes that would be committed. Finally git commit is used again to commit the new changes, and git diff is used to show the differences between the two committed versions of one of the files, showing that git diff can either compare two commits of a file or compare the current state of a file with some previous commit.

It's important to remember that while git commit permanently records a snapshot of the current repo state that can be reconstructed at any time in the future, it does *not* create a backup copy of the repo anywhere else, nor make your changes accessible to fellow developers. The next section describes how to use a cloud-based Git hosting service for those purposes.

> ■ *Elaboration: Add, commit, and the Git index*
> The simplified explanation of Git above omits discussion of the *index*, a staging area for changes to be committed. git add is used not only to add a new file to the project, but also to stage an existing file's state for committing. So if Alice modifies *existing* file foo.rb, she would normally need to explicitly git add foo.rb to cause her change to be committed on the next git commit. The reason for separating the steps is that git add snapshots the file immediately, so even if the commit occurs later, the version that is committed corresponds to the file's state at the time git add was used. We simplified the discussion by using -a option to git commit, which means "commit *all* current changes to tracked files, whether or not git add was used to add them." (git add is still necessary to add a new file.)

A.6   Getting Started With GitHub or ProjectLocker

A variety of cloud-based Git hosting services exist. We recommend and give instructions for GitHub and ProjectLocker, both of which offer a free account plan. GitHub gives you as many projects (repos) as you want, but all are publicly readable; ProjectLocker restricts the

http://pastebin.com/VzvRKmag

```
1  cd ~/.ssh
2  ssh-keygen -t rsa -C "yao@acm.org"
3  # when prompted for 'File in which to save key', press Return to accept
      default
4  # when prompted for passphrase, press Return to leave blank
5  chmod 0600 *
```

Figure A.2: Create an *ssh* (secure shell) keypair on Linux by replacing yao@acm.org with your preferred email address in these commands. After the second command, a message "The key fingerprint is…" indicates success. The last command changes the permissions on the key files so that only you can read them—a requirement for *ssh* to work properly. For the book exercises it's OK to leave the passphrase blank, but this guide from GitHub[20] explains the extra steps needed to use passphrases and why you should usually use them.

total amount of data but allows private repos that are off-limits to everyone except people you designate as collaborators. Both services allow you to lift their restrictions when using a paid plan, and your instructor may have a coupon or code that allows you to temporarily upgrade to a paid plan at no charge for the duration of the course.

Whichever you use, the basic concept is the same. You set up a **secret key** that identifies you to the cloud service as an account holder, and configure Git to know this key. You only need one key no matter how many different accounts or repos you have, so you only need to do the key setup once. You can then **push** your repo to the cloud-based service, creating a remote copy of the repo there that calls a **remote**. Other developers can, with your permission, both push their own changes and *pull* yours and others' changes from that remote.

You'll need to do the following three steps regardless of which service you use:

1. Tell Git your name and email address, so that in a multi-person project each commit can be tied to the committer:

   http://pastebin.com/hYtyQKVv

   ```
   1  git config --global user.name 'Andy Yao'
   2  git config --global user.email 'yao@acm.org'
   ```

2. Create an *ssh* (secure shell) key pair that will identify you to the cloud hosting service using the commands shown in Figure A.2.

To get started with GitHub:

1. If you haven't done so already, establish an account at GitHub[21]. You can select the free account, request a student account[22] if you're a full time student, or ask your instructor if he or she has a code available that will give you a temporary Micro plan (allowing private repositories) without the monthly fee.

2. Follow **only steps 4 and 5** of Github's instructions for adding your public key[23] to your GitHub account. (You've already done the subsequent steps about setting your name and email, and we won't need to set up a token, as the remaining steps describe.)

3. To create a GitHub repo that will be a remote of your existing project repo, fill out and submit the New Repository[24] form and note the repo name you chose. A good choice is a name that matches the top-level directory of your project, such as myrottenpotatoes.

4. Back on your development machine (the VM), in a terminal window cd to the top level of your project's directory (where you previously typed git init) and type:

http://pastebin.com/9aAw2txu

```
1  git remote add origin git@github.com:myusername/myreponame.git
2  git push origin master
```

The first command tells Git that you're adding a new remote for your repo located at GitHub, and that the short name origin will be used from now on to refer to that remote. (This name is conventional among Git users for reasons explained in Chapter 8.) The second command tells Git to *push* any changes from your local repo to the origin remote that aren't already there.

To get started with ProjectLocker:

1. Sign up for a ProjectLocker[25] account if you haven't already. The free plan is sufficient for the work in this book.

2. When logged into ProjectLocker, in the left-hand navigation bar click Manage Public Keys, then click New Key.

3. In the New Public Key dialog, for Name enter a memorable name for this key (for example, "SaaSbook" might remind you that it's the key you set up while reading this book). For User Name, enter the email address you used when following the steps in Figure A.2. Lastly, display the public key file with the command cat ~/.ssh/id_rsa.pub, and carefully copy and paste the *entire contents* of the file into the Key box, and click Save Public Key.

4. To create a ProjectLocker repo that will be a remote of your existing project repo, click Add Project from the left-hand navbar and fill out the form, noting the project name you chose. A good choice is a name that matches the top-level directory of your project, such as myrottenpotatoes.

5. Click on the User Home link in the left-hand navbar and you should see a list of your ProjectLocker projects, including the one just created. Note the field "Your Git Location" associated with the project. For user andrewyao and project minimax, the location will look something like git-andrewyao@pl5.projectlocker.com:minimax.git.

6. Back on your development machine (the VM), in a terminal window cd to the top level of your project's directory (where you previously typed git init) and type:

http://pastebin.com/aHPFbfZu

```
1  # replace 'andrewyao' with your ProjectLocker account name,
2  # 'pl5' with whatever appears after '@' in the My Git Location
3  # of your project on ProjectLocker, and 'minimax' with the
4  # name you chose for 'Add Project' on ProjectLocker
5  git remote add origin git-andrewyao@pl5.projectlocker.com:minimax.git
6  git push origin master
```

The first command tells Git that you're adding a new remote for your repo located at ProjectLocker, and that the short name origin will be used from now on to refer to that remote. (This name is conventional among GitHub users for reasons explained in Chapter 8.) The second command tells Git to *push* any changes from your local repo to the origin remote that aren't already there.

Command	What it does	When to use it
`git pull`	Fetch latest changes from other developers and merge into your repo	Each time you sit down to edit files in a team project
`git add` *file*	Stage *file* for commit	When you add a new file that is not yet tracked
`git status`	See what changes are pending commit and what files are untracked	Before committing, to make sure no important files are listed as "untracked" (if so, use `git add` to track them)
`git diff` *filename*	See the differences between the current version of a file and the last committed version	To see what you've changed, in case you break something. This command has many more options, some described in Chapter 8.
`git commit -a`	Commit changes to *all* (`-a`) tracked files; an editor window will open where you can type a commit message describing the changes being committed	When you're at a stable point and want to snapshot the project state, in case you need to roll back to this point later
`git checkout` *filename*	Reverts a file to the way it looked after its last commit. **Warning:** any changes you've made since that commit will be lost. This command has many more options, some described in Chapter 8.	When you need to "roll back" one or more files to a known-good version
`git push` *remote-name*	Push changes in your repo to the remote named *remote-name*, which if omitted will default to `origin` if you set up your repo according to instructions in Section A.6	When you want your latest changes to become available to other developers, or to back up your changes to the cloud

Figure A.3: **Common Git commands.** Some of these commands may seem like arbitrary incantations because they are very specific cases of much more general and powerful commands, and many will make more sense as you learn more of Git's features.

Confusingly, on return visits to ProjectLocker you cannot login from `projectlocker.com`, but only from `portal.projectlocker.com`[26].

The account setup and key management steps above only have to be done once. The process of creating a new repo and using `git remote` to add it must be done for each new project. Each time you use `git push` in a particular repo, you are propagating all changes to the repo since your last push to the remote, which has the nice side effect of keeping an up-to-date backup of your project.

Figure A.3 summarizes the basic Git commands introduced in this chapter, which should be enough to get you started as a solo developer. When you work in a team, you'll need to use additional Git features and commands introduced in Chapter 8.

A.7 Deploying to the Cloud Using Heroku

New cloud computing technologies like Heroku make SaaS deployment easier than it's ever been. Create a free Heroku[27] account if you haven't already; the free account provides enough functionality for the projects in this book. Heroku supports apps in many languages and frameworks. For Rails apps, Heroku provides a gem with the needed functionality, which is preinstalled in the bookware VM. Once you've created a Heroku account, login to your VM and type `heroku login` at a terminal window to setup a public key pair that will be used for Heroku deployments. You only need to do this step once.

Chapter 3 describes the three environments (development, production, testing) defined by Rails; when you deploy to Heroku or any other platform, your deployed app will run in the production environment. One important difference between your development environment and Heroku's production environment is that Heroku uses the PostgreSQL database rather than SQLite3, so you will need to change your `Gemfile` to indicate that your app depends on the PostgreSQL connector gem in production, but on SQLite3 in development. The excerpt below shows this change.

The concepts in Chapter 3 are central to this discussion, so read that chapter first if you haven't already.

http://pastebin.com/ud7PtCcP

```
1  # for Heroku, replace "gem 'sqlite3'" in your Gemfile with this:
2  group :development, :test do
3    gem 'sqlite3' # use SQLite only in development and testing
4  end
5  group :production do
6    gem 'pg' # use PostgreSQL in production (Heroku)
7  end
```

As always, once this is done, run `bundle install` to make sure your app's dependencies are satisfied. Once this is done, and you're satisfied with the state of your app, you're ready to deploy.

Essentially, Heroku behaves like a Git remote (Section A.6), except that pushing to that remote has the side-effect of deploying your app.

Heroku deployments are always from the `master` *Git branch. Branches are discussed in Chapter 8.*

1. Login to your VM, change to the root directory of the application you want to deploy, and be sure the `master` branch of your *local* copy of the Git repo is up-to-date, since that's the version that will be deployed.

2. `heroku create --stack cedar`
   This command is only necessary the *first* time you deploy a given app. It creates a new Heroku application with a whimsical preassigned name that also determines the URI. For example, if the preassigned name is `luminous-coconut-237`, your app will be deployed at `http://luminous-coconut-237.heroku.com`. You can change your app's name by logging into your Heroku account and clicking My Apps.

3. `git push heroku master`
   This command pushes the current head of your Git repo's `master` branch to Heroku, as if Heroku were a Git remote, and causes Heroku to run `bundle install` on its end to make sure all necessary gems are available and deploy your app. In this version of the `git push` command, we're pushing to the remote called `heroku` (rather than the default `origin`) and specify that we're pushing the `master` branch, since all Heroku deployments must occur from that branch.

4. `heroku ps`
   This command checks the process status (ps) of your deployed app. The **State** column should say something like "Up for 10s" meaning that your app has been available for 10 seconds. You can also use `heroku logs` to display the log file of your app, a useful technique if something goes wrong in production that worked fine in development.

Local (development)	Heroku (production)
`rails server`	`git push heroku master`
`rails console`	`heroku run console`
`rake db:migrate`	`heroku run rake db:migrate`
`more log/development.log`	`heroku logs`

Figure A.4: How to get the functionality of some useful development-mode commands for the deployed version of your app on Heroku.

5. `heroku rake db:migrate`
   If this is the first deployment of this app, this command will cause its database to be created. If this is the deployment of a new release, it's best to run this command just in case there are pending migrations (if there aren't any, the command safely does nothing). Heroku also has instructions on how to import the data from your development database[28] to your production database.

For subsequent deployments of the same app, skip step 2. Figure A.4 summarizes how some of the useful commands you've been using in development mode can be applied to the deployed app on Heroku.

■ *Elaboration: Production best practices*

In this streamlined introduction, we're omitting two best practices that Heroku recommends[29] for "hardening" your app in production. First, our Heroku deployment still uses WEBrick as the presentation tier; Heroku recommends using the streamlined `thin` webserver for better performance. Second, since subtle differences between SQLite3 and PostgreSQL functionality may cause migration-related problems as your database schemas get more complex, Heroku advises using PostgreSQL in both development and production, which would require installing and configuring PostgreSQL on your VM or other development computer. In general, it's a good idea to keep your development and production environments as similar as possible to avoid hard-to-debug problems in which something works in the development environment but fails in the production environment.

A.8 Fallacies and Pitfalls

 Pitfall: **Making check-ins (commits) too large.**

Git makes it quick and easy to do a commit, so you should do them frequently and make each one small, so that if some commit introduces a problem, you don't have to also undo all the other changes. For example, if you modified two files to work on feature A and three other files to work on feature B, do two separate commits in case one set of changes needs to be undone later. In fact, advanced Git users use `git add` to "cherry pick" a subset of changed files to include in a commit: add the specific files you want, and *omit* the `-a` flag to `git commit`.

 Pitfall: **Forgetting to add files to the repo.**

If you create a new file but forget to add it to the repo, your copy of the code will still work but your file won't be tracked or backed up. Before you do a commit or a push, use git status to see the list of Untracked Files, and git add any files in that list that *should* be tracked. You can use the .gitignore[30] file to avoid being warned about files you never want to track, such as binary files or temporary files.

 Pitfall: **Confusing commit with push.**

git commit captures a snapshot of the staged changes in *your* copy of a repo, but no one else will see those changes until you use git push to propagate them to other repo(s) such as the origin.

 Pitfall: **Forgetting to reset VM networking when your host computer moves.**

Remember that your VM relies on the networking facilities of your host computer. If your host computer moves to a new network, for example if you suspend it at home and wake it up at work, that's like unplugging and reconnecting your host computer's network cable. The VM must therefore also have its (virtual) network cable disconnected and reconnected, which you can do using the Devices menu in VirtualBox.

 Pitfall: **Hidden assumptions that differ between development and production environments.**

Chapter 3 explains how Bundler and the Gemfile automate the management of your app's dependencies on external libraries and how migrations automate making changes to your database. In this appendix we showed how Heroku relies on these mechanisms for successful deployment of your app: if you manually install gems rather than listing them in your Gemfile, those gems will be missing or have the wrong version on Heroku; if you change your database manually rather than using migrations, Heroku won't be able to make the production database match your development database. Other dependencies of your app include the type of database (Heroku uses PostgreSQL), the versions of Ruby and Rails, the specific Web server used as the presentation tier, and more. While frameworks like Rails and deployment platforms like Heroku go to great lengths to shield your app from variation in these areas, using automation tools like migrations and Bundler, rather than making manual changes to your development environment, maximizes the likelihood that you've documented your dependencies so you can keep your development and production environments in sync. If it can be automated and recorded in a file, it should be!

A.9   To Learn More

- The Git Community Book[31] is a good online reference that can also be downloaded as a PDF file.

Notes

[1]http://stackoverflow.com
[2]http://serverfault.com
[3]http://github.com
[4]http://projectlocker.com
[5]http://heroku.com
[6]http://pivotaltracker.com
[7]http://saasbook.info

[8] http://github.com/saasbook
[9] http://pastebin.com/u/saasbook
[10] http://vimeo.com/saasbook
[11] http://virtualbox.org
[12] http://saasbook.info
[13] http://saasbook.info/bookware-vm-instructions
[14] http://catb.org/~esr/writings/homesteading/cathedral-bazaar/
[15] http://content.aptana.com/aptana/tutorials/index.php
[16] http://www.barebones.com/produts/textwrangler
[17] http://noteplad-plus-plus.org
[18] http://saasbook.info/bookware-vm-instructions
[19] http://help.github.com/ssh-key-passphrases
[20] http://help.github.com/ssh-key-passphrases
[21] http://github.com
[22] https://github.com/edu
[23] http://help.github.com/linux-set-up-git/
[24] https://github.com/repositories/new
[25] http://projectlocker.com
[26] http://portal.projectlocker.com
[27] http://heroku.com
[28] http://devcenter.heroku.com/articles/taps
[29] http://devcenter.heroku.com/articles/rails3
[30] http://book.git-scm.com/4_ignoring_files.html
[31] http://book.git-scm.com/

Made in the USA
Charleston, SC
21 January 2012